Queerspawn
in Love

Queerspawn in Love

A MEMOIR

KELLEN ANNE KAISER

She Writes Press, a BookSparks imprint
A Division of SparkPointStudio, LLC.

Published 2016
Printed in the United States of America

ISBN: 978-1-63152-020-4
Library of Congress Control Number: 2016930021

For information, address:
She Writes Press
1563 Solano Ave #546
Berkeley, CA 94707

She Writes Press is a division of SparkPoint Studio, LLC.

To my mothers,
especially to Helen,
who insisted I finish this book
while she was still living.

Prologue

My best friend's sitting across from me, her dark, curly hair framing her pale face as she stares down at the ring instead of eating her share of soufflé.

"I never figured myself for that kind of girl but I can't help looking at it and thinking, *THIS is how much he loves me*," she says. "That's a lot . . ."

We stare at the ring together while she grins and giggles. The diamond sparkles with the light of a million girlhood fantasies.

We're in a high-ceilinged, noisy restaurant, Bottega Louie, in downtown Los Angeles. The din of clinking glasses and conversations at other tables makes us raise our voices even though we're sitting right next to each other.

"I have fun looking around and thinking to myself, *I bet no one in this room has as nice of a ring as me.*"

Jenny is yelling these confessions into my ear as I look down at my own fingers—nails freshly bitten and with month-old polish fading off of them, my left hand free of rings. All around us the wealth of the city is on parade. Designer shoes tap against the tiled floor, people ignore their dinner dates to update statuses on shiny tech devices, the waiters look like movie stars. *There might be some serious competition in this room*, I think to myself.

I am genuinely happy for her. Happy despite the fact that a

few years ago it was me who seemed close to getting married while she and her current fiancé were barely on speaking terms. At the moment their backs are turned to each other but touching. Watching them, I wonder whether I will ever get close to the whole marriage thing again.

It's been over four years since I got dumped, and I keep expecting to get over it—but I haven't. What if I really did miss my chance at true love? What if that ship has sailed? What the fuck happened?

It's funny because it's the same confusing feeling that I remember from the beginning of this mess—like I'm no clearer on male behavior and why men do what they do than I was at the start. It's frustrating, to say the least.

It might have been easier if I'd picked a simpler fellow—say, someone not serving in a foreign army. Or if I'd been less complicated; that also might have helped.

The great Joseph Campbell describes a hero's journey as a trip through a special world where the hero returns home transformed. Dorothy visits Oz and then goes back to Kansas a different girl. In my life it seems like I grew up in Oz and just visited Kansas for a while.

I look down at my dessert, hoping to soothe myself with sweets, but while I was lost in thought, my chocolate soufflé was usurped by my best friend's fiancé. His spoon circles the inside track of the dish like a NASCAR driver as he works on getting the bites of gooey chocolate from the crock. I look up from the ruins of the custard to catch what my BFF is saying.

"It's like having cancer—wedding planning is," Jenny complains. "You wake up and it's the first thing you think about. It's the last thing you think about before you go to bed. I'm totally obsessed."

We are the products of second-wave feminist mothers—in my case, lesbians, even. I have to remind myself of this. Us, the wedding-crazed lunatic and the self-pitying singleton.

Prologue

"We should order more soufflé," I say.

"Definitely," she says. "Two more . . ."

To be transparent, I am writing this book because I want my soul back. I'm writing it so that when I try to date people, I can sum the experience up in pat sentences like, "I was with someone for five years but it didn't work out." I think that if I can write it all down in a way that makes sense, maybe the right combination of words will unlock some sort of freedom in me—an understanding that will make the whole thing okay. I am searching for a way to tell this story that has an ending I can stand.

1

December 2001

*H*ome in California for winter break during my sophomore year of college, I'd spent the past three semesters at NYU trying to slough off any remaining high school naïveté through a formula of one-night stands, student poverty, and poor decision making.

My borrowed ID didn't fly in the Bay Area, which meant I was confined to house parties. Luckily, those had become novel again, since they didn't exist in my New York life. I was invited by an acquaintance to a shindig up in the Berkeley Hills at a craftsman house on a tree-lined street—an unassuming home for which the owners had probably paid the equivalent of what someone outside of Northern California would pay for a mansion, thanks to inflated local real estate costs.

Someone's parents' home, the wood-shingled bungalow spoke ambivalently of wealth. In the driveway, a forest-green, 1970s Volvo shared space with a lightly used Honda Civic sporting a Sierra Club sticker. From the look of the yard, the owners had told the gardeners that they wanted to preserve the "natural beauty" of the space.

Inside the house there was antique furniture, hardwood floors that creaked, loads of books, well used but pricey appliances in a remodeled kitchen, and ethnic art in each room. It was a house full of pieces that didn't really fit, an unplanned shabby chic in which nothing matched.

Walking in, I recognized almost everyone as a member of my tribe. We were upper-middle-class Jews in thrift-store clothing, overachievers, who'd gone to Hebrew school together through high school, despite the overhanging drifts of pot smoke we hung out beneath. What might have served as masks of rebellion elsewhere—the weed, the hip-hop—here were aped echoes of our parents' tastes. We stole from their stashes to get high, and our rap music was our equivalent of the African masks the host's mother had carefully placed on her walls. Here, if you really wanted to freak your parents out, you voted Republican.

Heading into the living room, I approached a wooden table strewn with handles of cheap liquor where people were milling about. *Red plastic cups—how nostalgic and quaint*, I thought as I took one. I scanned the room, priming myself for some good gossip.

In one cluster, kids in sweaters were talking about what they'd been up to at college, sharing about life outside of Berkeley. We were, as a group, arriving at an awareness of "the bubble," aka the noticeable difference between the Bay Area and the rest of the world.

"It's kind of amazing to see how quickly you can give into the prevailing apathy and ethos. I never thought I'd shop at Walmart, but three semesters into U of M and I'm beat," said one liberal refugee with a hyphenated last name.

I cocked my head toward the conversation on the other side of me.

"Isaac and Rachel B. broke up, I heard—that sucks, huh? But I guess being that far away at school and all . . . they had to drive sooooo far back and forth to see each other, so it kind of makes sense."

The gossip-bearing girl sipped from her drink and tucked her hair behind her ear. A boy in a plaid shirt passed her a blunt, which she passed to the person next to her. I took my place in the circle.

The subject turned to the war gearing up in Iraq and Afghanistan, and unlike in New York, where even hipsters were taking comfort in the flag, here there was a liberal uniformity to the discussion. No one supported going into Iraq, no one believed there were weapons of mass destruction.

I bragged that I had been out protesting the war not three days after 9/11. "They printed a photo of me and my roommate wearing big black signs that said, OUR GRIEF IS NOT A CRY FOR WAR in the British *Marie Claire*," I boasted. "You can tell it's us, even though the photo was taken from behind, because of our backpacks."

"Whoa, you were there, huh?" A guy in an A's hat who'd stayed in state for school looked at me with curiosity. "What was that like?"

September 11, 2001, is our generation's Kennedy assassination—our "Where were you when it happened?" moment.

"Uh . . . fine, I guess." I shrugged. "Weird. We had school off for like a month."

I recounted that back in New York, "vigiling" had become, for a time, the hip social activity. People gathered spontaneously with candles and pictures in public places and mourned, en masse. The fever-pitched emotion scared me, and I couldn't stand the immediate war mongering—the calls for revenge and instant security, the promises made to "get those who did this."

Here people understood what I was talking about. Here we were all the children of progressive intellectuals. We grew up attending communist party meetings, eating tofu, and boycotting grapes in solidarity with the farm workers. If not quite that radical, our parents were at least university professors. We were the children of those who rode the revolution's wave until it broke

13

on the shores and they set up camp there. It was a comfortable homogeny.

"You know we are going to hella hooride Iraq for all their oil. Their janky-ass tanks won't stand a chance," contributed another Jew with a forty-ounce bottle of Olde English malt liquor in hand.

Then, an interruption: "Speaking of wars. Did you hear Lior Gold is in town?"

Alicia Feldman's mention of that name made my insides light up like a pinball machine.

"You don't say?"

My mind conjured up Lior Gold, whose leg I used to rub under the table as a distraction from Torah study. Lior Gold, who, during text analysis of the Old Testament and Talmud, our holy books in front of us on the shared table, watched me steal sideways glances at him. Lior Gold, whose response was to raise his eyebrows in a gesture that was part surprise, part mischievous suggestion. Lior Gold, who'd skipped a grade and used the extra time to move away and join the Israeli Army.

"I heard he's part of an elite combat unit," Alicia continued, her eyes twinkling as she said it.

Not many Berkeley boys joined the army. When Lior did, the synagogue started including his protection in their weekly prayers.

Not that everyone thought Israel was behaving well. In the Bay, the old adage of two Jews, three opinions definitely applied, especially where Israel was involved. Former draft dodgers and pacifists almost came to blows outside shul during debates. With our collective ambivalent pride over Lior being a soldier, was it a case of hate the sin, love the sinner? I'm not sure.

Here is what do I know: When Alicia said that Lior was in town, none of this was on my mind. For all my antiwar posturing, the facts remained the same. My uniform fetish had kicked in. And thanks to being raised in the gay community, I knew what that was. All those poor ladies with firemen calendars have no idea. I wonder if they have ever given thought to what their attraction is about, as maybe I should have.

Lior Gold. Might as well have been named Lolita.

Back at home the next day, I looked up the number of Lior's best friend, Noah, in my trusty alumni ledger. Thank god he and I had gone to the same dorky private school. In the same fashion that my college was referred to as NYJew, my high school, CPS, was known as "Can't Play Sports."

I dialed Noah's number while I figured out how to phrase the invitation in my head. *Hey Noah, it's me . . .*I began in my mind, picturing the studious young man with the mop of brown hair setting aside his video game controller to answer the phone. Noah Reichenberg was the one person I could think of who could deliver my own private commando to me ASAP. I had to make this work.

He picked up on the third ring. "Hello?"

"Hey Noah, it's me, Kellen."

"Hey Kellen, what's up?" he said, clearly surprised to hear from me. Though CPS was a high school with fewer than four hundred kids, we weren't close friends, per se.

It was silent for a second, and then I managed to say, "Do you want to come by my house tonight with Lior and smoke?"

"Sure," he said. He knew it was not about him, but I guess he was feeling generous because all he said was, "I'll bring him by no problem."

I was favoring just-rolled-out–of-someone's-bed glamour as shown in flushed cheeks and slightly messy hair at the time, so I made sure my clothes were barely hanging on that evening, the strap of my top falling relentlessly from my shoulder. I pinched my cheeks and ran my fingers through the biggest tangles in my bangs and bobbed hair.

Noah and Lior came by my house after they'd each had dinner with their families. They were such good Jewish boys.

"My mom is sleeping in the front bedroom, so you should come back to my room," I said in a hushed voice. We padded through the unlit living room, trying to avoid its sharp-cornered furniture.

"How is your mom?" Lior whispered as we reached my room and turned on the light.

"Which one?" I joked. "The one currently sleeping in this house? She's all right."

Okay, let's handle the lesbians. When I was born in 1981, there were around a hundred other children of "out at birth" gay parents, according to COLAGE, the national organization for children with gay parents (an organization that didn't exist until I was nine). What does that mean? It means that only a hundred or so gay folks, nationwide, had decided, already being open and out and gay and all, to have kids. (As opposed to when the kids already existed, products of earlier, straight relations and not intended queer investments.) That's it, one hundred—just a sprinkling.

Why should anyone care? Because I'm uncharted human territory! There's all this hoopla nowadays about gay marriage, and someday having gay parents may be about as remarkable as being left-handed, but back in my day (cue grandpa voice), having gay parents meant something.

And not only do I have lesbian parents—I have four of them. The four best moms in the whole wide world. Seriously.

For the purposes of keeping track of them and not to indicate some sort of hierarchical order, we will say that my biological mom is Mom #1, her longtime partner is Mom #2, and the other two are Mom #3 and Mom #4.

The most basic explanation goes like this: Margery (#3) and Nyna (#1) were lovers when I was born, and Helen (#4) was Nyna's best friend. Nyna and Helen met through an ad Helen had placed in a women's bookstore, looking for help on her ranch. The three decided to parent together, and when Nyna and Margery broke up, when I was still a baby, they all stayed family. Then, when I was five, my mom married Kyree (#2), and they were together until I was eighteen. I can't really expect all that to make immediate sense, but I think the operative word is *abundance*—mother-wise.

Noah and Lior were both aware of my multitude of mothers. They may not have been able to name all four, but they knew about them. It takes me about thirty seconds into a conversation with a total stranger to bring it up. For some people it's a fascinating topic, but since these guys had grown up in Berkeley, they found lesbians generally unremarkable.

"Well, tell them all 'hi' for me," Lior said as he sat down on the floor.

Once in my room, I clumsily packed my swirled glass bowl, and we lounged and went about filling the place with weed smoke, just like we had in high school. Only now we were two college kids and a soldier.

As we talked about our previous year, I less-than-slyly checked Lior out—his close-shaved hair, the way his military posture hid behind the tied-dyed shirt he was wearing. I didn't remember him having the body of a man the last time I'd seen him. His shoulders had broadened. He'd put on twenty pounds of muscle. Newly-sprouted chest hair peeked out from inside his shirt. He raised his eyebrows at me.

It had been a little over a year since we'd last seen one another.

Like him, I'd also run off to Israel after high school. My version was attempting the socialist ideal with twenty-seven other kids, the culmination of many years of being groomed by a Labor Zionist youth movement (aka Jewish hippie summer camp). My ten-month stint in the Holy Land was spent mostly in trailers in the desert, where I developed a keen dislike for the concept of consensus. There's nothing like a seven-hour-long meeting to make one reconsider socialism altogether.

Partway through that experience, I'd managed to track Lior down and visit him, taking a much-needed break from the stifling intimacy that was communal living and the unforgiving landscape of sand dunes in the south.

He was studying Hebrew in an *ulpan* program up north on a wealthy kibbutz. The greenness of the land around made it seem all the richer. Green grass is one of life's greatest luxuries. I told him as much. I probably talked a lot while he listened.

On that beautiful, sunny day, we ate ice cream in the neighboring town of Zichron Ya'akov, known for its artists. The streets were lined with multi-story stone houses cut into the hillsides. The dessert came served in the hull of the fruit of the flavor you ordered—lemon in a lemon, cantaloupe in its half dome. Our spoons flirted in the pith.

He was making big decisions about staying in Israel and going into the army. I'd spent the past six months dissecting the political situation with too much input from too many people, so we didn't talk politics. We didn't talk about the future. Instead, he told me about dressing up the cacti they grew in the kibbutz garden in outfits made of cotton balls and felt, and I complained about the uptight girls in my group and the menial jobs I had to do on my kibbutz, like cleaning chicken feeders. Every once in a while I would look over and there he would be, looking back at me. Attentive. Solid. Sweet.

That night we slept side by side in his little twin bed, fully clothed, under the pretense that there was nowhere else to put me.

"We're friends right? It's no big deal," I said, edging my body infinitesimally closer. This was total subterfuge—and bad behavior, since I had a boyfriend at the time.

My body primed, I only finally drifted off after hours of lying still, waiting to see if anything would happen.

"I can't imagine you smoke much these days," I said to Lior, watching him fill his chest with air sucked from the pipe we passed between us.

"Naw, my commander would kill me if he found out about this, but actually they don't really test us. Maybe they would rather not know."

"So, what's the army like?" I crossed my legs and leaned toward him.

"Well, it depends on what part you're talking about. It feels funny to be out of uniform, wearing this, and to not have my gun on me." He smiled at me.

The more he talked about the army—the heavy lifting, the long marches they took with stretchers, and the physical trials—the more I desired him. I could barely run around the block, and here he could carry a guy on his shoulder for over a mile.

"Tell me more. You said you're a machine gunner?"

"Yeah, it's called being a Negevist, but mostly these days I'm sitting around getting fat, guarding the Lebanese border. I eat a lot of chips."

I could listen to him talk about the army for hours. I loved all the Hebrew words and the way he seemed so accustomed already to military life. It was like a movie.

"Tell me more about those chips."

Noah gamely put up with us as we carried on our flirtation. He was studying neuroscience, so I'm sure he was doing formulas in his head or something; also, I was keeping them both very stoned. Regardless, he didn't try to participate in the conversation. As we conversed, he stared politely into space.

"How's college life treating you?" Lior asked me.

The truth was, I was feeling rather unmoored.

"You know, I'm studying theater. Originally I'd planned to study political science somewhere respectable, possibly Ivy League, but my moms sat me down and said, 'We think you should study drama. Follow your heart.' That's so like them. It's not so bad, though, easier than writing essays. We roll around on the floor a lot. They put me in the studio program with all the weirdos—the Experimental Theater Wing."

"Imagine that."

I laughed. He smiled. His eyes crinkled when he smiled.

"In the army do they have generalizations like 'the weirdo studio,' or whatever?" I played with my hair, ruffling my bangs.

"Yeah—like, the paratroopers are all *tzahov*, yellow, like they're all Ashkenazi white boys, but, like, Golani, my unit, it's the unit that cab drivers and bus drivers rep, they all have Golani stickers on their windshields. It's the branch of the people. The motto is *Golani Sheli*, which means 'My Golani.'"

Later I would learn that the symbol of his unit was a green tree on a gold background. So peaceful, deceptively so. But back then I asked, "Why'd they put you there?" He had classic Eastern European good looks—strong jaw, dark features, a young Patrick Dempsey type.

"I guess they didn't need me in the paratroopers."

"They missed out not taking you. You know, I bet my theater program is a lot like the army because we also do a lot of crazy physical exercises, like power yoga, and we do intense group work—like, aren't we both in a group of seventeen?"

He nodded yes and smiled and I continued drawing parallels.

"I bet we are both sick of some of the people by now, and I feel like I'm learning this whole new language too. Like with you and all the army acronyms. Right now we are learning to dance like the fluids of the body."

He outright laughed at me. "Body fluids?" he repeated, as Noah started to pay attention, momentarily, upon hearing science come into play.

"Yeah, like arterial fluid goes *boom, boom, boom*"—I was stamping my foot on the floor in rhythm—"and fascia, the lining around the cells, dances all dramatic—you know, big sweeping gestures." I got up and swept my arms toward the ceiling, then dropped them with a flourish at my side.

"I can't wait to tell Menachem, our medic, how blood dances," Lior said, grinning. I showed him how cranialsacral fluid boogied, too.

It was getting late.

"Well, I should go," Noah said, standing up. He looked at Lior. "But don't let that keep you from staying." Behind him, my high school style was reflected on the walls in dried flowers, Nirvana posters, and a stolen street sign that read DANGEROUS CURVES AHEAD. My mom had yet to take any of it down.

"No, I have a lot to do tomorrow, so I'll head out with you," Lior responded, rising to his feet.

"I could give you a ride," I offered. "If you wanted to stay?" I was sitting on a bed with unmade covers. I did all but pat the mattress beside me.

The question sat in the air for a moment. *Crap! Distraction? Excuses?* I was at a loss for something witty to say.

"No. I should probably go," he said.

I couldn't come up with any further diversions, and they headed from my room in the back of the house toward the front door and the stairs. I caught them at the porch. I hugged Noah and he started down the stairs. I went to hug Lior.

"It was great seeing you," I said, pressed against him.

The time had come. As our bodies began to separate I looked at him expectantly. We were so close I could feel his breath on the tip of my nose. His lips were no longer in focus as I moved my head toward him. At the last second I closed my eyes, and for the briefest, electric moment, we made contact.

I opened my eyes to see him bounding down the stairs. It started with a kiss that barely got planted.

2

Nascence

tanding alone on my front porch, I thought, *Well, that doesn't usually happen to me.*

Kissed and then left? I mean that had *never* happened to me before; I'd never been rejected like that. Boys liked me, this I knew. I didn't have problems getting them—if anything, I had problems getting with too many of them. And Lior had come over to my house late at night, and he had definitely flirted with me, and he had kissed me for a second. I felt more than a little disappointed to see my crush bolt down the stairs and into the darkness.

I walked back inside and called Jenny, also home on winter break. (This was years before she moved to Los Angeles, back when her main concern in life was bossing around her younger siblings.) When she answered, she acted like it was normal that I was calling at 2:00 a.m. Embarrassingly, I have to admit that between the two of us, it kind of was. I used to wake up one of my mothers, but I was trying to be more mature these days.

"Hey, so I kissed him and he totally ran away," I started.

"Who?" Jenny said. I had clearly woken her up.

"Lior. Mr. Soldier. The one you went to preschool with at the JCC?"

"It's not like this is the first man you've ever been interested in," she said when I scoffed at her confusion.

"Yeah, but I thought we were getting along quite swimmingly, and then for him to—"

"So, he kissed you a little? And then left?"she asked groggily.

What charm had been missing? I wondered. *Men aren't supposed to turn down casual sex; they don't in movies or on TV.*

"Do you think he's not into you?" she questioned.

"No, copious sexual tension is our M.O. This time was no different."

"I'm pretty sure that means he's into you."

Then what the fuck? My pride was feeling bruised.

"Stop worrying about your lost mojo and get some sleep. If you don't get this one, there's always Fleet Week in May. I'm going back to bed."

I followed her lead and went to sleep by my lonesome— disappointed.

———

Less than twenty four hours later, he called. In the second before he spoke I wondered what he had to say for himself, and I said a quick prayer as his breath formed into words.

"Hey, you wanna meet up?"

That was how he told me he was now ready.

"I was worried you weren't going to call. You scared me for a minute," I said in what I hoped was a light enough tone. My eyes scanned from where I sat in my mom's living room with its sagging furniture—the cat-clawed couch, the cluttered sideboard by the central heating unit.

"I just needed a day to think it over," he answered.

Among our social circle in high school, the greatest use of free time was thought to be driving to one of the many viewpoints that dot the hills of the Bay Area. Lior and I had yet to graduate to a more sophisticated form of entertainment, so we took my car and wound up through the hills to a park that turned out not to have much of a view, thanks to the fog that had rolled in. Ignoring the fact that it was way past dark and hence illegal to be there, we walked in the damp midnight air, passing a wine bottle between us.

"I was starting to think you didn't like me," I baited.

"You're the one who stood me up," he said, referencing the last time we were supposed to have seen each other. "What happened?"

Touché.

After my visit to his kibbutz up north, we were supposed to spend New Year's Eve together in Jerusalem. It was the New Year of the millennium and there was a lot of trepidation, especially in Israel, as to how it would go down. Lots of people were experiencing "Jerusalem Syndrome," the madness that makes one believe they are the messiah. Crazy people had already been caught trying to sneak into the country. I remember reading an article on how folks thought the apocalypse was about to go down in the Holy Land and they wanted to come make sure it went as planned in Revelations, aka that the streets ran with Jewish blood. That *is* what those books say, after all.

Holed up on a kibbutz in the middle of a desert, I was as safe as could be—but what I wanted to do was meet up with Lior for the big event. Celebrating in Jerusalem became too much drama though, so, despite my promises, I ended up staying in the south and commemorating the millennium in a bomb shelter disco with vodka instead of champagne.

"So how come you ditched me on New Year's?" he prodded me.

"I'm really sorry about that. That guy I was dating totally wasn't worth it, but, you know, he was my boyfriend at the time, and you gotta have some loyalty. Plus there was that whole end of days business . . . I wish I'd been with you, though."I looked up at the immensity of the night."Maybe we can make up for it this year?"

It was a promise hiding behind an offer. I bit my lip and stared up through my lashes.

"Maybe," he said quietly.

The half-moon shone above in the clear sky.

"Do you see the old man or the rabbit?" I asked.

"I see both."

"Me too."

I took his hand and we walked back toward my car.

We were finally making out a little, *Thank the Lord*, when a cop car pulled up in the darkness behind our parked vehicle.

"Is that the police? That could be very complicated for me," Lior said as he untangled his body from mine.

No way, I thought. *The fun just began.*

My paramour didn't seem panicked, just occupied with thinking through the possible consequences and his plans to leave the country in a few days. Here we were—underage, drinking, in a car that smelled of weed smoke, and the lights behind us were doing a carnival march in our direction.

I started tearing off my own clothes, exposing skin Lior hadn't yet been privy to, with the idea that I could fool the police into thinking we were being more intimate than lawbreaking. Half-nude, I awaited the policeman's approach until it had been so embarrassingly long that I began to dress again so as not to catch a chill.

An owl hooted from a nearby tree.

"Well, now you've seen me naked," I said. "So much for a lady's modesty."

He laughed as I slipped back into my clothes.

In the beginning of a romance, there is no way to predict how it will turn out. The thing that began that night seemed at the time ephemeral, a long pent-up physical exploration of who we were to one another, a temptation finally given into.

Lior was home as part of being a *chayal boded* (a lone soldier). Israeli immigrants, whose family reside in their country of origin, are given a month off each year to visit loved ones. Lior was going back to the army in a few days, and we took those last nights as luxuries, each other's bodies unexpected gifts.

"I've been waiting so long to touch you," he told me as we lay in bed together at last. His fingers might have been making my cells vibrate as they slid over my skin. That was what it felt like was happening.

I made plans to see him the next evening.

"You can come over whenever." I tried to play it cool. My leg slid against his under the sheets.

"I won't make it over until late because after dinner with my mom, I'm taking my brother and sister to my dad's house," he said. "But I wish I could just spend all day in bed with you."

I told him I would be glad to wait in line. "As long as you're in my bed at the end," I said, in deference to his schedule filled with people who had worried about him constantly since he joined the army, those who'd waited all year to see him—unlike me, whose interest, though impassioned, was far more recent.

"Who would have guessed I'd be sleeping with Kellen Kaiser? This is quite the surprise."

I could hear my high school reputation in the way he said my name but I ignored it. "I feel quite the same way. I'm not used to having all these feelings about someone I'm just having sex with."

I tried to detach the sex I was having with him from expectations. By then I had developed a process by which I distanced myself from people I had sex with, one that involved thinking about any possible flaws they might have and inventing reasons why it wouldn't work out. Not having grown up around men, I can't claim to be a man expert, but I suspect that they employ similar techniques.

I tried this with Lior. I couldn't seem to come up with any flaws, so I worked on why a relationship with him wasn't viable. He lived across the world. He wasn't looking for a relationship either. *Stop thinking about him*, I told myself. If thoughts of him surfaced during my day, I tried to be Zen-like and just let them go. This wasn't going anywhere. There was nowhere for it to go. There was no point in day dreaming. I told myself to enjoy it while it lasted.

It was the third night we'd spent together in a row. Lior was on top of me. He put his hand around my head, reached behind the mattress, and found one of my Nyna's vibrators. With me gone at college, she had taken over my bedroom; apparently this was one of the side effects.

Lior knew about my lesbian moms; everyone who knew me did. But knowing that my mom was a lesbian and touching her sex toys were two very different things.

"Is this yours?" I could tell by the look on his face that he wasn't sure whether or not he approved. He was trying to be nonchalant.

"No, it's my mom's—put it back."

He dropped that thing like a live grenade.

I was lucky this happened in the throes of passion and not at a time in which he might have been more compelled to dwell on his interaction with my mother's sexuality. That I was naked and writhing beneath him was key.

The next morning, both Moms #1 and #2 were standing outside my door when I came out rubbing my eyes. Surprise! They were chatting amiably with my brother, Ethan, right next to my room, waiting to pounce.

"Hey Sissy, Mama said you have a boy in your bed and not to go in and wake you because you might be naked." He was a precocious ten-year-old.

"Well who is he?" asked Kyree (#2). "Do we get to meet him?"

Lior had put on his clothes while we'd been talking, and he came to the door behind me.

"Did you guys use a condom?" my brother asked him before even inquiring as to his name.

Lior blushed and mumbled something unintelligible but chose not to replicate our first speed bump of love by running out the door. That impressed me, considering.

3

New York in January

When Lior hopped on an El Al flight out of the country, only four days after I'd triumphantly lured him to my bed, he left me with a hug and a picture of him in army uniform. In it, he is glowing, and sweaty, dirt raked across his cheeks and forehead—a soldier Oliver Twist.

The photo came with me on my own return journey, nestled in my journal, which I kept with me on the airplane back to New York City, and then on the long subway ride on the L train and then the G line to Bedford-Stuyvesant, up past the Marcy Projects where JayZ came up, and then past the worn foyer and sagging stairs to where I lived—a little studio apartment with doorways shaped like the onion roofs of Moscow.

"Hey honey, I'm home," I sang out as I swept through the rainbow-beaded curtain that divided the kitchen from our living space in the apartment. My greeting was intended for my roommate and best friend at college, Cody.

Cody humored me by sharing a bed so I didn't have to sleep

by myself. I hated sleeping alone (still do), a problem I blame on my mothers' good intentions. They couldn't bear the thought of abandoning me in my last moments awake. Consequently, I got tucked into beds with others more often than not throughout my childhood. This has left me a heartbeat junkie—I rely on someone else's for my fix to fall asleep.

Between the single bed and the gay pride decor, Cody and I did little to combat the perennial rumors that we were a couple. Also, there's nothing like having gay moms to make people assume stuff about you. In middle school every time a girl got curious about bisexuality, she made a beeline in my direction. But regardless of the rumors, the love Cody and I shared was platonic.

"I had a wild affair," I shouted into the emptiness. Being that Cody and I had bonded partially over our mutual insistence that men not be the central focus of our lives, I was surprised by my temptation to brag about Lior. My eyes swept over the tiny rooms but didn't find her. She was either still in Maine for the holidays or out in Manhattan.

Listening to my neighbor's music of choice, merengue, pour through my wooden floors, I looked at the photo I'd brought back with me one last time before I put it down. I studied the man with the vibrant hazel eyes. The ones that perfectly matched his uniform. Turning it over, I saw that his address was written on the back, along with an invitation to write or send him pictures. That seemed harmless enough. Casual sex that resulted in a pen pal. Fine. Having never been able to keep up a pen pal friendship, I couldn't imagine that causing trouble.

But the more I thought about him, the more I wanted to write him. And what came out was basically a love letter:

Hey Lior, who knew you were such a stud? When you going to come back and see me, huh? How long till I get you back? Golani Sheli. Take care of yourself in my absence. I wish I could be with your unit. Huh-huh-huh . . . unit. Whoa—I

have a giant crush on you . . .talk about inopportune tim-
ing. I'll send you naked pictures of me and you can send me
Noblesse cigarettes and a blow-up Arafat doll, I hear they got
them in Gaza City . . .

Like a bug bite that begins to itch much worse once you scratch it, I also called him, thinking, *Hey, he couldn't mind my saying how much I enjoyed his company . . .* And I did it as a test, maybe. Only when I was on the phone I also said, "You never know, maybe I'll come visit you for spring break." He answered, "Oh, really? I'd like that a lot." And as I hung up I said, "I love you, bye" without thinking. Partially because I was used to hopping off the phone with friends and family that way, but partially because maybe I did love him?

I would have admitted, even at the time, to being in possession of a romanticism that made me believe that love could be as easily ignited by a dalliance between two near strangers as it could within the traditional dating scheme—but even so, I was surprised by my ardor.

After our first conversation, I bought a phone card to call him again but it proved to be really hard to get through. A little time passed. A few days. I went back to class. I decided to write him again.

Thus, we began a courtship resembling something from the past—one that would have made sense to any generation up until our parents': writing each other letters.

Turns out being in the army is like being in jail, in the sense your ability to communicate with the outside world is often out of your control. Not only was there a time difference, but my new lover also got up at five in the morning and was busy twenty hours out of every day. Not easy to fit in a phone call from overseas with a schedule like that.

You can write, however, from anywhere at any time, and on practically anything. I sent Lior missives on napkins; he wrote back on pillaged stationary from Palestinian municipal buildings. He wrote:

I feel I have so much to learn about you—who is this person I fell in love with? What kind of ice cream you like, what your favorite color is, all the little details. I usually go for a vanilla-based ice cream with chunks in it but no nuts. I'd say my favorite color is green, but since I went into the army, I'm not so sure about that. Everything here is green, from my uniform, to helmet, to vest, to the inside of this vehicle. It can drive you crazy. The one positive about all this green is it brings out the green in my eyes, not that there's anyone here to really care about my eyes.

Writing to you keeps me connected to something that is so different than the army. Your letters are like breathing fresh air after removing my gas mask. Like that analogy? I don't think its cliché.

I did something so corny, so dorky the other day that I wanted to tell you. I was lying in my tent, just having written a letter to you. The pen was by my side and without thinking, I wrote on the side of the tent, our initials. I'd never done that before, never even thought about doing it. In fact I'd always thought it was a dumb thing to do, and here I found myself writing on the inside of an army tent in the Israeli desert.

Despite my casual, can't-be-shocked facade, it turned out I was deeply sentimental. Reading Lior's letters made me smile until my cheeks hurt. I, too, found that because of him I was considering crazy things—like attempting long-distance monogamy.

"I suppose I should get rid of my other lovers, then?" I asked him during the next phone conversation we had. I was only half joking; there were a few guys who hadn't heard from me since Lior had entered—reentered—my life. Having dusted off the radiator that sat below the window frame, I was smoking a cigarette with my feet resting out on the fire escape, hanging in the Brooklyn night air. The metal was cold and wet, a symptom of the sluggish

New York January we were in the midst of. I could hear snippets of conversation in Hebrew coming from the other end of the line.

"Yeah," he said, "that'd be nice." Lior Gold, king of the understatement.

I wrote him:

Sometimes I think that it is the folks who spend the most time shielding their hearts that fall the hardest. It's like we spend so much time guarding ourselves that when someone gets to us, they really get to us. Can you fall in love this quick? Can it work this way? Who do I ask these questions to?

In another grand-scale commitment, I was considering spending my spring break in a war zone. A bizarre vacation choice. As I checked into plane flights after class two weeks into the spring semester, I wondered if I'd lost my mind.

That morning, Lior had managed to call. There'd been a bombing at Jaffa and King George Street, and he wanted to assure me he was okay before heading "into the field" for training. What a nice pastoral phrase—it was too bad he'd clarified that it meant "out of reception." On the phone, he seemed shaken and frustrated, and for the first of what would be a million times I wished I could reach him with my hands and have a chance to touch him instead of weaving words over the water between us.

The second time I was in Israel, Hamas blew up the very same block. A Pizza Hut on the corner. These explosions became echoes, like my voice did as it traveled across the international phone lines.

Everyone excels at something. One of my superpowers has always been sleeping. Once I'm asleep, nothing will roust me from my slumber—not noise, not lack of comfort. I can sleep in punk rock clubs and on concrete floors. Which is why when I couldn't stay asleep one night—not even with the faint thump of Cody's heart coaxing me like a lullaby from the womb—I was sure Lior had gotten to me.

My neighborhood—the Bedford-Stuyvesant that had raised Biggie Smalls and June Jordan, the Harlem of Brooklyn—went on through the night just as restlessly as always. The garbage truck took its noisy time, in competition with the argument of a crackhead and a wino below my window. This was where I had convinced Cody to join me, having lured her from the relative safety of the NYU dorms.

One regular midnight visitor, sporting a bowler hat and carrying a boom box from the '80s, sat on our front step to "guard" the place. My landlord had stopped the cops from harassing him a couple years back and his nightly visitation was repayment. He favored the R&B channel. Even with all the windows closed, the street seemed very close, almost breathing on my bare legs, in the form of a draft slipping through the floor.

I could tell anytime the downstairs door opened based on the change in volume of the street noise. On this particular wintery nocturnal stretch of early 2002, The African Village Café—the nightclub across the street, frequented by first-generation African immigrants—sounded like an operatic tropical hoedown. The sound almost managed to cover up the drag racing I swear was also going on.

Usually none of it bothered me, but on that night I felt like an old lady. *Keep it down out there!* I wanted to shout out the window. I heard the bus pull away toward downtown and felt my hours of rest dwindle with the lightening darkness. I missed having Lior's warm, strong body to hold onto. I put my arm around Cody, who shifted before I withdrew it, disappointed. I loved Cody and all, but the feeling was not equivalent. She had a lot less muscle, to begin with.

The next morning, feeling tired and twitchy, I called home, hoping one of my moms' voices would set my mind at ease. I receive counsel from all four moms on any number of things. I call them one by one until someone picks up. This time I got one (#1) on my first try. *Score.*

"So all that banging around coming from your room was love?" Nyna teased me.

"I can't stop thinking about him, but as hot as the whole soldier thing is theoretically, as a leftist I'm not sure I can take it in the long term."

"Well, you know what I think of the military—you'd be better off if he was just dressing up in the outfit for the bedroom, probably. It's people in power sending the less fortunate off to die in their wars," she said.

My mama Nyna's time in the navy had convinced her to raise me with a healthy mistrust for the military industrial complex. She had served stateside during Vietnam, spending her days off protesting the war in uniform.

That couldn't have gone over well with the brass.

They tried to kick her out for being a lesbian, said they had received information from lots of different women, but she wouldn't admit to anything. Proud of her honorable discharge, she bought our house with a VA loan but "wouldn't wish it on her children. Ever."

"On the other hand," she said, "Israel has a right to defend itself. You know I love Israel, and as a Jewish man I think it's honorable for him to go and serve. Since it's mandatory for Israelis, he's just doing the same thing."

Thanks Mom—way to present both sides. I sighed dramatically for effect, then hung up, grabbed a waffle from the toaster oven, and wrapped a scarf around my neck before hustling out the door.

On the G train, while avoiding eye contact with the rainbow of working folks who, like me, were headed into Manhattan, I considered that even if I could somehow get past my ideological concerns, like human rights and Palestinian autonomy, my overall anxiety would remain. I would be unsure of his physical safety until his service was through. I come from high-strung Southerners on one side and neurotic Jews on the other; my genes are poised for histrionics. I was setting myself up for one long-term panic attack.

The overweight middle-aged lady whose stuff was spilling into my space sighed like it was the end of the day and not eight in the morning. I tried to concentrate on other people's problems. What might be bothering her, for instance—too much borsch for breakfast? We shared the forty-five-minute commute in silence, outside of her heavy exhalations and the shuffle of people entering and exiting the cars. The subway shuddered and screeched as we reached the first Manhattan stop. My mind kept racing.

Lior wouldn't tell me much about what he was doing over the phone. Something about security concerns. I wished I'd asked more questions during our time together in Berkeley. What exactly was he doing over there? I got my visions from newspapers, the things I'd read about Israeli soldiers in refugee camps. He'd told me about the camouflage makeup they wore on missions to blend into darkness and scare people. I wondered who, exactly, he was scaring.

At school, up in the studios of my theater program, the teacher divided the room into five areas. Pointing to the edges of the space, she said, "Let's put anger in one corner, fear in the other, sadness in the upper left, and happiness in the upper right. Sex can be in the middle. Try to spend some time in each emotion but not get caught anywhere too long. Really try and feel where that emotion sits in your body. What does it look like on your face?"

What does fear look like on people's faces? My forehead wrinkled and my lips pulled back as I cringed and pretended.

4

Zionism

ior and I both took formative vacations to Israel when we were
thirteen—trips that bonded us to the land, inspired lifelong
relationships with its people, yadayadayada . . . Zionism. In his case,
Lior spent the summer becoming best friends with his cousins,
Talia, Benji, and Hadassah, while watching Benji prepare for and
enter the army. He saw how Israeli teens took on the responsibility
of defending their families and country, and he promised he would
come back and do the same. Then he actually fulfilled his side of
the bargain when the time came.

I, meanwhile, spent my thirteenth summer visiting Mom#2's—
Kyree's—parents with Mom #1 Nyna, and my little brother.
Grandparents aren't necessarily a given in gay families. A lot of people lose their relationships with their parents when they come out. I
didn't have many grandparents by that point, but in my case it was
more about them being dead. Even with four moms, at thirteen I had
four live grandparents total, and Inez and Sheldon Klimist, Kyree's
parents, were the only full pair. They had retired to Jerusalem.

In 1994, Israel was edging toward peace for the first time in its
existence with the signing of the Oslo Accords the year prior. That

peace treaty declared the Palestinian right to self-government, a first step towards statehood, which led to a temporary but palpable sense that maybe, just maybe, things were going to work out. It was a short-lived bout of optimism, but a sweet one. It seemed like a good time to visit.

Kyree's parents were culturally Jewish but vehemently anti-religious, which created some trouble for them because they lived on a street that edged the city's legendary ultra-Orthodox neighborhood, Mea Shearim. Their street ran like a vein of secular Mediterranean reality alongside the faux eighteenth-century Poland that the religious nurtured and inhabited. Posters wheat-pasted onto stone walls boasted Hebrew lettering but were actually in Yiddish. Women with scarves over their hair pushed strollers across cobblestones, trailing long lines of uniformly dressed children behind them. Black-hatted men with long-curled *peyes* framing their faces scuttled between doorways and down crooked alleyways, pulling their coats around them; they crossed quickly over the Klimists' sunny side street.

Every Thursday the surrounding Hasidic community put up metal street signs declaring the street free from cars for the duration of the Sabbath, and every Thursday evening my grandparents determinedly took the signs down.

Across the yard from where I practiced my Torah portion in anticipation of my bat mitzvah, warbling the melody I'd learned from a tape brought with me from the States, a collection of identical traffic signs rested against my grandparents' fence, growing in number by the week.

"How dare they tell us whether we can drive or not! Is it a city law? No. So they can't go putting up signs everywhere."

My grandfather, previously a labor lawyer, made the argument from a desk cluttered with papers.

"Smelly, mean people always trying to tell other people what to do," my grandmother huffed. She had emigrated from Germany in 1939 with her educated, gentrified parents and had no tolerance for the religious.

Glinting in the sun, the signs were a physical reminder of the back and forth between neighbors. Even on this one secular street, there was a yeshiva kitty-corner to us. We made up an unwelcome minority.

"The ultra-Orthodox are trying to recover a lost moment in time," my blond mother, Nyna (#1), said in reference to the hostile Haredim as she perched on the arm of a chair in the cool created by the thick rock walls of my grandparent's house.

"Before the Holocaust they had a whole world like this, now only this fragment remains."

Thanks to dreams of cattle cars that Nyna had before she'd ever met a Jew, way back when in Texas, she's pretty sure her last lifetime was spent among this ilk. Having grown up in the bars and bowling alleys of her poor Southern childhood, she had no reason to have otherwise heard about the Holocaust at all.

"They drive everyone crazy is more like it," my Jewish mother, Kyree, answered back. She rested her large frame in the chair on whose arm Nyna was perched. They were happy together then, relaxed and on vacation.

My toddler-aged brother, meanwhile, was building vast cities of blocks on the tile floor and then delivering their destruction. He was acting a lot like God does in the first part of the Bible, when he's still the wrathful, jealous deity. My brother still sported the long hair that, in following with Jewish tradition, isn't cut until a boy's third birthday. It would soon be time. Destruction aside, he was part of the reason for the trip; his grandparents hadn't set eyes on him since they'd flown out for his birth.

Staring out the window, I reflected on the elegant *peyes* of many of the religious men walking by.

"How do they get their side curls so perfectly done? Do you think they all secretly curl them?" I asked the group. No one deigned to answer.

The idea of those serious men standing in front of mirrors holding curling irons vastly amused me. For my part, I had taken on my shiksa mother, Nyna's, voyeuristic delight in the ultra-Orthodox.

Seeing boys barely my age pour out of the yeshivas, I was curious as to what their lives must be like, so opposite from mine. Did they wonder about my life when they looked through their hands and shot glances my way? Even with the long skirt that I wore—thanks to the signs suggesting "modest dress" that the Haredim posted all over—it was clear I was not one of them. We stood out there. I wondered if they understood the relationship between my parents as we all strolled down their streets.

Every day, as I struggled with the Hebrew for my Torah reading and its musical tropes, I was ever more tempted to knock on the door of the yeshiva across the street and ask for help with how to sing it. But I knew that the ultra-Orthodox don't let girls read Torah, or have bat mitzvahs.

"What do you think they would say if I knocked on the door and just pointed to where I need the help?" I asked at dinner.

I was answered with caustic laughter.

The Zionism that grew from my experience in Israel found a different outlet than Lior's. Rather than swear military allegiance when I came home with the sights and smells of the exotic and historic plastered in my pores, I promptly signed up the next summer to attend the same Labor Zionist youth movement summer camp Kyree had gone to as a child. There, instead of archery and fishing, we participated in activities like a mock Knesset (Israel's legislature), where we practiced conducting parliamentary democracy and forming coalitions, and a midnight activity in which all the children woke up and pretended to be Jews sneaking into

British-controlled Palestine. There, between campfires, make-out sessions, and Hebrew songs, I learned to love Israel in the way only a progressive leftist might.

Oh, I love Israel—I love it so much that it drives me insane! Because I love Israel, I want to make it better. It's like a sort of geo-political codependence. A codependence that led me to work for Hillel, "building a left-wing Zionist community at NYU," in 2002.

Hillels are like Jewish clubhouses that come with college campuses. Old, rich Jews donate money so that little Shmulik, while away from home, has the opportunity to attend Shabbat services or seek counsel from a rabbi or possibly attend the annual Purim party and meet his future wife.

I wandered into Hillel, after that momentous winter break when I met Lior, hoping to find some like-minded liberal Jews. Cool, social justice–oriented, party-with-a-purpose types. I figured that at a school of twenty-five thousand there must be some. The earnest and yet matter-of-fact programs coordinator told me that if I could find such people . . . well, they'd pay me to drag them back there.

"We have an internship opportunity that could totally fund that sort of community building," she said with a smile that should have warned me away.

I guess they couldn't find anyone quite as idealistic or dumb as me to fill the position. I took it because 1) I was idealistic and dumb and 2) heck, I was already thinking about Israel all the time thanks to Lior. I figured I might as well institutionalize it. And I knew I could put the thousand-dollar stipend to good use. A bagel and coffee in New York costs twenty bucks.

Very quickly, I found out that my new job was, for the most part, miserable. It combined the social anxiety of sales cold-calling with the religious division that fueled the crusades. In theory, I was supposed to convince the strata of liberal Jewry at my school to unite together for Israel; in reality, I was pretty much universally hated.

It felt a lot like the seventh grade. That was the year I switched to a fancy girl's school and was instantly relegated to the ranks of the unpopular. A school where I ate my sorrows away in the form of pumpkin pie every day for two years. I thought I'd left that phase of my life behind, but this whole left-Zionist-community-building gig here at NYU seemed to be going about as well.

Rooms often silenced when I walked in. When I showed up with fliers for an event featuring an Israeli activist from Peace Now, the looks I got suggested I smelled like poop.

Most of the New York–bred Orthodox kids at the kosher cafeteria thought I was a traitor to the Zionist cause. I just didn't fit in among the Israel advocates. Maybe it was because that portion of the Jews in New York were a different breed than I was used to—aka racist Republicans—and they had an all-or-nothing stance with Israel: either you were with them or against them, no shades of gray. If they made aliyah and moved to Israel, it would mean America had one less douchebag.

However, my new soldier boyfriend did buy me a certain amount of popularity with these people. They were always interested to hear about what was going on with him, which worked out because it was all I wanted to talk about, if I was being honest with myself. The boys got an envious glow in their eyes and talked about how they'd considered aliyah and army service. Thanks to Lior, they couldn't claim that I didn't care about Israel or didn't understand security concerns. When they introduced new people to me, it was often with the caveat, "She's dating a combat soldier," like that might make up for my loony leftist political beliefs.

Lior became my street cred with the right—but a liability in the burgeoning antiwar community. The leftists—those I'd determined were Jewish and therefore my targets for bringing into the fold—thought I'd gone batty and wouldn't set foot inside the Hillel building regardless of the event. I couldn't solve the Middle East crisis on campus, let alone in real life. All my years of growing up a peacenik did not stop me from generally wanting to hit people in the face.

In lieu of Jesus, I rely on the elevated moral senses of my godmother, Margery (#3), in scenarios like this.

She's a great resource for anything activist related. She's a lay ordained Buddhist from a long line of well-bred Quakers who also became a human rights lawyer. When she's not freeing hostages through diplomacy, she's advocating for asylum cases. I therefore employ "What would Margery do?" while envisioning her rosy cheeks, closely cropped gray hair, and uniform of black pants and maroon, plain blouses.

In this case, I called her for direct intervention. I dug my cell phone out of my overstuffed purse on a street corner off Washington Square, and within seconds her voice was asking me what was going on. The blustery wind made me shiver before answering.

"It seems like doing the right thing isn't very much fun," I said. "I'm trying to help create peace and everyone hates me. Remind me why I'm doing this again?" My foot shuffled a piece of trash along the sidewalk.

"Resistance to change is part of what makes the path of nonviolence so difficult. And if you're really good at it, they often kill you." She said this with a hint of humor, but I knew it was only funny because it's true.

"Do you think it's wrong for me to date an Israeli soldier?"

Lior and I had been together for barely a month, and I'd since dived into Middle Eastern politics in both a personal and professional sense.

"I think you know enough about the situation to decide for yourself if he has good character." I could imagine her cradling the phone, resting it against her bespectacled, round face.

When I was little, whenever someone complimented my looks in Margery's presence, she would make sure to correct them gently—"What is most important is that she is a good person. She has good character." As a child I wondered whether she was insisting I wasn't that cute, but by then I knew the wisdom of her words. Good Character.

On a crisp late January day in 2002, I attended a peace rally despite the frigid temperatures. The rally's connection to the Free Palestine Movement made it less fun than it had been in the past. Everywhere I looked, signs declared ISRAEL—THE BIGGEST TERRORIST COUNTRY ON EARTH in bold red, green, and black lettering. ISRAEL: THE 4TH REICH read another. There were pictures of Ariel Sharon's face with swastikas all over it. At least a third of the signs on display were bashing Israel, and many protesters were adorned with kaffiyehs—the checked red or black scarves made popular by the Palestinian Liberation Organization. In theory, we were protesting the US invasion of Iraq.

By this point in my life, I was a veteran protestor. I'd protested the first Gulf War with my family. I'd protested for Tibet, Burma, reproductive rights, racial equality, and gay rights, and against the IMF, the World Bank, and the World Economic Forum. I'd spent some serious time recently advocating peace in Israel, too, but I felt shut out of the antiwar community in New York City. It was a tricky thing: I desired an incorporative left-wing alternative to the current paradigm as much as the next kid, but I wasn't willing to offer Israel up entirely for sacrifice.

I've never understood how people can believe in autonomy for folks like the Palestinians and the Tibetans and then demand Israel's demise. If you believe that every people who feels the need to have their own space deserves it, then a two-state solution is probably the answer.

The current situation is like watching an abused boy beat his puppy. There is a power imbalance, but you should feel bad for both. After all, the conflict was born from two despised peoples being set at each other's throat.

The Jews post–World War II were hanging around Europe with nowhere to go, the Palestinians were the red-headed step children of the Arab world (if you want to see unbridled brutality against them look toward Jordan and Black September), and the British were colonialists with a history of stuffing hostile tribes into arbitrary borders and rescinding responsibility. Both Jews and Palestinians had existing populations in Palestine so for the British it must have made sense in their minds, like dividing Africa did to them, I guess. Probably it shouldn't have been done that way, although what all those post–Holocaust Jews should have done with themselves otherwise isn't clear. But Israel exists now and I think arguing for its destruction is a waste of time.

I guess I also just didn't see the black-knit-beanie-wearing, secretly upper-middle-class, cigarette-smoking faction around me as the people who were going to figure it out either way. When some kid practically decapitated me with a swipe of his END ISRAELI APARTHEID poster on a stick, I was ready to leave.

While I'm not sure Lior's existence had totally ruined it for me with the antiwar kids, the antiwar thing had been ruined for me. I was mad at the antiwar kids—angry that they had the comfort of certainty, the luxury of feeling righteous. They didn't have to serve and go to war anywhere, so it wasn't their problem.

Here were the people I found myself instead identifying with: crew-cut-bearing recruits and their worried mothers, those people who have SUPPORT THE TROOPS bumper stickers on their cars. I wanted to tell them that I understood, that I was part of the club too. I had felt this way before—the longing to announce my membership in a club that otherwise wouldn't assume I'm a member. Before, it had come from my desire to have some sort of a gay community calling card. Funny that these were the two groups I wanted into simultaneously: gays and military families.

Too emotionally entangled with it all to be able to stand and debate Israel's role in the Middle East, I just went home. As I walked away from the crowds, a tough wind swept down the corridor of buildings, catching a torn section from the *New York Post* and carrying it off to some other street, along with a few leaves from an unseen tree and a handful of tears from my eyes. The force of the gusts made the trash rattle against the gutter. I pulled my jacket tighter around me, tucked my head toward my chest, and continued onward.

During my long subway ride home, I mulled over what I was doing, wondered about my motives in undertaking this relationship. Played the chicken or the egg game. Which came first: my desire for Israel or my desire for Lior?

Sometimes I felt like a woman who'd chosen to marry a death row inmate. How did they frame the events of their lives in their minds? I wondered how much of their choice to commit was about the man and how much was about participating in something larger than themselves. The 9/11 attacks and the ensuing war seemed to have filled people here in the city with a sense of purpose. I wondered if by attaching myself to Lior I was doing the same thing.

After hopping off the G train at Bed-Stuy, I climbed the stairs that reeked of urine, walked past the bodega, past the big brick Marcy Projects and the bar whose owner was a notch on my headboard.

Then I climbed the stairs to my apartment—and in a hurry, because there were envelopes waiting to be opened once I could sit down. I saved the best part of my day—the chance to rifle though my mail—for last. Waiting for letters from Lior felt like being underwater; opening them was like breaking the surface to breathe.

In what felt like a statement on my current political schizophrenia, thanks to my peace work, I was being mailed things like opportunities to be a human rights observer in the territories. The pamphlet told me to come see what was "really going on" under Israeli occupation. Maybe Lior and I could run into each other there, like some kind of absurdist romantic comedy. I'd be there in the refugee camps and just when I was about to get shot for being in the wrong place at the wrong time, he'd recognize me and we'd both laugh. It's too bad life doesn't have a laugh track like in the sitcoms.

I read the whole pamphlet and then threw it in the trash (okay, the recycling). Then, gingerly, I opened the letter from Lior, which was encased in a legal-sized envelope. There were smaller sheets cut from a notebook inside, their edges frayed.

> *It's been a tedious and busy week. I miss hearing your sweet voice on the phone. I feel like I want to get as much of you as I can. Even though I don't get to see you, writing to you and talking to you as often as I can partially sates my enormous appetite for you.*
>
> *By the time you get this letter, I will have started my sojourn in the territories. It is such a gray situation now, there's no clear right and wrong. I understand that we are an occupying army, keeping down a weaker people, and in the end we will withdraw from most of the West Bank. But also, we are defending Israeli citizens from terrorists bent on destroying us. It's hard to balance these two things.*

There are roadblocks all throughout the territories which are designed to keep terrorists out of Israel and make it harder for them to travel, and soldiers are instructed to be hard-asses, asking for ID, searching cars, etc. But the other effect this has is slowing down people trying to get to work, or get to the doctor.

It's hard to figure out where to draw the line. Especially in the army, where it's demanded of you to give up most of your personal views, politics, and become part of a collective, take orders.

So being in the army definitely changes you. Makes you think about things you'd never imagine and shuts off thinking about other things entirely. It darkens your view of people, of hope, of peace. Questions morality, "civilized" countries, and forces you to learn about yourself.

I think to myself, *Now here is someone else who understands that the world is complicated.*

5

Violence

S tanding in sweatpants meant for movement class, I was smoking a cigarette outside of school on a day when smoke and steam looked the same, thanks to the cold, when suddenly I saw these plainclothes cops chasing a guy who ran right down the corridor under the building's ledge.

They tackled him right next to me. He was a black guy in his mid-twenties. Wads of money in his hand, he was resisting arrest and these two fat NYPD officers took him down to the ground. One of them started punching him in the head.

The cop stopped beating him when the guy gave in, so it was to subdue him, I guess, but even so I wasn't sure that was acceptable. The guy kept saying, as his head fluctuated between fists and concrete, "Why you punching me, man?"

I brought it up in my next phone conversation with Lior. We'd gone back and forth on the violence issue. The only common ground we could find, as far as permissible use of force, was in the World War II resistance.

"Nazis get what's coming to them," I said, pirouetting around on the wood floor of my apartment for emphasis. It was too bad he couldn't see me.

"I'm pretty sure that if I had been alive during the war I'd have been fighting the Nazis, although everyone wants to think that, right?" he said.

"Habonim Dror, my youth movement, they were totally behind the Warsaw Ghetto Uprising. I'd have met you there." Momentarily, our fantasies of a previously shared life came alive, shimmering and simple. The Nazis were asking for it. But everything else seemed less clear-cut, more ambiguous. Everything else included the things that populated his every day.

I thought about how people are walking steaks—chunks of meat, really—that can be wiped off windows the same afternoon they walked down the street, if enough explosive is involved.

When 9/11 happened two weeks into my second year in college, I thought to myself, *A huge terrorist attack has finally hit America.* I thought it was the kind of thing that would change the way we lived our lives. I thought that somewhere there was an Israeli thinking that finally everyone would get how it is.

The big reaction began that very day: lots of racist propaganda on TV. They said a Palestinian group took responsibility but then retracted it, or perhaps more accurately, the story disappeared. Lots of finger-pointing at the Arab world. All-day, all-channel news coverage. Watching the carnage and smoke over and over again.

I was stuck in Brooklyn. Thanks to my time in Israel, it all seemed vaguely familiar to me—that numb sense after a bombing, the calculating of human damage. And despite my overwhelming concern for those affected, I also wondered how the crisis would affect my schedule, the audition I'd been preparing for. That damn monologue I had just memorized.

I didn't feel entitled to grieve for the New York that had been lost, as I barely knew it; so far the reaction the city had most often elicited from me had been overwhelm. My teachers though, all of them NYC veteran artists, were a mess. For a month after 9/11, every class dissolved into tears. When the students were finally at the point where they could keep it together, the faculty was still nowhere near able to resume.

By February of 2002, New York City was slowly lifting itself to its feet. People hesitantly smiled at each other on the subway, despite the cold, despite the groups of police on guard with submachine guns that had become suddenly the norm.

One day class was pretty empty. A girl said it was because on the news the night before they'd said there was a threat of a terrorist attack and now the country was on high alert. The information had come from one of our detainees in Cuba.

Greetings from Guantanamo.

I couldn't imagine Israelis not going to school because there was a "threat of attack." No one would ever get educated. From my desk in the abandoned classroom, I watched America relate to terrorism, saw how sheltered we were as a country, how fearful and naïve.

Death pervades everything once you start to look for it. It's like sex that way—omnipresent, essential, uncomfortable.

My mama Nyna's (#1's) sister Darlene was found dead on February 4, 2002. I made immediate plane reservations. When I arrived, it was to a neighborhood of tract housing with chain link fenced yards, screen doors, and children's toys left out on the sidewalk. Nothing was over a story high. It was my second time in Louisville and my second funeral there.

We pretty much only visited when someone died.

The car pulled up to a house that smelled like stale cigarettes and had clearly been decorated in the seventies—Darlene's house. Inside were women who watched soap operas and had feathered hair and bad teeth. They came attached to silent men with large belt buckles and baseball caps. There were towheaded boys still wearing bottle cap–thick glasses. The only thing we seemed to have in common was a penchant for naming dogs Smokey.

The last time I was there, my grandmother—who I'd met once before, who'd kept a college savings fund of two hundred dollars for me and sent me five-dollar JCPenney gift certificates every couple Christmases—had died. This time it was my mama's older sister. Darlene had passed away in the middle of the night, lying next to her husband of over thirty years. He'd rolled over to find her dead beside him. He called my mama "Fruitcake," as a sort of backhanded endearment. I think he must have been indelibly sad, unable to come to grips with what had occurred.

Silk flowers and posh fabrics decorated the Louisville funeral home. We'd been there five hours so far that day. A routine had been established: walk back and forth to lounge, eat deviled eggs and potato salad, put ranch dressing on everything, drink coffee, smoke cigarettes with the family. Darlene had died of smoking-related heart disease and emphysema, but that didn't stop anyone. I inherited a carton of American Spirit menthols, left over when she died, from Dickie, her husband. He referred to them as her "health food cigarettes" because in Louisville you could only buy them at the health food store.

"Can you believe they sell cigarettes at that kind of store in the first place?" I asked my mom.

She shrugged.

During the Baptist service, Nyna surprised us all by trying to climb into her sister's coffin. Instead she collapsed, sobbing, into my arms.

I felt for her—I had never seen her like that before. My mom was different there, more Southern. It was strange to imagine her young in this context, to place her among these people in my mind. It was strange to look vaguely related to them myself. But they seemed to feel no such awkwardness.

Everyone was super friendly at the reception, almost confusingly so considering the situation. With that characteristic Southern hospitality, they embraced me instantly, tucking me into big sweaty bosoms and manly bear hugs.

"When y'all coming back?" they asked me. "You don't have to wait for a funeral next time."

The children who ran through the house and out the back door were easily twice my size, both in stature and width. I wanted to show Lior this, to have him here with me. What would he think of these people? Would he cringe slightly at each mention of Jesus, as I did? I wrote to him about it, and he wrote back:

> *I'm sorry to hear your aunt died. All this thinking about death has made my own experiences with it become clearer, sharper in my mind, and it's not like I don't think about death here. Violent and random. My own death is something I ponder quite frequently. Not that I am searching for it—I have much to live for now with you in my life. But I know that I am living by the gun these days and that it is dangerous. I'm sorry if I'm scaring you. This letter was meant to be a comfort, but I've been overwhelmed by my thoughts. It's like a little door has been opened to the little room in my mind that contains all the little death thoughts.*

6

Spring Break in a War Zone

In class we practiced "living truthfully under imaginary circumstances." We worked ourselves up toward crying with memories of traumatic personal events. We created exercises in which we imagined our loved ones' lives on the line.

Outside of class the emotion came more freely for me, and people's lives really did hang in the balance. What relation did the two spheres have to one another? My existence in acting school felt superfluous and meaningless; I'd begun to question what place art played in social change, and what I was doing in acting school at all. Maybe I should have studied political science?

Instead, if I'm being honest, what I was really doing was majoring in love, as cheesy as that might sound. I didn't care if it made me a bad feminist. Neither art nor politics were as immediate. I planned meticulously for my spring break trip to Jerusalem. Twenty days in advance of leaving, I began a countdown. Day thirteen involved missing my alarm, rushing to studio and then rehearsal, and having drinks with classmates after. Day ten I realized the actually-going-back-to-Israel part hadn't sunk in yet. I wondered if I'd cry on sight of him. The morning of day eight brought a phone message from Lior saying that he'd be out of touch for a few days but he loved me. Another form of the waiting game began. I had no idea I was so patient.

On my plane to London—perhaps in an effort to provide some comfort in these *harrowing* times—the airlines asked for an "emergency contact number" should something happen to me. Might as well have asked where to send the body. You'd think I had a death wish the way people were saying good-bye to me. It was not the same way they'd send you off to Cancun for spring break.

I, meanwhile, felt like a mail order bride on the way to meet her betrothed—blushing, nervous, a little dirty knowing what was in store. I had been to Israel before, lived there even, but never in the midst of a long-distance affair, and never for one week in March that was a test of whether what we had felt earlier was lust or something more.

I got off the plane to a welcome greeting of hot air and cigarette smoke, an outdoor cancer sauna that felt oddly like a homecoming. I endured the lines for customs, returning for the first time in two years to the Middle East, this time without socialism—or twenty-seven other Americans—to insulate me. And then I stepped into the usual hustle of the Ben Gurion Airport, where a million greetings were taking place all at once.

Hands were gesturing, smoking taxi cab drivers were sitting out front, all of them parting like the Red Sea to help me find Lior. What a delight seeing him come forward from the crowd, tan and handsome, clad entirely in army green. To top it all off, he'd come to get me in uniform. All my soldier fantasies had come to life. It was like I was in some personalized porno flick.

I had been worried briefly that I wouldn't recognize him, but there he was. We embraced—like in the movies, except it was real. Our climactic meeting was happening so shortly after we had each admitted we thought it was love, and then had committed to the relationship—me by purchasing a thousand-dollar plane ticket, him by taking time off from the army. And now here we were, amid cell phones and people pushing carts and each other, orthodox women pushing strollers, life pushing me and him into a car borrowed from his family, then back to his apartment and into his bedroom.

I was raring to go when we got to the apartment, but he had one last bit of business to take care of. Once he'd locked the front door, he took off his M16, removed the ammunition and locked it somewhere separate from the gun, then checked the empty chamber and put the rifle away.

Finally, I could undress him.

Upon inspection, his uniform was made of a shirt and pants in slightly different shades of olive green. He had slipped his beret (dark brown with a military pin) into one of the epaulets on his shoulders.

"The paratroopers have red ones," he told me as I studied how I might unfasten it. "It's joked in a song that it's *machzor al ha katef*—a period on the shoulder."

The next thing to be done was to slip the beret out and set it carefully down. Then the shirt could be untucked from the belt, which was made of the same material as the seatbelts in racecars, tough and synthetic. I unbuttoned the green plastic buttons of his shirt, one by one, my heart pounding. The white T-shirt that he wore underneath stretched over the muscles of his chest. Lifting it over his head, I could see the soft fuzz of his buzz cut peeking out before the shirt caught a little on his chin and we both giggled. We'd been otherwise silent for this ritual.

I undid the Velcro of his belt and the buttons of the fly on his pants, feeling my girl parts slicken with anticipation.

"You forgot to take off my boots," he said. I looked down and remembered that to get his pants off, I would have to deal with his boots first. I got down on my knees and undid the laces. He sat down on the bed, me in front of him, and I slipped each heavy, black, mud-flaked shoe off him. Then I peeled off his socks, unperturbed by their rank smell, and grabbed a hold of the sturdy green fabric of his uniform.

"Off come those pants."

There was something about undressing him that felt like unwrapping a gift—one that had been battered along the way, according to his bruises from recent training. Being tough, it turns out, is not about dishing it out but about being able to take it. Think of all the Rocky movies—the hero taking a beating and coming back to win it in the final round. Lior was perfecting these skills, but the practice did leave marks.

I was gentle with his body in a way the army was not.

That night—pumped up on romance, lying naked in bed—I heard fireworks, a perfect mirror image of my inner state. Thousands of shells bursting midair, thunderous explosion.

"What was that sound?" I asked, breathy. I walked to the window expecting to see a show in the sky.

And then came the ambulances.

Lior said it was a suicide bombing—not the spray of light I'd had in mind at all.

It was not the first terrorist attack I'd been close to, but I wasn't yet innately primed for the noise of the blasts, or the imminent wailing of sirens that followed. *What do we do?* I wondered, eyes welling with tears, before closing the curtain, tucking my body into the warm safety of Lior's strong frame, and trying to get some sleep.

When I woke up in the morning, the news reported that our local brunch spot, Moment, was gone. The morning before it had been a restaurant full of people eating toast and drinking coffee, and now blocks away it lay deconstructed; its elements a collage of metal, glass and concrete, turned to rubble.

That was the start of my visit, the big welcome celebration.

Lior rented us a cottage up north on a pastoral moshav called Amnun for a couple of days as a getaway from the stress of the city. We were staying in a *tzimmer*, an Israeli setup wherein a family rents out an adjoining space in their home, making a tiny hotel for two. A love shack guesthouse.

We stopped by a falafel stand on the way there. Next to it stood a giant billboard bearing pictures of patriotic pioneers—a girl in a kerchief, a boy in utilitarian blue pants with a scythe in hand, both laden with fruits and veggies. The youth on the sign looked down at us like we were supposed to do right by them somehow, figure the whole mess out so they could farm and grin and look purposeful. Fluffy, milk-colored clouds sprinkled a robin's egg blue sky above them.

Inside the glass-walled Pita Hut, crunchy balls of spicy flour were served under a pile of toppings not seen in most versions sold in the States: cabbage salad comingled with french fries under a tangy yellow sauce. Tahini dripped down my fingers and onto the tabletop until Lior licked the rest off of my hand.

"You start licking me and I'm not responsible for where it ends," I teased him.

"Maybe we should take some tahini home and I'll lick it off you . . ." He raised his eyebrows.

"Trade that for ice cream and I am sold."

The cottage we rented, though built in the plain architecture of socialism (somewhere between dorms and bungalow), did come equipped with a hot tub. Because despite characteristic Israeli informality, this was a romantic getaway—no matter the easy-to-squeegee plain stone floors.

"It's beautiful. Let's go test the strength of the boxspring," I said, pulling him into the small bedroom.

They had left mints on the nicely made up bed. I'd brought us tabs of ecstasy to share, a reminder for him that life back home was about partying and talking and having your feelings.

"I didn't know you could do this outside of a rave," he joked to me.

"We can dance if you want to," I said, my hips starting to swing.

The drugs made my skin tingle even more when he touched me. We sat in the hot tub until we couldn't stand the sensation of water, gave each other massages, wandered to the edges of the moshav holding hands. Words tumbled out of my mouth with all the effort of a rain shower until finally we were watching the sunrise. As the horizon blushed, I sat in his lap and told him about my life in New York.

"So tell me about this girl you live with . . . Cody?"

I nodded.

"How'd you end up living with her?"

"Well, you probably heard about me getting kicked out of the dorms last year?" Good gossip traveled fast back home.

"I heard you got an ounce of weed sent to you in the mail from Humboldt," he confirmed. "What did you do when you got caught?"

A warm, balmy breeze swept by us, rustling the trees. I wanted to capture this moment—the way the sky was changing color before my eyes, the day new and beginning. I took a deep breath as the drugs ebbed.

"I feigned innocence. Come on, this face? Plus they thought I was planning to sell it, but you know what a snob I am. Quality like that was all for me."

"So . . . Cody?" he said again, refocusing the conversation.

"Well, after I got kicked out of the dorms I had nowhere to stay and no one wanted to be my friend. She let me stay in her room under my fake ID and then I convinced her to move to the ghetto with me."

"That's pretty sweet of her."

"I've never met anyone so brilliant and original in my life. Plus we share a bed, and she's a dominatrix for extra cash."

"Seems like a great girl."

"I think she might be my soul mate." The ecstasy vibrated under my skin.

"Oh yeah? What about me? You don't think I am?"

The sun had taken full control of the skyline. We'd decided talking was more important than rest. It was amazing what a great listener he was. Being so talkative, I was used to people's varying attention spans. I could babble on for hours, but I understood that people could only take so much. But Lior was a trooper. Such endurance. Such stamina.

"So before we go to bed," he said in the lull between one story and the next, "I'm going to be honest with you: I'm not sure I can tell your parents apart. I mean . . . um . . . I'm having trouble keeping them 'straight,'—wrong choice of words, obviously, but how do I figure out which is which?"

For me it was simple because they were all so different, a grab bag of social class and generation. But it was hard to explain. It would have been easier if there were just two of them—some semblance of the nuclear model most people are used to—and for a moment it was tempting to try and make them all fit. Two parents (Nyna and Kyree) got married when I was five, one short, femme, and blond, the other tall, strong, and brunette. But then where did the other two fit? I was closer to both of them than most folks are with either of their parents. I mean, Helen (#4) and I shared a bedroom for seven years.

I explained to Lior that Helen paid my dentist bills and called to remind me to go. She gave me all my spending money and used to indulge me with trips to the perfume counters in the mall where we would douse each other in excessive mélanges of scent. I told him Margery gave me the deposit on my current residence, and that when I was in her area we had a standing commitment for dinner on a night of my choosing, anywhere I wanted.

The look on his face reminded me that drugs and confusing family situations might not mix.

"Life's complicated, but you know that, Lior. Look at us. We're both the children of divorce, right? Explain your family. Why did your parents break up?"

They had both seemed like nice enough people when I'd met them briefly in high school.

"They hated each other."

"Well, that explains everything." His brevity amused me. "So when did it happen?"

"They broke up the first year I was in Israel and then got back together and then filed for divorce the first year I was in the army." He looked noble in the growing rosy light, like he was covering the feeling of being wounded with a brave face.

"So you left and your family fell apart, just like mine. Around the same age, even."

"I mean, kind of. I guess you could say I was the family peacemaker."

Sitting in his lap, I could see it. He was shy but steady and confident at the same time; he was somehow able to be solid and yet flexible and sensitive.

"But sort of similar situations, right? Like we were keeping the family together." I told him how my parents broke up three days after I left for my trip to Israel at 18. They kept the news from me for a whole month to make sure I wouldn't just fly back. Then one day I called home only to be told my couch had just been seen heading out the front door.

"That must have been hard for you," he empathized.

"Being in the army and hearing your parents have called it quits couldn't have been easy either." Around us, the earliest-to-rise folks were getting up. The bustle of morning routine was beginning to reach my ears.

"It wasn't, but I'd been planning to go into the army for a long time, so it didn't affect my decision. I'd made that promise when I was thirteen."

"You always keep your promises?" I asked him.

"I try to."

I thought about other promises and commitments. "Marriage seems hard to live up to. I doubt I'll ever get married. I'd rather be a mistress. The way I see it, there's little difference between marriage and prostitution, outside of social stigma. It's all the same, perhaps a more abstract version of the transaction . . . Anyway, mistresses get better presents."

In response, Lior scooped me up and carried me over the threshold like a newlywed. We were finally going to bed.

"Maybe I'll convince you otherwise about marriage," he wagered.

7

Introductions

ivorce ran in Lior's family, just like mine. He had found in his mother's brother and his wife a set of surrogate Israeli parents, and Lior's cousins were like siblings to him. So when his aunt and uncle got divorced, he took it nearly as badly as he did when his own parents split. He had preserved his relationship with both relatives, however, so our weekends were divided between the two of them. If we did the Shabbat meal at one house, we did Seudah Schlishi at the other the next day.

Lior's aunt and uncle had each remarried, and their children, though grown, were usually in attendance at any given meal. Benji had curly hair, wore glasses, and often came late, usually distracted by whatever physics theorem he was working out in his head. Hadassah, the baby of the family, looked like a California surfer girl and wrote for the army newspaper as her national service. Talia was an artist. The table was always set for at least six, and every meal was a celebration, a feast. There were always at least three different types of kugel on the table and usually a roast chicken.

From the first night I shared a meal with them, they were rife with questions for me.

"So do you mind talking about your family?" Lior's aunt asked. "I mean, I don't want to bother you if you don't want to talk about it."

Barbara was blond like her children and had held up nicely for her age.

"No, I'm more than happy," I said. "What would you like to know?"

"So . . . how do you have four mothers?" The eternal question.

This is not a normal number, I know—even for people with lesbian parents it's two too many. I tried to explain. "Well, there was an original three, and then a fourth married in."

"So the three of them were romantically involved?"

"No. It's easier to draw it all out, really."

"No, no, explain it. Go ahead."

"Well, when my mom decided to get pregnant she was together with my godmother, Margery, and Helen was Nyna's best friend. Helen was already fifty-five and had always wanted to have a kid, but, you know, since she was gay . . ."

I gave them time to finish that line of thought in their heads.

"So they all decided to parent together. And then Margery and Nyna broke up when I was like six months old, but continued to raise me together. Then Nyna met my other mom, Kyree, and they got married."

"How?" asked Benji.

"In a synagogue, with a rabbi."

This seemed to delight them.

"And your dad? Who is he?" Hadassah asked. She had left the dinner table and was participating from the couch, where she was flipping through TV channels with the remote.

My relationship with my father is of prime concern to most people who are overly worried with how having gay parents has affected me. Even the most well-meaning of liberals eventually give voice to their anxieties about my relationship to men—specifically to that one big man, *Dad.*

I told Lior's family I was the product of a one-night stand. Nyna had been planning a tour of Europe, and in discussing the trip, the three original ladies decided, why not get pregnant while there? My father, one Elliot Cohen, approached Nyna as she sat on a bench outside the Louvre. They enjoyed each other's company, and feeling out of sorts abroad, they each found the familiarity of another American a comfort. Three days passed. On the third night, enamored, Elliot asked Nyna back to where he was staying. She demurred, saying she was a lesbian, but he insisted, saying that it was no bother to drink red wine with a lesbian.

Prior to meeting Elliot, Nyna had arranged to meet a different man in Paris—an Italian who otherwise might have been my dad. But he stood her up, so, not wanting to let her ovulation go to waste, she was happy enough to bed my witty progenitor. And there I came to be, in the city of romance, on the single night my father conquered Sappho, not realizing the joke was on him.

There's some confusion as to how such an otherwise brilliant man managed to be so obtuse as to not use precaution, but the story goes that when he asked whether she was on birth control, my mother replied she was a lesbian, and he took that as good enough. I tend to think perhaps the wine confused him, or love overwhelmed him, or he thought lesbians were immune to disease and impossible to impregnate. This was all before AIDS, of course, a time when people generally felt more at ease when sleeping around.

This all made Lior's family smile. I felt a little like a circus animal, but they were nice and I'd answered these same questions a thousand times. From a young age I had been a media darling of the gay community—precocious, articulate, and very political. This was just another interview. My "spokesperson" switch—located close to my liver—had been flipped.

"And your dad, you know him? Are you in contact?" asked Talia.

"We have an on-and-off relationship," I said. "My luck is that the guy she slept with was from Berkeley."

My dad found out that I existed when he called my mom two years after they met in Paris. Why he was checking up on a one-night stand two years later, I'm not clear; this is not a common practice among the men I've slept with. But while checking in on my mother, he heard me in the background.

"You have a kid?" he asked.

She confirmed that, yes, she had a daughter.

"How old is she?" he asked—and when she answered, he said, "Are you still a lesbian?" When he found out that she was, he suggested we all have dinner.

Nyna was nervous about this—Elliot was a divorce lawyer and lesbians were not well protected under the law. He could easily have sued for custody and won, even in liberal California. Children have been given to convicted murderers as opposed to their gay parent. So seeing him was a risk. And she wasn't looking for him to have a financial or parental role in my life. Why should she dare him to action by flaunting me in front of him?

For some reason, we met up anyway. Elliot remembers that everyone waited endlessly while I decided which coat I wanted to wear.

"Why doesn't someone just put a coat on her so we can go?" he asked.

But no one did. At the restaurant Nyna let me hide under the table, and he didn't approve of that either. She told him that she wasn't worried about my not using utensils.

"If she can't use a knife and fork by the time she goes to college, we'll talk."

Things went well enough though that a three-layer cake was produced once Mom admitted that I was Elliot's child, and he became one of the people with whom we shared holidays—the real Jew at our Chanukah parties.

He remained a holiday fixture and occasional visitor until I was six. Nyna and Kyree had been married a year, and we were settling in as a family. His life seemed to be charting a parallel course. He, too, had gotten married, to a woman with a daughter a few years older than me. He would get to parent in a day-to-day fashion, even if the child wasn't biologically his own. And since things seemed to be working out in his newfound role as a father, he now wanted my visits to be without my mom, so he could incorporate me into his new family life. Up until then when he and I had spent time together, Nyna had always been there with us.

Back then, Elliot was pretty much the only male in my life, outside of teachers, and this was the mid-1980s—a time filled with day care scandals, milk carton kids, and warnings of "stranger danger." I had been well briefed on the fact that there were men out there—with vans, usually, but not necessarily—who would try to steal me away. They might offer me kittens or candy. I was not to accept either; this was made very clear. Secrets were not to be trusted. If someone told you not to tell, it usually meant something bad was going on.

In light of this, my father—who was not quite a stranger, but who I still didn't know very well—began to strike me as suspicious. Why did I have to go alone? Why didn't he want my mom there too? Anything he wanted to say to me, she should be able to hear also, right? I just wasn't ready to hang out solo with him. Nyna, of course, said that she respected my feelings and felt bound to honor them. He said that it was his way or not at all.

I offered a much briefer version of all this for Lior's assembled family. Even after my long-winded response, they still had a lot of questions. As I answered, they all nodded and clucked approvingly. They were a great crowd.

We had *parve babka,* a kosher cake, for dessert, and then coffee, and when we left they all hugged me with greater force than before.

——————

When Lior and I visited the army base that same week to meet his fellow soldiers, they had their own set of questions.

"Nu, so have you ever been with a woman?" asked a kid with an M16 dangling at his side.

"Sure, I gave it a try, but I like the dick, what can I say?"

After translation, raucous laughter greeted me.

Between the Israeli straightforwardness and the level of maturity in the army, I felt like I fit in with his unit. They seemed to appreciate that I was a guy's girl who could joke about smoking and premarital sex. In my summer dress, surrounded by all that army green, I felt a little like the USO. Showing up, looking pretty, brightening their day. Eventually, I would come to know some of them well, but on that first visit it was all surface.

——————

Upon first sight of the whole army base business, the word "strapping" came to mind. So strange to finally see Lior within the context he inhabited most often, to meet the men with whom he spent his time, each wearing the uniform that made them all but indistinguishable to my untrained eye. About half wore *kippot* and were identifiably religious. Slowly, names I'd read in letters and had heard mentioned over the phone became attached to actual faces.

I met Menachem, the religious Bolivian who drove the rest of the guys crazy; Yossi, a hulking and hairy Bulgarian with a Portuguese girlfriend; Gal, who had sensual features and professors for parents; and Yair, who was slight and played the cello but was tough as nails. Physically, they were a mix—tall and short, light and dark. Yossi had a paunch. None looked like Arnold Schwarzenegger, or really anything like what I'd imagined an elite combat soldier to look like. They came across as nice Jewish boys—outside of the wrestling and homoerotic behavior they constantly engaged in, which didn't lapse for my sake. Despite getting teased about being possibly gay, Amit jumped onto one of the other guys and humped him while shouting in his ear something about his mother conceiving him with a donkey. There was lots of ass grabbing, dick flicking, and nipple tweaking. Their average age was eighteen.

On a picnic table, they set cups of Nescafé and *vaflim*, the waffled wafer cookies that I used to break apart to eat as a child. As the girl Lior had foolishly attached himself to in the States, the other soldiers joked to me, "Why would someone move to Israel to fight in the army and then fall for a girl from his hometown?" But they also said they could tell Lior was in love with me from the moment he got back. My boyfriend blushed and rose to leave the table.

Lior took a minute to talk to his commander, Itamar, off to the side. Itamar was a religious, ginger-haired sprite of a man, a hero to his team. I liked watching them interact. I liked the cool confidence with which Lior handled things. The way he touched his gun reminded me of my body, of how it felt for him to touch me. I knew that he was this version of himself more often than he was the version I saw in bed. It was strange to recognize the man in the soldier and the soldier in the man.

Here are the things I learned about the army that trip: They wrap their dog tags in black electrical tape to kill any possible glint. They arrive at the war zone in rented tourist charter buses. They watch action movies like *Independence Day* on the way there. Does Will Smith know the boys get pumped up with him on their way to fight? What does it mean when pop culture and warfare intertwine?

Toward the end of the week, the army pulled a cruel joke and called Lior back into service. They wanted him to guard a set of armored personal carriers.

"I'm so sorry, baby, you know I wouldn't do this if I didn't have to," he said to me as he was packing to go, already in uniform. "It's been such a beautiful week, and the only place I want to be is next to you, but you know the army. It's like a jealous wife; it doesn't like to share." He stuffed a set of graying socks into his duffel and kissed me on the forehead.

His leaving meant I would be alone for my last night there after having traveled all that way. They needed him at some base near Bethlehem. Those armored personal carriers were taking precedence—the needs of machines being put before those of people. He wouldn't be back in time to see me off. I would need to order a cab to the airport the next morning. The self-pity set in.

"The taxi number is on a *petek* sitting next to the phone. If it gets lost you can always look in the phone book."

When he stared back from the door, I was crying. He hugged me. We exchanged the first of many tearful, army-born good-byes to come. I went to bed without him. And then, like some black-and-white TV Christmas miracle, I woke up to find him by my side, kissing my cheek.

"Hey baby, do you know you look like an angel when you sleep?" He brushed my tangled hair off my face with his hand, "How did you manage to do it? Are you going to get in trouble?" I asked, my voice husky.

He said Menachem was covering for him, and he thought that it'd be okay as long as he got back early on Sunday morning. "Besides," he said, "they can take me to jail—I had to see you."

My heart pounded, telling me that he was THE ONE. The word in Hebrew is *bashert*.

War

Less than two weeks after I left Israel, a bombing at the Park Hotel in Netanya killed thirty people. Termed the "Passover Massacre" in the media, the scene of the disaster was a crowded ballroom dance floor full of people celebrating the holiday, Holocaust survivors among them. It was a bloody month. In "Black March" alone, one hundred Israeli civilians were killed in fifteen terrorist attacks, one occurring about every two days. The Park Hotel bombing wasn't the first, but it was the biggest one yet.

In response, Israel called up twenty thousand reservists for Operation Defensive Shield, known in Hebrew as Homat Magen, the biggest military operation in the West Bank since 1967.

With Lior part of the action, for days I followed the developments in the headlines instead of through the comforting tones of my lover's voice. By that time we'd gotten used to talking on the phone every day, and I was spending almost as much on phone cards as I did on rent. But the war forced us back to writing letters. And in the absence of calls or letters, the newspapers were often my best source of information.

On March 29, 2002, the *New York Times* reported that Israel had invaded Ramallah, then six other cities. For the next month or so, Lior was all over the West Bank, and I would often only know his location based on what was going on in the news. By the time his letters arrived, he was always somewhere else.

The major points of conflict in the ongoing "large-scale coun-terterrorist operation" to which I seemed to have attached my life were Bethlehem, Jenin, Ramallah, and Nablus. I wondered con-stantly which of them he was in at any given moment. It was a little like *Where's Waldo?*—only with war and someone I was in love with.

I began to develop an order of preference between the four places. When I found out he'd been in Ramallah, it was not much of a comfort. But even Ramallah seemed great when I compared it to the next stop, Nablus—called Shechem in Hebrew. What did it say about the place that they couldn't even agree on a name?

Baby. Writing this on my third? night in Shechem. It's being written on occupied paper and an appropriated pen. I'm not sure exactly what building this is but it's huge. It's like the center for the city. Electricity, telephones, who knows what else, are all controlled from here. It's empty, except for about eighty soldiers, who are camped out here for the evening. We're hearing some automatic gunfire. Most of the fire is a comfort, as it is ours. Occasionally we hear the distinctive pak-pak of AK-47 Kalashnikovs (AK-47s) that are the Palestinian weapon of choice.

Baby, by now everyone has asked me what I am doing here writing to you. Someone even said something about me writing to "Mrs. Gold." I thought about explaining about how you're keeping your name but then thought better of trying to explain that to a chauvinist Israeli. The last sentence out of his mouth was "Dear Kellen, I would like to suck your pussy but I'm stuck in Shechem." I swear he can't say five sentences without saying something dirty or offensive. Not that the sentiment he conveyed wasn't true. He told me to put a naked picture of you on the inside of my helmet so I can always look at you whenever I want. Not a bad idea. Just reread this letter and it is so disorganized. I guess that kind of reflects my state of mind. Quick, hurried, jumping from one thing to the next.

My life, it turned out, was no less jumbled than his. Interesting note on the moral structure of this relationship: it had put the fear of God into me. In general, my vision of God had always been one of an all-loving Earth-birther, but these days I was trying to hedge my bets. What if God was a little more like the Old Testament version? That thought had made me become a tad superstitious. Why not avoid stepping on the cracks in sidewalks? It couldn't hurt to be extra careful.

After a day of advocating peace and getting nowhere, I stepped out to a hookah bar in the East Village with some other kids from Hillel. My nerves were shot from waiting for the mail each day, watching the twenty-four hour news cycle and checking my phone every five minutes to make sure I hadn't missed a call from Lior. I hadn't heard from him in three days.

The ambience of the place wasn't helping matters. The hookah bar was full of Arabs, but all the Hillel kids were oblivious, talking loudly about what had happened in Jenin. That day seven soldiers had been killed there. But there were also reports of an Israeli massacre. My companions were refuting this as a possibility. I wished they would stop talking, mostly so I didn't have to think about any of it.

People kept buying me drinks, and between the frustration associated with my campus evangelism and my anxiety over Lior's whereabouts, I had a powerful urge to get wasted. Having a boyfriend at war had turned out to be a great excuse for drinking. Folks tended to be very sympathetic no matter how loused I was.

War

After four more drinks, the lighting in the bar began to seem a little too strong to all of us, so—ignoring the pleasant spring weather and the promise of breathable air outside—we switched to a skeezy college bar with a packed back room. There, drink in hand, I headed to the dance floor with a tall, dark, and handsome fellow I worked with.

"I can dance with you, right?" I slurred. "You know my man's got a machine gun, so you won't try anything."

"You're safe with me," he promised. "I'll even protect you from all the other assholes."

The crowd at the bar was all kids; looking at them, you'd never know the legal drinking age in New York was twenty-one. I listened to 50 Cent rapping about partying like it was someone's birthday. Heads bobbed in and out of sync with the music. Got to love white people dancing.

A few more songs passed, and then the crowd on the dance floor pushed us close and jostled a sip from my drink onto my shirt.

"Oops, can't hold my liquor. Rather literally, huh?" I dabbed my chest with a napkin.

Tilting my head down sloshed my brain around in my skull in a way that changed the weather; from beneath my lashes, I started making eyes at my companion. Those drinks had finally made their appearance in my bloodstream. The bass in the music, the alcohol and my loneliness had triggered a familiar warmness between my thighs. The anonymity of the city beckoned once again.

If I kissed someone, would God take it out on Lior? If I gave in to what I wanted in the moment, would it, like butterfly wings in the chaos theory, create some effect across the sea? I wanted to kiss the real live, touchable, tangible man in front of me. I wanted to taste the alcohol on his breath.

"Maybe you should kiss me?" I suggested. It would be so easy. Lior would never have to know.

75

"I think your boyfriend would rather I just make sure you get safely home," my coworker said. "You're stressed out and drunk."

The moment he said it, I realized what I had so narrowly avoided—the irreversible act of betraying Lior's trust.

Fucking good guys always ruining my good time, I thought, and then I started to cry.

At home I got down on my knees by my bed, like they do in the movies, and made a deal with my God and all the other options: if they would just protect Lior, I would stop being such a slut.

The next morning I woke up with a pounding headache and a guilty conscience. Without much hesitation, I decided I would never tell Lior how close I came to cheating on him. What good would it do him to know?

This is another part of being with a soldier. You're supposed to be the Penelope to his Odysseus—ever faithful, ever patiently waiting, chaste. While the warrior is away, he needs to be unfettered by concerns of his mate's virtue. *I may not be cut out for this*, I realized. I'd never felt that sort of moral pressure before. I didn't come from monogamous stock. My maternal grandmother married five times.

What about Lior? Was he tempted? When he went drinking on the weekends, home between missions, did he sit with these questions? Did he feel like his actions would affect me, the way I worried mine might affect him?

His letter arrived that day.

They just started shooting not very far away. That's the thing—it can be quiet as fuck for a few hours and then shooting like mad in a matter of seconds. Never allows a moment of relaxation. Even when sleeping you never know when you're gonna get woken up and told "go, we gotta take a new house," and then the heart starts pumping quickly again and the nerves tingle throughout the body. I guess that's part of what makes war so tiring. Even if we are getting some sleep, it is never good relaxed sleep. I want to crawl into your arms, have your body to protect me. I feel so safe with you, nothing can hurt me. I know this is supposed to be my (male) role, protector, but I feel like we protect each other. I am so excited for our life together.

I imagine us in some little apartment. How are we going to decorate it? I want to play with lambs with you, see our children play with them. Am I going to be a terribly overprotective parent? I'm so protective of you. I just couldn't handle it if something ever happened to you. I begin to understand how it can make you feel, powerless to prevent harm to me. I've been on so many operations by now that fear hardly registers anymore. So much depends on luck. There's only so far professionalism and being a good soldier can take you and I have so much to live for.

Whenever I didn't answer the phone, Lior worried. I told him how silly it was that he, in the field, should worry about my safety, but he said knowing about the dark side makes you worry more, not less.

We just had to make it through this whole war thing without him dying or me ruining everything. Praying became part of my routine.

April

In his absence I developed relationships with his family, independently. When his mother visited New York on April 3, we met up in Union Square. It was a sunny, warm spring day, and the place was awash in people. I strained to remember what she looked like from long-faded high school memories. When she approached me from within the milling crowd, both our faces showed relief at having successfully recognized one another.

"Deborah?" I hesitantly asked.

"You must be Kellen," she happily answered.

She had a steel-colored halo of hair and the sweet dumpling body of a prototypical Jewish mom.

"Now we can at least be anxious together," she said as she drew me close for a hug. This put me a little more at ease.

I had asked Lior to brief me on how to behave with his mother the last time I'd had him on the phone, but he hadn't been particularly helpful. I think he might have felt nervous as well.

"Just be yourself," he told me, but like he wasn't sure that was actually the best idea.

Ultimately, Deborah and I had to rely on our desire to get along and the social skills God gave us. Mostly we talked about worrying, how we were mutually perfecting the form. We exchanged the facts we had at our disposal—the details Lior had gifted us over the phone and in letters. It was strange to realize that I knew things she didn't about his condition and whereabouts, or that Lior talked more candidly with me about his feelings and fears than he did with her. His mom felt really ambivalent about his having joined the army, and I wondered if it had made him present his experiences differently to her, if it made him want to show her less ambiguity than he showed me.

"I told him over and over that it wasn't a good idea. I love Israel, but this is my son we're talking about. I will kill them if anything happens to him." Her face showed me she meant it.

One by one, as Lior's relatives visited New York, I met them. I went out to dinner at Ruby Foo's with his Aunt Karen and Uncle Steve, in from North Carolina and San Louis Obispo. Over eggrolls and fried rice, I marveled that we had this instant relationship. It was not one person I'd become attached to, but a string of them. It was a whole community that was revolving around someone terribly far away. Steve told me to trust Lior's sense of safety, and I finally understood what my mama Nyna meant by, "I do trust you, it's the rest of the world I don't trust"—an oft-repeated phrase in my house while I was learning to drive. I did trust Lior. But what about everyone else?

Spring semester of that year, all my classes seemed to relate somehow to my romantic preoccupation. We were reading Frantz Fanon in my postcolonial theater class—in fact, in a case of interdisciplinary overlap, I'd been assigned his seminal text, *Black Skin, White Masks*, in two classes, and excerpts of *The Wretched of the Earth* in a third.

Fanon explicated for me something I had already instinctually known—that people define themselves in relation to an Other, a "that which is not me," and that we endow that difference with all that we can't stand to accept about ourselves. We load it onto "The Other" so that it can't possibly be ours to carry. Only the more we say, "I am different; I am better than you," the more entangled we become, until disgust and desire are intertwined. Fanon talked about black men and white women, and I thought about the Jew and the Arab, my uniform fetish and my boyfriend.

When I was growing up, soldiers were presented as, at best, a necessary evil. Toy guns were banned from my house. Male aggression on the whole was held suspect. We didn't watch sports; we supported women's shelters and took self-defense courses. The uniform that swathed my boyfriend was a symbol of many things I disagreed with, and yet if I was honest, it also made me totally hot.

How did all this apply to what was going on? What did it mean about Lior's relationship to me as a woman? What about the colonization of the female body and the desire/disgust complex of slutdom? What exactly were we doing with each other? My brain felt like I'd been sucking down ice-cold Slurpees at warp speed. I developed a sense that I'd forgotten some small but important detail, and no matter how many to-do lists I made, I couldn't remember what it was. It was the feeling of overload.

When Israel occupied Hebron the first week of April 2002, I thought back to my visit to that city in 1999. Pulling up as part of a busload of American kids on a field trip from our dusty kibbutz, we piled into one of Judaism's holiest sites, smothering laughs, slightly annoyed that we had to defer half-finished conversations until we re-boarded our chartered vehicle post-tour. We paid no real attention to our surroundings—physical locations worth killing and dying to preserve, places that housed the graves of our ancestors. Our tour guide castigated us for not being properly reverent, but it didn't make a difference. We were eighteen. I remembered wandering off from the group to buy cigarettes at a Palestinian corner store identical to the Arab-owned corner stores in San Francisco. The shelves carried similar products but with different names. Children ran in to buy candy while I was paying at the counter.

How was either side any different from the other? The same man who blew himself up at our favorite brunch spot was probably eating hummus and joking with friends earlier that day. His mother maybe chided him about cutting his hair, being careful, not getting too involved. She knew that it was dangerous, but then again, so did I, and like her, I sent my own man off with kisses nonetheless. Now they were both humans making choices that might end their lives.

When Lior called and told me he'd been pulled out of the navigations he'd been temporarily returned to and was being sent to the territories, it felt like old news. He couldn't tell me where he was headed, but he did say he'd been there before. I made a list of possibilities and tried to rate them as my roommate, Cody, made me dinner.

"How's that list going, sister?"

"Please tell me, Cody, that I have at least convinced you to be a Zionist, that at least one person has been convinced by all my rhetoric."

"Sure, you can call me a Zionist," she said, "I'm all for the IRA, but I'll side with the Jews on this one."

She put down her Gaelic homework, scooped up one of her two pet white rats off the floor—either Mary Kate or Ashley (I couldn't tell them apart)—and strolled into the kitchen to check on the Tasty Bite Indian food in a pouch that we were boiling.

"Hey, do you think you could do the dishes?" she called from the other room. "I have to head out to the dungeon in a minute."

From where I was sitting at the table, ignoring the essay on community organizing I was supposed to be writing, I responded, "Who'd have thunk it—me all settled down and you doing all this kinky stuff as a Dom after having slept with what, all of three people?"

She came back into the living room still wearing her day clothes—a dress layered over jeans.

"I have such a hard time imagining you being dominant. What does that look like?"

She gave me an impression. "Well, I have to wear these really high heels, and I can't really walk in them so I sort of toddle around." She raised herself onto the balls of her feet as though she was wearing high heels. She looked a little bit like a T. Rex, her arms propped up in front of her and her body tilted slightly forward. Her lank blond hair crowded her face. She whipped her head around. "And then I dare them to look at me!"

I burst out laughing.

"Last week I had to peg some leaky old Asian dude, which was disgusting, but yesterday I just had to smoke cigarettes while some guy rubbed my feet. Then I had him write me a poem about being a sissy maid." She returned to the kitchen, sans rat this time.

"It's really too bad the one rule my mom has for me is no sex work, because that sounds great," I said. "But do you think it's warping your view of sexuality?"

"Well, I will never look at a Hasid the same way again." She brought two plates out, mine with my food the way I liked it—nothing touching—and hers mixed into a multicolored mush. "I saw one in Victoria's Secret and I just knew he was there buying something for his mistress."

We ate at our one rickety table, unfinished homework lying on top of an ashtray as company. A passing car played strains of 50 Cent's "Wanksta."

"If I could be assured it would only be Hasidic dudes as clients, I would break the no sex work rule and come join you."

"You say that, but you've never heard them babble in Yiddish while their balls are in a vise." Giving up on dinner, Cody rose, grabbed a bag full of shiny clothing, and slipped her headphones into her ears. I could hear Elvis Costello's "Everyday I Write the Book," which she had, for days, been listening to on repeat.

"Love you Cody—have a great night at work," I shouted.

"I'll call you if it's slow and we can make top ten lists over the phone," she said, bobbing her head. "You can start without me: Reasons We Shouldn't Have Built the Interstate. Go!"

In an NYU class about communal strife, someone brought up the situation in Israel as an example of the ultimate community conflict. I tensed up, ready for a fight. I wanted so badly to talk about it, as it was totally consuming me, but any chance that came up seemed dangerous. I had visions of myself running, sobbing, from the classroom.

The problem (or advantage depending on how you look at it) was my heart had yet to harden. Outside of the occasional small dose of homophobia thrown my way, I had grown up in the deliciously liberal bubble of the Bay Area. The effect of so much love in my childhood appeared to be an intense fascination with pain and why one person would hurt another. I'd been swiping my fingers through flames ever since. Maybe Lior and I shared that. Maybe we both felt like we'd had it too easy. I think we were both children who asked hard questions.

"Mama, how come some people get privileged lives and others get such hard ones?" I'd once asked Nyna.

I imagined little Lior asking, "Mama, why do people go to war?"

In my theater and therapy class, we studied posttraumatic stress disorder (PTSD). People put their traumas up for show. Drama kids love that stuff. Our teacher asked us to bring up difficult experiences, and we shared our secrets on cue. We all claimed to be uncomfortable expressing our emotions; then we spread them out like a Sunday buffet.

I wondered whether Lior would exhibit any signs of PTSD when his service was over, whether that would be the tie that bound him to American veterans serving in Iraq and Afghanistan. Our teacher talked about the phases that occur in therapy: rage at having been hurt, shame at having hurt others, and then, finally, empathy. Over the past four months, I had tried to ensure that Lior kept some empathy with him already. In a class discussion about challenges to treatment, we discussed how a bunch of old men could be convinced to play "make-believe" in drama therapy. I wondered what would happen if a drama therapist came to work with Lior's unit.

Thanks to school, I spent most of my time thinking about what Lior was up to and doing nothing of much consequence. Lior was over there in real life. I quickly grew tired of buzzwords like "ontology" and "performativity" and started to refer to college as the "thought aquarium." While Lior was fighting to gain control of Palestinian civilian territory, block by block, and trying to determine who were combatants and who should be left alone, all around me people were sitting in buildings discussing war as metaphor, politic, dialectic. I couldn't hold on to both realities equally. My academic classes became structured time for me to spend with a notebook, writing to him.

————————

Coaxed into Manhattan on a day I didn't have class to attend a party held in one of NYU's dorms, I spent the hour-long ride there musing about how New York seemed like a city that would be a lot of fun if I lived in Manhattan, made thousands more a month, and didn't have to work all the time. I tried to convince myself that this was what college was about: being broke and going to parties. (Never mind the New York-induced paranoia that no matter how cool any given party is there is probably something way cooler going on somewhere else.)

Lately, my main requirement in a social function was distraction. A steady stock of alcohol helped with this. Upon entering the party, I scanned the room for drinks and located a metal tub that I suspected held ice and beers. On my way to get a drink, I got way-laid by my one friend there.

"Have you met Kellen?" she said with gusto to the stranger accompanying her. I shook the girl's hand and forgot to let go until she gently removed her hand from mine. I looked up; her acne-scarred but well made-up face stared back. She seemed to be wearing head-to-toe J. Crew.

"You theater kids are crazy," the stranger said. She may have been referring to the nascent threesome on a couch to my right. At that point I was so sick of the kids in my program that they would have had to set themselves on fire for me to pay them the slightest bit of attention.

"Give them one beer apiece and they strip to their skivvies, I swear," I said. The room smelled like smoke and cheese.

"What, you don't want to join the orgies?"

We were becoming prudish buddies quickly.

"Naw, I gave Mindy's cervix a going-over during our naked yoga class last week," I half joked.

The stranger's eyebrow shot up like an electrified caterpillar, but she seemed comforted to have found someone else in the room that wasn't sold on group sex.

If only she knew me back when, I thought, but what I said was, "Plus, I have a boyfriend."

"And where is he tonight?" she inquired.

My friend got up to get herself a fresh drink.

The threesome to my right had morphed into a postmodern improvisational dance. Having fallen off the couch, a tangle of limbs stretched into bodies surfing across each other over the hardwood floor.

"We're long distance. He's serving in the Israeli army."

"Wow. That must be so hard for you—what's that like? I mean, you must be so worried all the time." Her face registered real sympathy as she brushed her bangs out of her eyes and leaned forward.

I always felt a sticky-sweet satisfaction when I got this reaction, predictable as it was. I didn't want the attention and pity—no, I *did* want the attention and pity. Who the hell was I kidding?

"What does he do there?" she asked, twirling a straw in her drink.

"He's a combat soldier."

I heard in my serious tone the smallest hint of pride. She had no idea what it meant to be a combat soldier. Neither did I, really, but I'd come closer than she had. I'd touched his warrior body. I had come to know things from his scrapes and bruises. Or so I told myself.

"So does he, like, kill people?"

"I very much hope he doesn't have to," I said, solemn.

"Well, of course."

I excused myself to the bar, where I escaped another "Oh my god, your boyfriend's in the Israeli army, that's so scary" conversation with a stranger.

As much as I wanted to talk about him, there were also times I'd rather have skipped it. The director of my most recent play had started to give me notes framed within the context of Israeli society and the current conflict. She'd even gone so far as to say *bev-akasha*(please) in Hebrew. If I was supposed to be tough in a scene, she'd suggest pretending I was a soldier at a checkpoint. I didn't know what, exactly, to make of her behavior. Or mine, really, either.

There were times when I was made speechless by the sound of Lior's voice as it flowed through the telephone, after I'd picked up on the first ring. Once, I was chewing bread and spat it out half eaten so I could try to speak.

"Baby?"

The bread ball was wet in my hand.

"Hey there," he said softly. Maybe he was trying not to wake anyone else up. "It's so good to hear your voice."

In these moments, my heart swelled and made me aware of its location. When we spoke, he covered up the scary goings-on of his day-to-day life with anecdotes, poured honey-like over the line. We shared details with each other that we had saved like leftovers, started sentences at the same time, cursed the poor reception. Hung up. I conjured his breathless invectives at the phone company in the pale of my room.

———

As school headed toward the long-awaited destination that was summer, I was ready for it to be done. My nerves were shot, and by that point the only thing that soothed them—outside of Lior's voice—was walking through the Jews. More and more often I skipped the transfer to the G train from the L and elected to walk through the Satmar ultra-Orthodox neighborhood that existed between the boutiques and coffee shops of the hipsters and where my apartment lay.

If I walked all the way down Bedford Avenue, past where gentrification blended into the barrio with its Puerto Rican flag–painted apartment buildings and cafés that served black beans and plantains, and then past the freeways that ran raised above the street, I came to where the Jews scurried by on their way to and from synagogue. They were very insular, and I knew they were anti-Zionists, but I loved them anyway, even after one gray-bearded scholar propositioned me for sex.

Sometimes just the sight of a mother with a scarf over her *sheitel* would bring me to tears—even though, as an outsider, I was only good for use as a Shabbas goy in their minds. When I said I was willing to turn off the lights but that I was Jewish, I got pushed right back out the door. They didn't want to encourage another Jew to break the Sabbath.

Walking home down the streets of brownstones took an hour longer than the subway but reminded me of Jerusalem and Lior. The residents there wore the exact same black wardrobe as my grandparents' ultra-Orthodox neighbors. No one spoke to me, even on the occasions I had tears running down my cheeks. The invisibility made it a perfect place to have my feelings.

Everyone would look away from me when I'd take a seat on the stoop of a brownstone. Hunchbacked old men would walk by, twirling their *peyes* as they shuffled along their way. It could just as easily have been 1920 in Kiev; the rosy cheeks of their young children belied no modern reference point. It was like a Jewish renaissance fair there, and a great comfort in my time of need.

I likewise stalked Israelis all over Manhattan—the guys selling sunglasses on West Fourth Street and girls waiting tables at midtown cafés. Men, who claimed to have served in the very same unit as Lior, let me babble away as they unselfconsciously put the moves on me. "How do you speak Hebrew?" they'd say, and then I would tell them my situation and they would give me the sympathy I craved.

When I wasn't being creepy around Jews of various stripes, I knew I needed to do the things that were the backbone of my life in New York, but all of it seemed blurry, to the point of barely existing. It surprised me when surfaces didn't yield, when I found that I couldn't glide right through them. I sleepwalked through my classes and social engagements.

It didn't help that it had been a rainy spring. Everything was misty, but even rain couldn't make New York City seem clean. The puddles collected cigarette butts and the streets flooded with muddy streams, litter carried in the current. I slogged through my days.

My feelings for him seemed more real than the world around me.

10

Juliet in Jerusalem

Lior and I decided I'd come to Israel for the summer of 2002, despite all the violence. My friend Jenny's parents forbade her to come with me. My youth movement had also canceled their yearly six-week trip. I seemed to be the only one stupid enough to go.

The spate of shootings and bombings in downtown Jerusalem didn't faze me; neither did spending thousands of dollars and making my family, little brother included, worried sick. I was steadfast, resolute, impervious.

Throughout the seventeen-hour flight to Israel, I imagined all the time I would get to spend with him and went over the quickly devised rules my parents' had given me about where I was allowed to go in Israel and how I might get there.

Though I had shaved my legs before boarding, by the time we landed there was stubble. My attempts to refresh myself were limited to what one might accomplish in an airplane bathroom.

When security finished questioning me, I searched the airport for Lior, my hair already messy from having shoved my way past people in an attempt to reach him quicker. Then there he was. The buzz cut, the soft-framed eyes that scanned the passengers looking for me, eyes that matched his uniform as they took me in.

"Hey there, beautiful."

The drive home was thick with our physical need for one another. I couldn't wait to tug on his chest hair, breathe in his scent, and taste the salt of his dried sweat.

In his apartment, the fans worked their heavy rotations over where we were tangled in the sheets.

"I can't wait to wake up next to you semiregularly," I murmured, as if the word "semiregularly" could possibly be romantic. "Have I told you lately that you are perfect?"

He shook his head to say both, "No, you haven't" and "Come on, now."

"I don't need anything but you to entertain me," I insisted.

He nodded and ran his hand over my hair. "I agree," he said. "I think we could have fun in a cardboard box."

We fucked until our parts were too sore to continue. And there were no bombings on my first night there this time. *Thank God for the little things,* I thought. It was fun to seduce him, to convince his tired body it was worth the effort. His desire transformed my self-esteem. If I never left this bed again, it would be all right.

Only upon the third day's arrival did I realize, with a shock, what the drill was going to be: He would leave me for five days a week. I'd wait for him to come home on the weekends. And on some weekends, he didn't even do that.

Our routine for his departure also took getting used to. The new Jerusalem bus station was bright and shiny, with metal detectors at each door. Every Sunday morning, a rush of soldiers flowed through those doors to go back to the army, Lior among them. After a kiss good-bye, he'd join the churning sea of army green, hundreds of young people pushing onto the buses. I'd turn away and board a cab instead of a bus of my own.

I was "allowed" to take buses that went from city to city but was told by Lior's family to avoid the ones that operated within Jerusalem itself, because they were the ones more frequently blown up. I bent the rules one day midweek and took a bus to the mall—a bustling place that was itself replete with metal detectors at the entrances. The next morning that same bus line was blown up at 8:00 a.m., full of schoolchildren.

You never get used to something like that.

———

There is a particular aloneness that one feels upon moving to a new city. I was not used to living by myself, having been raised with constant companionship: four mothers providing for my every need. But each time Lior went back to the army, it was just me and his things.

How strange it was to prepare to go to sleep in his bed, and to then wake twisted in his sheets, without him beside me. Daily, listening to the hollow click of my tongue on the top of my teeth, as I tasted my morning breath, I had to overcome my desire to languish in the heat and stare at the trees outside. These lazy days were punctuated by the sounds of cats fighting outside, as they poured through the garbage like rats do in New York City, I touched Lior's clothes in the closet. Smelled him on them. His laundry soap. His scent.

The small space seemed vast and quiet. I roamed the apartment looking for distractions, making lists of tasks I needed to get done. Get up, make breakfast, maybe if I was lucky there would be some missing ingredient and I'd have an excuse to walk to the *shuk*, where I might buy hummus, peppers, pita, olives, cheese, or chocolate *rugelach* as a treat, and see people in the outside world.

On the street, people were routinely going about their lives, whereas I, surrounded by all the foreign languages and exotic smells, felt like I'd been dropped into someone else's life entirely. I would listen in on strangers' conversations in Hebrew and, based on facial gestures, imagine what was being discussed: *You wouldn't believe what she said to me . . .*

Being there without Lior made me feel very grown up; after all, I was turning twenty-one that summer, across the world from everything I knew. A kept woman in a Jerusalem apartment, I didn't have to work. I could stroll through the streets of the world's holiest of cities at will. In my lonelier moments, this freedom would fill me with a pride that, to some measure, made up for the hardship I'd undertaken for the summer. (Let's be honest. It wasn't that hard. What did I know of suffering?)Nonetheless, at least weekly I called someone I knew well to chat, check-in, have a chance to say how much I really cared.

"I'm in Jerusalem, but I really miss you!"

Cody, thousands of miles away, snorted at my affection.

"How's the weather in New York these days? What are people wearing?" I inquired.

"It's fine. You've been gone all of three weeks, for Christ's sake. Everyone is wearing the same things," Cody said.

"Well, here it's super hot, but Jerusalem is just not a town where you can rock booty shorts, if you know what I mean."

She couldn't have known what a lifeline that was to me, discussing the mundane with someone who knew me.

Late on Friday nights, I felt like Sleeping Beauty, waiting for Lior's touch to awaken me. After the slip of the lock on the front door, the light would turn on, and my eyes would pry open slightly to see him drop his heavy pack and gun to the floor. Roused from my half-dream state, I'd watch as he checked the gun and stored the ammo separately, then came to the bedside to begin his undressing routine, the first button of his green pants already undone. By the time he was naked, I was fully awake.

"Hey there," I'd whisper. "Welcome back."

In the morning, when the sun spread through the curtains, we'd lie in bed intertwined or read the paper with my head tucked against his chest and his arm around me. We'd sleep in late and only leave the house to visit with family or go to movies at the mall.

It was heaven.

More than once, I waited all week for Lior only to be told that he was not coming home, that it would be another seven days. It felt like being thirsty and having water offered and then rescinded. The situation made me very selfish. When the bombing of a bus in Megiddo, the biblically determined inception point for the apocalypse, killed seventeen people on June 5, my first thought was *What? Now he'll be sent to fight in the territories instead of coming home for the weekend. How unfair!* Compassion for the dead and their families seeped in bashfully only after.

One Saturday afternoon, without Lior home, I wandered the verboten downtown, unable to resist a taste of the forbidden (after a rash of recent shootings, the official word was that it was unadvisable to go without armed guard). I've never been great at following rules. The sidewalks edging the sand-colored stone buildings were largely empty. When Lior was home on the weekends and we went out together, he wore his gun even when he went out without his uniform. Alone, I had no such protection.

Across the street from me, a man was walking in the opposite direction, clearly in town visiting from the *shtachim, the occupied territories.* He had the knit *kippa* and ragged *peyes* of a settler. A modern cowboy on Jerusalem's lonely streets, he had his M16 slung against his back, two handguns at his side, and a knife strapped to his boot. He seemed a more apocalyptic sign than any I'd seen. I wasn't sure if I should feel safer with him around, guns or no guns. He looked like a character from a video game I might have been playing back home with Cody if none of this had ever happened.

***

The weekends the army kept Lior I visited his family, splitting my time between his divorced aunt and uncle's houses as he did, feeling like a foster child in each.

They were nice to me but they were not mine.

"How are things going for you?" Aunt Barbara asked me when I was in her home. "Do you want more broccoli kugel?"

She offered me the kugel dish before I had a chance to answer either question. Often the dinner conversation was all in Hebrew. They'd remind each other to speak in English, and then quickly slip back into their preferred language, occasionally translating certain words, but usually the simple ones I already knew. They'd say what was, to me, a string of nonsense and then translate, "You know *shel,* it means 'of'?"

Meanwhile, on the TV, which they kept playing in the living room as we ate, the news showed the army's progress through some shell-shocked Palestinian town and then split to a commercial in Hebrew with a catchy jingle.

One day, Lior's cousin Hadassah piped up that she'd seen me on the street and recognized me by the way I walked. "You had such a spring in your step," she said. "You were clearly not from here."

Despite my sense of melancholy, I stuck out like a bouncy sore thumb in tense Jerusalem. I smiled too much, laughed too loud for the bleak atmosphere the city was coated with that summer.

***

After the meals at the uncle's house we "benched," which means we said the Birkat Hamazon, the postmeal prayer, which I only vaguely knew the words to since it's said in Conservative and Orthodox homes but not in Reform households like mine.

I mumbled the words under my breath, catching the tail ends of most of them, self-conscious about my technical non-Jewishness. It was different in Israel. Back in California, I was the most Jewish person most of my friends knew. Here, I didn't rank in the top one million, if I ranked at all. I knew Lior wanted me to convert officially. See, although I do have a Jewish mother, Kyree, she is not the one who bore me. My biological mom is Nyna, the blond Southerner, and even though Nyna is the one always dragging us to synagogue, here that gets me nowhere. Also useless is the fact that the guy she chose to sleep with was Jewish. Thanks to Jewish law, that's not what counts. As per usual, I'm half in, half out of the box.

I thought back to my bat mitzvah. After having not spoken with my dad for seven years, I decided at thirteen to extend an invitation for him to read an aliyah as part of the ceremony. I figured it made sense since he was the reason Nyna had raised me a Jew. He was even a Cohen, whether or not that status officially trickled down to me. But his experience of Judaism and that of my raucous, celebratory, queer congregation bore little resemblance to one another. His was the only East Coast Yiddish pronunciation, all *s*'s at the end of words instead of the modern Hebrew *t* sound that strung the rest of the aliyot together. He said "Nasan lanu" instead of "Natan lanu" and "Nosein" instead of "Notein." Up on the bimah, looking more stereotypically Jewish than the rabbi, he looked pasted onto the scene, cut out from some other service.

Pre–and post–bat mitzvah, I had attended Sunday school and then after-school Torah study and my Zionist summer camp, and now I was working for Hillel, all the time knowing I didn't fully count—although, thanks to the varied branches of Judaism, it did depend on whom you asked. I'd be welcome to move to Israel, under the law of return, since they base that on the Holocaust-era

Nuremberg qualifications, which I fit under thanks to my biological dad. But I still wouldn't be considered legally Jewish if I lived there, since that's decided by the religious establishment.

In my conversations with Lior's family, we commiserated over the unfortunate power the ultra-Orthodox wield in Israeli government. Lior's uncle was a Conservative rabbi, and in Israel this is less respected than it is in the States.

In the United States there is a rainbow of types of Jews: Orthodox, Conservative, Reform, Renewal, Reconstructionist. In Israel, it's more black and white. You are either Orthodox or not. If not, perhaps you were raised religiously, and so then you are at least traditional, but that's still seen as a downgrade rather than a legitimate choice. Conservative Judaism in America is pretty religious. In Israel it's considered a poor excuse. So Lior's family got my situation's absurdity, but then again they didn't—not really.

"So why didn't your mother just convert?" they asked me when somehow we became entangled in another discussion of my religious status.

I shrugged and said that my biological mother, Nyna, while Jewish enough in practice, refused to convert on the basis of not wanting to give up her other Gods. How crazy must I have sounded when I explained that? I didn't mention Lior's recent concession to my multifaceted spirituality: he'd started carrying around a piece of jet, a feather-light black stone that my mom's witchy friend had blessed for him, even though he insisted the religious guys in his unit would flip if they knew he was smuggling pagan amulets.

July

In late June, I decided to get an internship to pass the time. Through the lady who ran my program when I came to Israel the year after high school, I got in at the Jerusalem Rape Crisis Center. Mama Nyna laughed at the news—"Like your summer wasn't gonna be depressing enough." Still, I looked forward to the nice long walk from Lior's apartment to the nondescript building whose address was only revealed to me once I got the job. I enjoyed studying the straw-colored Jerusalem stone of the sidewalks, the multihued throngs of people waiting for buses I wasn't allowed to take, my reflection in the shop windows with signs I could barely read.

Since I wasn't fluent in Hebrew, I couldn't actually talk to rape victims, so I was tasked with fundraising and compiling a report on sexual assault of people with intellectual disabilities. I informally referred to it as the Retard Rape Report, because rude or not it was an exact translation from the Hebrew. Israelis have only one word for the developmentally disabled, *mefager*, and it is used interchangeably as a school-yard slur and a technical term. It took me awhile to get used to this idea.

Thus began the season of the best (read: horrific) phone calls

Lior and I ever had, during which I would recite facts like, "You know who rapes the intellectually disabled most often? The people who transport them. You gotta keep your eye on the bus drivers."

To which Lior might reply, "Jesus . . .well, um, Jenin is different this time. Whole blocks of buildings are gone. We're searching the same houses as last time though. In one house I saw a portrait on the wall of a martyred son, a freedom fighter sent to heaven, and as we talked to the grieving mother, I recognized the son as someone we killed the last time around."

My jaw would drop at statements like this, and I'd be glad he couldn't hear it over the phone. Lior had been in combat for three months by then. There seemed to be no end to the violence. I didn't know what to say about what he was going through, so I tried to keep it light. And usually failed.

One day, as we were talking on the phone, my eye caught on a title of a book sitting close to me on one of the piles: *Honor Killings in the Occupied Territories.* I had skimmed its first few chapters.

"I've also been reading a bunch about honor killings," I said. "Did you know that literally thousands of women are killed by their family members for things like leaving their abusive husbands and having unknown numbers in their phones? And I take it so for granted that I can sleep with however many people I want . . ."

"Hey there, not while you're with me you can't," he said.

We both chuckled.

Black humor was our only defense against the onslaught of tragedy around us.

My days at the rape crisis center reminded me of my first work experience. Some people get a paper route. Not me. When I was ten or eleven, Margery (#3) offered to let me help around the congressman's office where she worked in exchange for spending money. She was always happy to hand me some cash, but she was especially gleeful about doing so if I was willing to earn it.

July

A cardboard box full of files was put in front of me with instructions not to read them, just to sort them alphabetically. No sooner had the adult stepped out of the room than I opened a file in my lap and read away. I had been tasked with organizing the asylum seeker cases, and so my days were filled with cramming my brain full of horrifying atrocities—Tibetan nuns raped with cattle prods by Chinese prison guards and such. I didn't dare tell anyone what I had read for fear that they would take the task away and I would be prevented from further immersing myself in the gore. If I had been in any way naïve to the evil of the world before then, this internship did the trick. No surprise that I became a declared human rights advocate on the spot. As a middle schooler.

It felt even more crucial in Israel—being a human rights advocate, that is. I felt like I finally had a right/obligation to weigh in on political matters since I was there experiencing the consequences. My arguments with Lior suddenly involved more real-life dilemmas. I wanted to go protest in the territories. He forbade it, and reminded me that I had promised my moms I wouldn't travel there.

"I wouldn't have to worry about dying in the army then," he said, "because your family would kill me."

We compromised on a Rabbis for Human Rights–led trip to East Jerusalem to take testimonies around house demolitions. Joining me were the requisite rabbi and an old English couple, whom I found funny and naive. The husband spoke very little Arabic, badly, and made a big deal out of using it. "*Shookran, shookran*"— (Thank you, thank you)—he endlessly repeated, first to the driver, and then to the man who led us into a two-story concrete house.

As we shuffled through the front door I was overwhelmed by the decor. Fake flowers offset plastic trees; the living room was fulgent with gaudy nylon and frilly lace tablecloths pinned down with filigreed tea sets. The walls were hung with gold-sequined calligraphy on black velvet; tiny blinking bulbs festooned every available space, as though the sheer clutter improved the ambience. *My mothers would like it here*, I thought.

We sat on brocade-covered couches among the kitsch and listened with a delay as the Arabic being spoken was translated to us. Through a local activist who'd volunteered to help, it was explained that the Israeli government makes it pretty much impossible to get a permit to build if you are Palestinian. So people build without permits, and then the government orders their houses demolished.

The home we were in had a demolition order on it. The government could decide to knock it down with very little notice. The owner explained that he had saved up for twenty years to build his house. He paid taxes. If they demolished his home, he would have to move back in with his father, where nine people lived in two rooms. He looked at us plaintively, as though we held the power to fix the problem in our hands, and dabbed tissue at his watery eyes. The tissue box was sequined. I was unsure what our note taking was accomplishing, but I was glad to have something to do on his behalf.

On the way out, the Englishman said "*shookran*" a bunch more times. I went home angry yet didn't feel I could bring it up to Lior. But that made me upset, too, so I decided I had to try.

"Baby, I think the Israeli housing policy is a racist piece of shit," I exclaimed that weekend, when he was casually reading the paper.

"Me too," he said.

I was pleasantly surprised to find out that he agreed with me, and for a second it all felt more doable. I had a momentary fantasy where the government handed control over to me and Lior and we hashed out the Israeli side.

12

August

I've always felt more at home surrounded by community. My mom(#1) believes in strength in numbers and passed that along to me. I figure that's one of the reasons why I have four mothers. She always tells me whenever I move somewhere new to find the gays and Jews, as though I can just walk into any synagogue or gay bar in the world and be instantly accepted. Yet there I was, thousands of miles away in the Holy Land, playing army wife—and that's what I was trying to do.

In my copious free time I attempted to explore Jerusalem's tiny gay scene, stalking the familiarity of the San Francisco Bay Area at Lulu's, the city's only gay bar. Lior had introduced me to a gay acquaintance, Ben. He took me out on a night when Lior was away at war and I was lonely, a month after my twenty-first birthday.

"I bet some fags will make you feel better," Ben encouraged. As we walked up to Lulu's, there was no sign that it was a gay bar other than the unisex crowd of guys in line outside. In Israel most guys have that Euro/metro look, so their dress code wasn't a giveaway.

"You'll love it here," Ben said.

Inside it was dark and intimate and the DJ was playing mostly

American dance music. Men talked close to be heard above the sound, and they ground against each other on the dance floor. As Boy George inquired as to whether we really wanted to hurt him, I sucked back a cheap vodka drink and scanned the room.

I knew my mother would be happy I'd ended up there.

An Israeli man approached me and Ben. "Eh, don't you know this is a gay bar?" he said.

"Yeah, I like gay bars. My moms are gay," I retorted. Ben put his hand on my shoulder in support, but I didn't need it.

"Really? I have never met someone whose moms are gay, why—that is so cool. Let me buy you a drink." His demeanor had an instant makeover as he hustled me toward the bar.

It was a good time that night, even though Lulu's had balloons scattered all over the floor—debris from a birthday party—and every time one popped it got all tense, like it was gunfire. Jerusalem is not a city known for its good parties, but we tried to make the best of it.

Israel, in terms of geography, is like California but squished: woods at the top, rolling green hills in the middle, and desert at the bottom. When Lior returned to the army one week, I ventured on a road trip down into the Negev desert, back to Mashabei Sadei, the kibbutz I'd lived on for six months when I was eighteen. Only three years prior.

Jerusalem sits in the hilly middle of the country, and so as the bus passed into the desert, everything flattened and expanded. From my view through the wide bus windows, I saw Bedouins herding goats on the side of the road, the tents they lived in visible in the distance. When cities sprang into view, they seemed out of place. More often than not, the bus dropped people off at signs along the road that didn't seem connected to anywhere at all. The desert struck me as unchanged since my last appearance there, which was strange, because *I* felt so different. Looking around, I noticed all the soldiers on the bus with me. Watching the never-ending transport of soldiers everywhere, I was reminded of the magnitude of war-the reality my lover faced every day. We arrived at the bus station in Beersheba just in time to see a bomb detonation crew considering whether to blow up some suspicious bags, a popular Israeli pastime. Everyone had crowded a safe distance away to observe as one guy geared up the explosives. Watching from within the crowd, I could see that they just exploded something near the bags to see if that would set them off. It didn't. A relief—we were still alive.

Afterward, the surge of people into the bus station was intense, a rushing river of bodies. That would have been the time to detonate if the terrorists wanted to do some real damage. I'd begun to see everything with an eye for security flaws.

———

Mashabei Sadei was a nostalgic green oasis in the sand. While I hardly recognized anyone, I was happy to amble over the property like a tourist, taking pictures, high on memories of my time there. *There's where I puked out front of the bomb shelter disco! There is the water tower where Emily lost her virginity!*

The third day in, I tried doing some work in the *pinat chai* (the animal farm—like a petting zoo).

A few of the kibbutz kids came in after me, jabbering away in Hebrew, possibly plotting my destruction. One of them was Dar, the daughter of the family that was assigned to be mine the year I lived there.

When you volunteer on kibbutz, they assign you families that you're supposed to bond with. I have heard stories about people forging lifelong connections, but mine involved a few awkward afternoons at best, a couple of them with me drunk. Still, it was enough of a connection for Dar to recognize me and take advantage. She looked at me from under dark, full lashes.

"Eh, I remember you. You come to my house. I know you. Lemme show you the best part over here," she said in a childish Israeli accent. And with that, my kibbutz "little sister" convinced me to hand over the keys to the animals' enclosures.

Immediately, it became clear it was a bad idea. Children running around touching things and putting their hands into cages—and then the ferrets were having sex, which upset the children, who then tried to detach the ferrets from each other with water and words and a stick. All I could say was, "*Zeh Ahava*, it's love you are witnessing." Amidst the escalating chaos, I thought, *I'd like to bring Lior here to hold the baby bunnies.*

After I hustled the kids outside and left most of the mess for someone else to deal with, I took a walk around the perimeter of the kibbutz, along the sandy track that divided the Eden-like village from the barbed wire fence that enclosed it. Outside, visible through the chain link, were the desert, dunes, and a scattering of spent ammo. The warm, still air wrapped itself around me.

Despite the impromptu sex ed incident, the visit felt like a nice respite from the tension of Jerusalem. Somehow it always felt safer in the desert. Even with the evidence of army exercises nearby, I knew there was not much out there worth bombing; that kind of thing was less tempting without the huge crowds of people. Out there, they practiced for war elsewhere.

As the end of the summer approached, I began to panic at the thought of leaving Israel. The five days of waiting for Lior every week were somehow all made worthwhile at the moment I heard his key turn in the lock. It was a better ratio than the three-months-to-one-week pattern we had been operating on back when I was in New York. I pondered whether I should make aliyah and become a citizen, or at least defer college for a year.

On my daily walk around Jerusalem, I made lists of pros and cons for living there in my head. Things I liked about Israel: the kaleidoscope of culture, men selling shawarma off turning spits, the thousand-year-old walkways. Things I could do without (not counting the conflict, because duh): people not stopping for ambulances in traffic, diapers strewn in nature areas, old ladies who cut you off in line.

By the *shuk*, I watched two old women haggle in Russian over a pile of red and green peppers while a bearded man smoked a cigarette and swept the street. A stray dog made a wide circle around him and crossed my path. This new aliyah plan would not go over well on the home front. It was not really an option. Realizing this, I wanted to dunk my head in the spice bins, suffocate in turmeric. Take a layer of it back in my lungs.

Later in the evening, I passed my boyfriend's sleeping form as my bare feet slid across the floor and out into the Jerusalem midnight. From the porch I saw a city that had been witness to two millennia of lovers—a city whose story is greater than all those people, but made by them still. As an American it is almost inconceivable, the history there. The thoughts made me feel smaller, compressed not only by gravity and space but by time, extending from my body backward and downward from the stone under my feet. The mewling of the stray cats, with whom I shared the inky darkness, punctuated the quiet.

13

Human Failings

Back at NYU, the well-meaning Hillel rabbi assured me that this was the toughest part.

"Goodness," he said, "if you can survive having him at war, why, marriage will be simple."

I knew even then as he said it, still in the throes of long-distance romance, that he was wrong. No marriage I'd seen up close could be considered easy. If his was, that was foreign to me—something I could look in at but not understand.

If anything, it seemed to me like the success of our relationship might be bolstered by our being long distance. When we saw each other, the compounded longing from the in-between time meant we were too busy slinging extra affection in each other's direction to argue. "Who cares about what restaurant we go to as long as it's together"—that sort of thing. We let a lot slide. Also, with that whole war business forever looming, trailing what-ifs behind it, the "What if you die tomorrow and I called you selfish over some petty nothing?" thing came into play.

We didn't have a real fight, one where feelings got hurt, for the first nine months. Then Lior called one day—the day after

the one-year anniversary of 9/11—and asked how many people
I'd slept with. "I need to know the number," he said to me, serious. A knot of dread formed in my stomach. Turned out he'd been
obsessing over it for the preceding week, throughout his many
hours of guard duty, and hadn't brought it up. There was danger
right there—all those hours standing around, getting caught up
in obsessive thought patterns. He was up by the Lebanese border
again, tasked with stopping the drug trade, but he didn't give a shit.
Instead he cared about my chastity.

With apprehension, I told him the truth and tried to convince
him my sexual history was reasonable.

"I mean sex is really great, right?" I said. "And everyone I slept
with was a consenting adult."

"And you?" he pried.

"After the first few years I was legal."

It was an expected point of conflict. Boys had never been able
to accept that I slept with whomever I wanted. And now I found
myself defending my past behavior to Lior, who hadn't shared my
upbringing, and who, despite his having taken women's studies
did not see my promiscuity as a sign of assertiveness and feminism. The issue seemed not to be that I had slept with so many
people, per se, but that I refused to voice regret over my previous
choices. He wanted me to be shameful and secretive about what
I'd done.

In Lior's mind, the past was to be left out of conversations,
and for the most part, that happened. As in many relationships,
what cannot be integrated must be set aside. All the other lives you
might have lived are sublimated to support the one you've chosen.

I hoped that we could move past it, but a couple of days later,
when we talked again, he told me, "I spent all of Kol Nidre services
thinking about it."

Kol Nidre is the service that takes place the night before Yom

Kippur. It's your last chance to get the mistakes of the past year taken care of and have your name written in the book of life—a holy moment in which the gates of heaven are open to hear your prayers. It has always represented for me the best part of religion, the self-reflection and seeking. The thought that he'd spent that time worried about my past "transgressions," to use the words of the liturgy, disappointed me. While he was thinking about my past, I'd been thinking of our future, of his safety, praying that he would be inscribed in the book of life.

I tried not to let our argument make me feel bad about myself. I refused to be forced into shame. Sex *was* great. I knew it. The gays knew it. Everyone else would have to catch up while we led the way. Like usual.

I'm not saying I didn't get treated like shit by some guys along my journey. Some men feel the need to punish you for being easy by being cold and mean afterward, even though they benefit from your generosity of body and spirit, but usually I was able to understand that their behavior was culturally motivated, an unconscious move to police women's sexuality. I never thought, *This guy is treating me badly; it must be because I'm unworthy of respect.* And that is a victory. One point for sexual liberation.

Part of the credit for that is due perhaps to my being raised by lesbians. Since I was already marginalized, I had less to lose if I refused to play by the rules. Damned if you do, damned if you don't in my situation.

"You can't turn a ho into a housewife," I'd often heard my male friends say.

"It's lucky I don't have any interest in being a housewife" had always been my reply.

I tried to explain all of this to Lior.

It appeared he understood intellectually what I was saying when I proclaimed my promiscuity to be a political statement—but that didn't change his mind. He couldn't shed his feelings any more than I could shake my past. It didn't change much that, according to me, women who are sleeping around aren't necessarily looking for love in all the wrong places.

"I know what the feeling of being loved is," I told him. "I am one of the most overloved people on earth. If I enjoyed sleeping around it was for the anonymity as much as anything else."

"Uh-huh," he answered.

When I talked to Cody about it she was flabbergasted that I'd told him the real number in the first place. She twirled a strand of her blond hair and looked at me like I was dumb.

"Guuurl . . .you gotta lie about that kind of shit. Guys can't handle the truth; their tiny little jealous brains won't let them. So you just pick a number between six and ten and stick to it. Only add into that serious relationships will have to be explained based on photos."

"But I want our relationship to be based on honesty and respect. If we're going to spend the rest of our lives together he should know 100 percent of me—who I really am," I countered.

"Okay, but don't blame me when that doesn't work out. Dudes are controlling douches by nature," she insisted.

It worried me that she could be right and that the virgin/whore dialectic would be too ingrained in my boyfriend's psyche for me to do anything about it. Between us, we had two very different sex educations, and it showed.

I was a textbook case for sexuality in the children of lesbians: according to a national study, I was conforming to the general trend of teenage promiscuity and bisexual experimentation, followed by serial heterosexual monogamous relationships.

"Yeah, you slept around—but so did half the folks we know,"

my friend Jenny reminded me when I told her about my conversations with Lior in disbelief.

Still, I knew my family approached sex ed with a uniquely progressive spirit.

My younger brother got to come to my socialist summer camp a year earlier than usually allowed, since I was a counselor, and it'd gone okay until I got word that he'd been selling condoms at five dollars a pop to older boys. The Moms had thought his curiosity about sex was a beautiful thing and sent him to camp with bunches of them, like a tiny ambassador of information. Alas, his inner salesman had gotten the best of him.

Even in such a radical environment my brother's condom-selling business raised some eyebrows—and not just because of the capitalist bent of the whole thing. I mean, why does an eight-year-old come to camp with a rainbow assortment of rubbers? Personally, I wasn't all that surprised; I recalled experiments around how much water condoms could hold in the bathtub and making balloon animals with them at an even younger age. But I had the same parents he did.

My mothers taught me, through a scientific, antisensationalistic approach, the workings of the human body so early that by age three I already knew that a penis usually had to enter a vagina in order for a man and woman to conceive. I promptly attempted it with the son of an acquaintance at the ranch Helen (#4) owned. Very much in charge, I commanded the young fellow to stick his flaccid member inside me. We were just figuring out positioning on the top bunk of a bed in a back room when we were discovered by adults.

According to a poem I wrote in high school, that situation ended with a telling off for me and a spanking for him, but years later my mother assured me we'd only been sent outside to play, no lecture given. While my friends were being filled with the preciousness of virginity, I was being raised on the idea of empowerment. I could share my body with whomever I liked, receiving pleasure as I may.

Lior hadn't been raised by Puritans by any means—Berkeley Jews are known for their sexual permissiveness—but he had been raised with the idea that sex was about love and that anal sex and other juicy bits should be kept for people you really cared about. And all the social pressure of adolescence had only partly ripped away this notion. It still took him a day to decide to have "casual sex" with me, and look how that had turned out. (Insert many sighs here.) But then he wrote to me:

My love,

> *I am sorry if I have caused you pain or discomfort. I don't mean to or in any means desire it. Since I've spoken to you I've had plenty of time to think and while I haven't come to any major conclusions, I have had some ideas.*
>
> *I guess I wish I could possess your past as well, share it with you. Been born next to you, grown up side by side, but I wasn't that lucky. We had to wait almost twenty years to be together. The past is out of our control and I need to accept that. And I will often try, struggle to understand you, and try to see the world through your eyes... I guess I realize we won't always agree on things we both find important and that is scary as well. I feel like I've harmed you, taken away some of the innocence of our love by my silly problems with your sexual past. I want to offer you again, as for the first time, my body, soul, and heart.*

All that talking had finally got me somewhere. His letter deserved a call to a mama. I told Kyree I was sure he was the man for me.

"I mean Mama, I was worried for a second with this fight, but who else took women's studies in high school—not that it's offered outside the Bay Area, but still? And how many other hot soldier types grew up around gay folks? Like me, he can't ride a bicycle, likes frogs, and is a Liberal Zionist. He even has a T-shirt that matches my *Wild Women Don't Get the Blues* bumper sticker; these must be signs."

I've spent my whole life trying to read ciphers to make sense of an overwhelming world.

She chuckled.

"Plus, it's not like he doesn't like sex. He wants it like three times a day—and he blushed, but didn't balk, at the guide to cunnilingus Nyna gave him last Christmas."

That one made her giggle.

"Your mother is quite the lady," Kyree said. "If he can handle being around her, he must be something."

The fact that he could keep up with the unending oddness of my parents astounded me. More important than that, even, he approached my family with no sense of novelty. A lot of otherwise cool guys had approached my family like we were the next hipster trend or some sort of collectible. I could see the gleam in their eyes when I said the words "lesbian parents."

And on Lior's side, his family seemed to be getting used to me too. Back in California, a year after our whirlwind romance began, I spent a day while I was home for winter break making the best of the nice weather at an outlet mall with his dad and sister. How's that for normal? While we were there, Daniel, Lior's father, bought me running shoes, which Nyna took as a serious sign in our relationship.

"His family has accepted you. They are clothing you. That is a sign of investment," she said to me when I showed her the light blue sneakers.

14

The Struggle

The best friend I made during my years in college, my almost lesbian lover, Cody, left for a semester abroad in Dublin as I returned to New York for my last semester in 2003. This was her right, I understood. College roommates don't plan their lives in order to stay together.

Besides, I was the one who had made the break in our parallel lives: I had committed myself to a man. It is so taken for granted that this is done, that it makes sense. It is heteronormative—a word I have become obsessed with. You'll have to excuse me when I use it repeatedly. It refers to aspects of "straight culture" that are forced upon everyone as though they are just part of life. It's why people think life goes like this: boy meets girl, boy and girl settle down, boy and girl have kids . . . repeat cycle in perpetuity.

But here I was, part of a couple, ready to do it myself—blend seamlessly into that narrative, playing the girl role. There is no living with some other straight chick forever. That doesn't happen—not often, anyway. Someone was eventually going to bail. And it was me, not Cody, who did it first by running off with Lior. Still, I felt abandoned once she was gone.

In an attempt to keep busy and stave off loneliness, I decided to try and take school more seriously. That lasted for about a week; soon enough I was floundering again for activity. Then I was approached by a girl I recognized faintly from my Berkeley Jew circle.

"Rabbi Siegel suggested I speak to you," she said. "I'm interested in setting up a dialogue group around the Israeli–Palestinian conflict and he said you might be a good person to help with that."

I was tired of preaching peace and social justice to the Zionists and Zionism to the peace and social justice crowd, but I was open to new ideas. In pretty much any form.

"Yeah, I mean, I support dialogue," I sputtered. "How do you feel about Israel?"

She shifted her weight and exhaled before saying, "I wouldn't call myself a Zionist by any means. I believe the Palestinians deserve a state and that they are being unfairly persecuted."

"Yes, well, so do I . . ." I countered.

Perhaps I can bring her into the fold, I thought. *Yes. Success will be mine after all.* The Nobel Peace Prize started to loom before my eyes.

"I'm not sure you're not a Zionist," I said. "I am, and I agree with all those things you said. And I'd love to help out. Sign me up."

So began the most significant feature of my college career: the start of Foundations of Dialogue: The Israeli–Palestinian Conflict and the NYU Community.

Trekking over to the local copy shop together the next week, we printed out a flyer.

Join Jewish, Muslim, Israeli, Palestinian, Arab, and other NYU students in an effort to create a safe place on campus where we can begin to break down barriers and build trust and positive relationships through dialogue.

We met with our counterparts in facilitating the group. The Arab Student Union secretary ended up being a half-Jewish, half-Chaldean Christian who grew up in Palau. It was interesting to me that she had chosen to ally herself with the Arab kids. She told me that the Jewish kids at the Bronfman Center were cliquish and mean to her. I knew what she meant. We laughed about how conservative most of them were, like our grandparents (or more so, in my case).

The other facilitator, a Lebanese girl, decided after our first planning session that it wasn't for her. "I don't think I can listen to people say things I really disagree with and not interrupt them or say something back," she admitted before leaving.

I had a feeling that wasn't going to be easy for me either.

Halfway through our first meeting, Lior called. Two of the guys in his best friend's unit had died. His voice cut through the laughter of the conversation I'd been having. I sat silent, cradling the phone after he hung up. I couldn't decide whether leading this dialogue group seemed more relevant given my conversation with Lior or less so—a bunch of college kids sitting around talking and achieving nothing while other people died.

As facilitators we weren't there to express our opinion but to help people communicate theirs. Our contributions were thoughtful questions, gentle coercion to make sure people obeyed the dialogue precept of respect, and the keys to the classroom where we met. With the exit of the fourth partner, it was one Jew and one Christian for Palestine's side and me for the Israel side. It was unclear who was "winning."

Now it was up to us to recruit from our tribes.

There are a million clubs at a university the size of NYU: the ballroom dancers, the Agape Christians, Students for a Free Tibet, etc. There were clubs for the Latinos and the black kids, and there was a club for the Jewish kids and its counterpart, the Arab Student Union (ASU). The school wasn't necessarily a hotbed of identity politics; it was more like the sheer size and overwhelming location led folks to try and funnel themselves into any niche that looked cozy and welcoming. In a city with such a vacuum of connection, any tenuous bond seems like a foundation, a promising starting point.

With twenty-five thousand students and sizeable factions of every political persuasion, NYU reflected the atmosphere of the city as a whole. As events played out on a global stage they were mirrored in protests held by students, often screaming at each other, red in the face. With all that was going on in Israel, each group—the Jews and the ASU—regularly confronted each other in Washington Square, faced off at each other's events and generally fussed at one another.

Thank goodness everyone loves Chinese food. If only peace were as simple as loving kung pao chicken. We met once a month, drawing people with the prospect of free halal/kosher food. It turns out that if food is kosher, it's halal—but not the other way around. So we usually went with kosher Chinese, because it was popular. So popular that the group occasionally brought out people I suspected didn't know or care about the conflict at all.

"Who invited the squatters?" I asked a co-facilitator as I watched a white kid with gnarly dreadlocks fill his plate.

"Want to bet that, if anything, they are pro-Palestine?" she shot back. "Even the homeless have some sense."

One more point for their team.

We had decided the format should be democratic, with the public deciding the topics and then discussing them with little other structure. In that vein, we brainstormed a list of topics with the crowd at the first meeting and scheduled them so that one month we would discuss Jerusalem's division, and another, "Violence: Is It Ever an Option?"

Violence was my favorite session yet. We had everybody line up, with folks who believed that violence was never the answer on one side and folks who were all for "just arm us all and let us go at it" on the other. Then we split the line, like chunks of a worm, into groups. That made it so all the gentle folks were together and the war birds were in their own corner.

At last people were well matched regardless of their political loyalties.

"Yeah, I say let's just go for it. You know, if the Palestinians want war, we will give them some," said a fellow in a polo shirt and a black *kippa*. "My grandpa didn't die in Auschwitz for us to give up Jerusalem."

"Israel operates under a 'might equals right' assumption," said a kid from the pro-Palestine contingent.

"So what if it does," said an Orthodox kid with a paunch and a Brooklyn accent. "What of it? So does the rest of the world."

"Well then, that same logic justifies terrorism. Israel is engaged in an imperialistic land grab supported by our government and our taxes; the only choice the Palestinians are left with is violence," the first kid replied. He was wearing a vintage NWA T-shirt.

As long as they weren't interrupting each other I had to keep my mouth shut. Over time, I'd begin to develop an appreciation for the rainbow of opinion. It was shock therapy perhaps, treatment through intense exposure.

"Oh, and then there's the support of the Arab world—they funnel arms and money to the Palestinians the same way the US does to Israel." The kid in the *kippa* was practically foaming at the mouth.

The violent folks all agreed that the only answer was the other's destruction. Everyone appeared content to bomb each other into oblivion. I wanted to blame it on their lack of proximity, but I knew that many people living through the violence themselves felt the same way. I wandered over to a circle full of sane people.

"It's so clear a two-state solution is the only way both sides will feel like their interests are being acknowledged," intoned a pretty girl in glasses.

"I agree. If the Palestinians get a state they are much more likely to acknowledge the Jews' right to one too," said a girl in a headscarf.

The pacifists were sure they could solve the conflict then and there, if given the power. I wished there was a way to give it to them.

If only there was a way to divide the world like this, I thought. *Then all the people who want to go to war could fight each other and the rest of us could live in peace.* Only I was in love with someone who had chosen to go to war. Which group did I really belong in?

I knew that on both sides of the conflict, the majority of people were moderates who wanted peace. The thing was, we had to deal with the extremists—and both sides had them. In my ideal world, the extremists could live their little uptight lives separately; but in this world, that wasn't possible.

"What are the answers?" asked a stringy-haired postpubescent in mushroom-colored corduroys. "There's no way I'd stand around and let fanatics kill my family."

"What do you expect the Palestinians to do when Israeli soldiers do the same thing?" someone else piped up. Nobody wanted to take the blame. I didn't want to associate my lover with words like "murderer," "war crime," "oppression" and "imperialism." When I heard how horrible the Israelis were, I tried to picture his face.

I regularly left the meetings brimming with a panoply of emotions. *Why did I find myself always having to defend those I loved?* I had grown up feeling constantly under attack. It's something me and the Palestinians and the settlers had in common. Flashback to me being five and no one believing me about my parents getting married. Watch me lecturing classmates about their homophobic slurs. Watch me repeatedly defending the people I love now and then.

Unconsciously, I internalized on some level the idea that the world was against you—that no one was going to stand up for you, you had to stand up for yourself. Like that Holocaust quote:

When they came for the Jews,
I remained silent;
I wasn't a Jew.

. . .

When they came for me,
there was no one left to speak out.

That same semester, although I had mainly given up on acting, a friend asked me to be in the play he was directing. It was a befuddling honor for anyone to want to work with me, especially on a production that was costarring a girl who was on the PBS children's show *Ghostwriter*.

The play was about a group of miscreants whose lives revolved around a bar in Queens. I played a crackhead named Chicky. Typecasting.

The night before my last play of college opened, Lior called to tell me that six soldiers from his unit had been injured the night before on a mission in Gaza. *Why is it whenever I accomplish anything, he has army drama?*

"I'm so sorry, baby . . ." I sympathized.

"Uri and Harel both have shrapnel injuries and here I am watching TV at home." I could hear the bitter tone in his voice. He sounded pissed off and reticent, not wanting to talk even though he was the one who had called me. The next morning, it came out that the mission had killed thirteen Palestinians, including a twelve-year-old and a toddler.

I told him this seemed like a terrible mission, and thank God he wasn't on it. Then he said he wished he had been there. Due to his coming to the States for my graduation, he wasn't with his unit. I said I wished I could be there to hold him and make him feel better, and he replied, "I wish I was in Gaza."

"You'd better get used to not being on missions. You don't have much time in the army left," I snapped.

Lior would be done with the army in less than three months. The fighting would go on without him. We had been dreaming for so long about being together, and now he seemed regretful that the time had come.

For him it was about not having been there with his friends when the shit went down. But while I considered the whole thing a tragedy, the mission was considered a success. Was it a question of distance or morals? If I were in his place, would I feel the same way? I told him that if I didn't love him I'd hate him. I meant that if I didn't know him as a person, my pacifism would overtake my affection. He didn't take it well.

The more I thought about it the more upset I got. But when I called Nyna, she told me to let it go.

"War is a terrible thing," she said. In the background I could hear the hum of her TV playing an episode of *Law and Order: SVU*.

"He feels guilty that he couldn't protect his friends, that he wasn't there to suffer with them," she continued.

"But he wants to be part of this larger monstrosity. I am dating a neocolonialist!"

"This isn't anything new for you," said my mother matter-of-factly. "You knew he was a soldier."

I wished I was a lesbian, or didn't have a uniform fetish, or dated guys who were more like girls.

"They must convince themselves they are doing the right thing to stay sane," my mother said.

War is an evil thing.

I then tried calling Jenny for advice. Recently neither of our boyfriends had been acting ideally; it was very bonding for our relationship. She said I should stand my ground, morally speaking, but wait until I had seen him for the big blowout. "See how you feel once you're in the same room," she said, and then she reminded me that I was in a highly emotional state owing to my impending graduation. As we spoke I paced my room, agitated, scraping grooves into the varnished wood floors.

———

Nearing the end of my last semester, I had so much to do that the day to day finally subsumed my larger reality. Lior called one afternoon and I picked up late enough that my voice was caught on the answering machine. When I listened to the recording later, I sounded so terse.

"Hey," I said brusquely, "I'm headed out the door to catch the subway to class. I thought you were going to call this morning. I can't talk now."

The amount of work that stood between me and graduation made me feel all the more estranged from him. Without having seen each other in months, more and more, our relationship seemed like an agreed-upon illusion, like we pretended to be the people we thought the other wanted over the phone. It scared me. We had been living separate lives, with only memory to remind us of the person we knew.

15

About Our Future

In May of 2003, I graduated from my fancy acting program. At the ceremony, held in the same wood-floored, wide-windowed studios that we had had all our classes in, I felt like the kid who fell through the cracks—but upon reflection, I guess I didn't invest myself as much as most, either. While everyone else was immersed in art, I was focused on politics. I'd judged them all as we'd pretended the studio was filled with honey or pudding and waded, dragging our heavy, sticky feet, or imagined our loved ones dead to dredge up emotion. Art had felt selfish, masturbatory. But on that last day, I was the one who ended up feeling alone.

The view from the windows was the same as it had been over the past few years: a set of water towers that looked like rockets ready to take off from the rooftops. The newly blessed actors were emotional, lots of crying and ass kissing. Everyone seemed very attached to one another. At the end of the ceremony each of us received a pocket harmonica and a picture of the graduating class that I wasn't in. Guess I hadn't attended class that day. The end of an era.

Love über *alles*—including college, right? I was following in the great tradition of women who had prioritized their relationships over their education. I mean, how many women dropped out of school to get married? Hundreds of thousands, likely. Millions, maybe. I was at least graduating. The more I said it in my head the weirder it sounded. Who the hell had I become?

———————

The next day, as I drove to the airport to pick up Lior, all my conflict blended into a mixture of terror, anxiety, and unqualified lust. Both my guts and my girlie parts were churning. Upon sight of him, everything but the lust faded into the background.

"Hey there, handsome," I purred.

In the first couple of days, which we largely spent reacquainting ourselves through sex, all planned arguments were postponed.

I took him on a tour of the main campus building where I'd spent the last few years. We tried to have sex in the twelfth-floor bathroom, but someone knocked and we panicked. Then we went at it awhile in one of the acting studio rooms, but it was clear we wouldn't have enough time. So we gave up and went back downstairs to where, it turned out, Nyna and her new girlfriend, Val, had been patiently waiting for us so we could all go out for dinner. In my desire for genital interaction, I had forgotten they were also in town and expecting attention.

All four moms had been out to visit in the preceding month; this was the last wave of visitors. So many mothers . . . so little time.

When I explained what our situation was, they let me and Lior borrow their hotel room for our quickie.

"So you don't have to take the subway all the way back to Brooklyn," Nyna said with a wink.

"Normal people's parents don't do this," Lior asserted upon arriving to their room.

"I know, isn't it great?" I said, beginning to shed clothing.

"I think it's a question of boundaries and perspective," he said.

"We just won't do it on their bed," I compromised.

I could tell Lior wished there were another option, but not enough to stop him from getting laid. Guys can compromise a lot in the name of some ass.

Afterward we went out to eat at a Cuban place. Nobody but Lior seemed to think there was anything out of the ordinary about everyone being aware that we'd just had sex.

For my part, I felt gleeful to have so many of my favorite people in one place. They acted so damn cute together. Nyna demanded to feel Lior's muscles.

"Oh—they are even bigger than the last time I saw you."

Lior blushed and averted his eyes. He treated my mother with the same good-natured tolerance as he did me. She, in turn, played the mischievous girl teasing and trying to get a rise from him. She pulled at the chest hair peeking out from the collar of his shirt, then said, "You are such a cute little bear!"

You'd hardly have known she was gay.

The next day, as part of the graduation festivities, there was a huge fireworks display put on by NYU.

"So that's where all my tuition went," I joked.

Lior gripped my hand tightly.

This was my first glimpse of the postarmy version of him in an urban American setting. The bright-colored waterfalls of light did not mitigate the unease he experienced at the sound of the explosions. The city's cacophony shocked him. New York City operates at a constant roar. He jolted at trucks clanking over manhole covers and construction noise. He patted his thigh occasionally, looking for the machine gun that usually hung at his side.

"It's not there, baby," I reminded him. "But I'll keep you safe."

Taking his arm, I led him through the throngs of people, my

hand firmly entwined with his. I wondered if he would ever enjoy the Fourth of July again, and if this was common among vets. How ironic to be unable to enjoy the most patriotic of holidays because you yourself had served as a patriot.

Lior wondered aloud whether he could be medicated for occasions such as this, like they used to do for his family's Australian shepherd when he was a kid.

In New York, people asked him all the time whether he had killed anybody. Perfect strangers posed this question casually, like they were asking him what he ate in the army. With the same naive curiosity behind it. People asked me the same thing in his absence. Neither of us knew how to answer.

"I just don't think it's appropriate to ask someone that—and why should I dignify it with a response?" he said after one such incident. He had met some of my colleagues at Hillel and it had been one of their first questions.

I heard a vet on the radio compare it to asking a woman whether she's been raped—the question being similarly intrusive. He said the two experiences were alike in that going through it changed you; you never forgot it. When Lior had arrived home in bad shape the summer before, I had asked him the same question. I had also wanted to know.

The summer I'd spent in Israel, where Lior fought five days out of the week and then came home most weekends, had taught me that the concept of war there is different than in America, where soldiers go away for many months at a time and then come back shockingly different. Still, there were times when Lior came home and I sensed a shift, another layer of innocence had dissolved. Sometimes his eyes had changed or he looked suddenly older after just a week away. And when I'd ask if anything had happened at work that week that I should know about, he'd answer, "Same old stuff."

It's characteristic of Israel that the "battlefield" is so close.

There it's all about proximity; everyone is overlapping. Distance makes it easier to excuse the actions that populate war. We can pretend to some extent as civilians that it doesn't exist. No such luck in Jerusalem. No one says, "What happens in Gaza stays in Gaza" for a reason.

As I wondered if Lior would be able to re-assimilate once back in California, I couldn't believe we were almost there at the finish line, close enough for these doubts to come into play. When I said good-bye to him at the airport it was with far fewer tears, because I knew that when I said good-bye to Bedford-Stuyvesant, I would be headed his way.

When you're in New York, no matter how miserable you are there is always the comfort that you are in the middle of everything—the center of the world. It feels like to leave would be to ditch the party early, when all the fun stuff is still on the way, before the strippers arrive. Moving away from that city felt like it took the strength of a rocket breaking through and out of a planet's gravitational pull. Lior said he would consider living in New York, but I was insistent on leaving. Residing there was like being on a carousel you could never get off of, the painted ponies turning at a dizzying pace.

So we would go home to the West Coast together. Never mind that since I seemed to have failed at the whole acting thing, I had no idea what I was going to do with my life. The plan was I would finish school and he would finish the army and then together we'd start the rest of our lives.

It demanded a celebration. Too bad my boyfriend was thirty thousand miles away.

Luckily, I was up one party companion since Cody had returned from her semester abroad in Ireland. She was moving back into the apartment as I moved out. She was still blond and tan and blasé.

"Look at all those windows," she said as we hung out on the rooftop of our building, staring at the myriad dark squares that littered the walls around us. "All those terrible lame people living their awful lives. I'm glad that my pet rats ran away while I was gone. Glad for them, really."

We drank cheap champagne mixed with Chambord while smoking lots of cigarettes.

I employed the "drink mine, drink hers, pour new drinks" technique that had become a tradition with us. This was how we used to do things. I felt a beautiful nostalgia. I also felt like I annoyed the hell out of her, having forgotten what she was like in her absence. I had to remember it was her nature to be taciturn.

"Are you excited about being back in New York?" I asked.

"No," she said.

"Are you excited about your summer plans? Starting out your senior year? Getting juiced for the future?"

"No, but I bet you are." Her tone was mocking, but she was nice enough to bait me. She knew I was about to burst.

"Yeah, you know I am. Just a few more weeks and then I will be with him for the rest of my life! I'm just so excited to finally have a chance to live together and share a bed and fuck and fight and do all that stuff that normal people do."

She was making snoozing noises like she had fallen asleep.

"You guys are pathetic. You are just like the rest of them in the end. I bet you'll have kids, too," she said, studying her glass of champagne. Zero population growth was one of the many causes with which we had always allied ourselves.

As I prattled on about my future with Lior, it struck me that Cody found my relationship with him repulsive. She was disgusted by our mutual need for one another. She liked to pretend that she didn't need anyone. It was part of her fake autism routine—the one that she used to get out of movement classes in college, claiming she couldn't stand to be touched. Despite the fact that she had happily shared a bed with me for years, sometimes I believed her, and it helped me to justify leaving.

"Feelings are for losers," she said. There had been a time when I would have agreed with her.

She helped me take the last of my stuff to the post office for shipping but refused to take me to the airport.

"I have to unpack my stuff, set my room up," she explained. "It can't be about you all the time." Her expert use of emotional distance made me burst into tears.

"I love you, Cody, I'm going to miss you so much. I don't know what I will ever do without you . . ."

I was playing Dorothy at the end of *The Wizard of Oz* when she's talking to the Scarecrow. *I'm going miss you most of all . . .*

"You'll be fine. You'll have Lior and get all famous and shit, get married, have babies, and die. Don't you worry about me."

I hugged her for a good three minutes, until she pulled away.

I got on the plane and left.

16

Sayaret Kellen

L ior had always intended to come back to the States for college. The Israeli university system is more European in style, in that they enter into school with a decided major, emphasizing depth over breadth. He wanted the classic liberal arts education, the "find myself through study" version. I had gone the opposite direction at NYU with my specialized theater degree, but in my last year of school I had begun to understand the appeal of his ideal, even as I was itching to leave the academic arena for good.

Diploma in hand, I flew to Israel to collect Lior as my prize. Very similar to the old caveman-style, knock-them-over-the-head-and-drag-them-home approach.

Upon arrival I immediately went to work ushering in our new life together. To commemorate his first day out of the army, I made up a contract subscripting him into Sayeret Kellen. Sayeret Matkal being the name of Israel's most elite unit, I thought it was cute. His roommate, however, who'd been out of the army for almost a decade by this point, balked at the idea.

"I think the last thing he wants to do is sign his life away, today in particular," he said to me. But I refused to believe it was a bad thing—this was, after all, the beginning of our future together.

Turned out there was a lot of other paperwork that needed to be done as well. I wasn't the only one who wanted Lior to sign on the dotted line. Countless forms followed. Equipment needed to be returned and signed off on; the army protocol demanded that you first return their materials of war, and then they'd give you back your person. Pieces of paper served to disconnect you from the life you'd been having and certify you for the one you were headed for.

As one last errand for the army, we returned Lior's gun and flak vest to his unit. They were based in Hebron at that moment, and so to reach them we had to drive through the territories and a succession of Palestinian towns. They were dusty and unremarkable, surprisingly tranquil. We passed a child in a loudly patterned sweater and turquoise sweatpants leading a donkey along the side of the highway. Otherwise the road meandered primarily through undeveloped valleys. Hard for me to believe people were fighting over this barren land.

Lior was wearing his soldier face, and he made me promise not to tell my mothers that we'd ever taken this trip. Halfway there, on a road winding between short brown hills scattered with rocks, he showed me how to use his gun.

"If someone shoots at us, they'll try and take me out, since I'm the driver. If I'm shot, you'll need to know how to use this."

He gestured to his M16, which rested placidly between us.

"I'm pretty sure that if you get shot, I'm fucked, regardless of the gun," I said.

But he was serious, and so we went over its basic mechanics. I repeated aloud the steps he described one by one. I thought about the unlucky souls who get killed in ATV accidents or shot on roads like this one right after getting out of the army, so close to making it out alive.

We made it there. While he took care of the nitty-gritty I chatted with his boys, invited them to our wedding. No one doubted that there would be one. They gently rode me about taking him away, stealing him back to the States.

"What, you don't like Israel? I thought you were a Zionist," Yair said. He was wearing the floppy fisherman-style hat that the army issues. The brim hung over his pretty eyes.

"Why don't you move here instead—we'll teach you Hebrew," offered Gal.

I imagined myself with a baby at my breast at a barbecue, with all these men as pseudo family, and briefly smiled. The hills behind them shone with the amber light of approaching dusk.

I apologized profusely for spiriting Lior away, and we left.

Just days before we flew home, terrorists blew up Café Hillel in the German Colony—Lior's old stomping grounds. It was supposed to be a "safe" area, and Café Hillel was practically Starbucks; it intentionally exuded a separated-from-the-chaos-of-the-world vibe.

The awkward calm that descends over Jerusalem in the hours after a *piguah* made the air thick in my throat. I thought about how my time there with Lior had been bookended by brutal violence. From the first night we spent together in Jerusalem to this last bombing, the acts of violence were strung together like a strand of pearls.

I felt guilty to be leaving for the ease of the States. One look at Lior's face confirmed that he was wallowing in a similar depression. We both wanted to go back home but felt like chicken shits for doing it. We knew that we had no control over the violence, but we couldn't help but join the collective local consciousness sitting impotent at their dinner tables.

On the way to the airport, I was unusually quiet. A Mizrachi song played on the taxi radio, the lilting wail sounding like Arabic but sung by a Jewish voice. The driver smoked a cigarette with the window rolled down, his bald spot visible over his head rest. A Golani tree printed on cardboard twirled on the rearview next to a picture of Ovadia Yosef. A Chihuahua bobble head sat on the dashboard and nodded in our direction. We watched the land roll by and I knew we were both wondering how long it would be until either of us returned to Israel. All the excitement that I'd brought to swaddle Lior in, to help prepare him for the journey home, seemed to have momentarily escaped me.

From then on we would be living together, facing the hurdles of life as a team. When we got on the plane, he'd go back to being mostly American—speaking English, applying to college, and getting a job. That line of thinking made me nervous for him. I reached over and put my hand on his thigh. I wanted to tell him I would make everything okay but I wasn't sure that I could deliver.

"I love you," I said. My hand squeezed his leg.

17

Approaching Adulthood

*O*ur plan was to spend a couple of months in the Bay Area, where we had cheap rent thanks to my mom Nyna's willingness to play landlord. We'd get jobs and save money while Lior applied to schools, and then we'd move wherever he was accepted. In the meantime, we were moving into the San Francisco house I'd lived in until I was twelve.

After Nyna (#1) moved out of Margery's (#3) and into Helen's (#4) house when I was a baby, she bought a house of her own. It was one of four attached houses climbing a hillside that the Department of Housing and Urban Development had built for low-income, first-time homeowners. Above us was a Eurasian family and below, a black family and a Chicano family: rainbow row.

Since Helen rented next door to the site, we watched the little brown shingle-sided houses with brick-red trim and black tar paper roofs get built. When the houses were ready, Nyna, Helen, and I moved in, leaving the rental next door and dragging our belongings less than a hundred feet.

This was the house that defined childhood for me. Upon returning, I recognized the spot on the brown carpet where a neighbor girl had poured sticky syrup when I was four. But the home's proportions had changed with my own, and there was a disconnect between what I saw and what I remembered so clearly from childhood.

When we moved across the bay to where real estate was cheaper during my middle school years, Nyna hung onto the house, renting it out in the interim. The last tenants had been a Guatemalan family who had up and disappeared one day, leaving all their belongings behind. Nyna said she had known that they had marital problems and that the husband was a drinker.

Because of this, part of Lior and me moving in involved getting rid of massive amounts of that family's things. It was eerie sifting through the minutia of someone else's life: a single shoe kept company by a broken board game, a man's jacket strewn over televisions in triplicate. I reminded myself that Lior had searched a multitude of houses and so was probably less affected by this odd task than I was.

Nyna, of the poor white Southern childhood, asked us whether we needed any of the Guatemalan family's items for setting up our new home.

"There's no point in going and buying dishes at Goodwill for you and then taking their dishes to Salvation Army, you know," she said, arms elbow deep in strangers' clothing.

"Yeah, but at least when you buy it secondhand you don't have any idea of where it came from, or whose it was," I countered. "The karma gets wiped off in the resale. Who knows what happened to these people?"

"Everything has a history," she said.

I wasn't sure I wanted to taint our new life with the evidence of another family's collapse. Still, they were free dishes . . .

Approaching Adulthood

Lior and I were finally getting a chance to be a normal couple, setting up a home together. Our eventual wedding registry would have to be filled with superfluous gadgets—mixers, juicers, and the like—because we were gathering the essentials now. Those that the Guatemalans hadn't provided us, that is. Our collective troop of parents helped with most of it, and Lior's younger brother and a visiting army buddy helped us cart stuff over to the house. Our new couch came up the stairs with ease, gliding on the strength of men who could take over a small country.

Lior's army friend Avishai had been released at the same time as him, ahead of most of the unit, and was in the States making money so he could travel somewhere more exotic—a common practice among post-army Israelis. Go to any mall in America, head to the kiosks in the middle selling bath salts or remote control airplanes or aromatherapy eye masks, and odds are the person doing the sales will be Israeli.

Now that I know this, I await the accent that accompanies the pitch, "Ma'am if I can just have a minute of your time." I look forward to responding in my much-improved Hebrew: "*Achi, ein li zman*" (Brother, I don't have the time.) Israelis take advantage of the average American's weakness to the hard sell. We can be persuaded to buy anything if someone tries hard enough. So they come and help folks unload their pocket change, and then they take that cash and make it last six months to a year in places like India and South America. I really can't object to the redistributive economics at work in this system; it's like being Robin Hood and vacationing all at the same time.

Lior was hoping that this practice would result in more of his army buddies coming through town.

We'd be better off living near the Mall of America if that's what you're hoping for, I thought.

Between the visitors, phone calls, and pure habit, Lior was speaking Hebrew half the time. Because of this, mine was still improving, even now that we were home in the States. But Lior still worried about losing his in the long run.

"After all the time I took to learn it, it'd be a shame to let it go," he said on a day when, thanks to Avishai, he'd spoken as much Hebrew as English.

It was no surprise that Lior felt conflicted about his time in Israel coming to an end. It meant leaving everything he had built there, not to mention proving right those who had said he was just coming to enlist in the army and not really making aliyah.

Sometimes I took his melancholy personally when it seemed like he resented me for bringing him back to the States. *Maybe we should have stayed there and I could have adapted*, I thought. *That way if things were hard I could have blamed him for bringing me there instead of the other way around.*

The day of our move, after the last of the boxes had been brought inside the house, we dragged our sore muscles over to a bar in downtown Berkeley to meet up with some friends for drinks. We took over a black leather booth, and eventually the banter turned to Israel and politics.

The play about Rachel Corrie, an American girl killed by an Israeli bulldozer while protesting in the territories, had premiered, and we were discussing the circumstances of her death. Had it been an accident, as the driver and the army claimed? Or had he run her over intentionally? We all seemed to think that the latter was a possibility but differed on the meaning we took from it.

"Morality is totally relative," I said. "People act differently under stress. Mistakes get made. Anyone can kill an innocent person." I returned to sipping my margarita.

"An 'innocent person'? Define that," challenged Lior's friend Josh.

"A baby, whatever. A total innocent."

"That's a very extreme situation. You mean accidentally?" Lior attempted to clarify. He shifted in his seat.

"Accidentally or intentionally. Anyone put in the right situation can kill a baby. You never know what you're capable of until you're put in that situation."

"I don't know that I agree with you," Lior said.

The rest of the people at the table watched to see how the argument would pan out. Over by the bar, a man in Oakland A's gear was hitting on a girl with a high ponytail and dangly earrings. "Are you calling me a baby killer?" Avishai asked.

He misunderstood the point I was making. He thought I was referring to the toddler that had died because of their unit.

"No, I was saying that I think anyone—not you but me, *anyone*—is capable of killing a baby when put in the worst sort of circumstances. I mean, think of in the Holocaust, when mothers smothered their infants to keep them quiet. People act very differently based on context."

"That's a very specific example." Lior tried to push back.

"That's my point, though," I insisted. "That in theory everyone is a potential baby killer, until put to the test."

Someone else at the table insisted that we switch to more bar-friendly conversation. "Anyone heard how the A's are doing this season?"

Avishai glowered at the repeated use of the word "baby killer." It was less theoretical for him. He didn't seem convinced that I had not insulted or perhaps accused him. Lior started explaining in Hebrew what I had said and I think he apologized for me, though I couldn't quite follow.

I felt bad for striking a nerve. It was true, though, that circumstance dictated behavior. I was sure of it.

In our new home, Lior and I played house. We dressed as grown-ups every morning, even though it felt silly. We laughed at each other's struggles to maintain the part—his fight with his tie, my constant running of pantyhose. Lior was doing security for Jewish day schools and wore a suit, along with an earpiece, secret service-style. I happily noted that the suit was an acceptable replacement for the uniform, fetish wise. I liked the way his muscles sat under the crisp cotton and light tailored wool. It said power, money, people in charge, even though his perspective was more working class than Wall Street.

He came home describing the luxury cars the wealthy Jews drove and the Juicy Couture sweat suits on the firm bottoms of the gym-toned moms. I smiled and told him he sounded like my mother Helen, kind of.

By then Helen was living on her property in Mendocino County, all by herself, without electricity, using kerosene lanterns and sleeping under a thin blanket with her dog for company. She's proud, in a self-deprecating way, of her German heritage, to which she credits her stubbornness and work ethic. She says the Germans taught the Jews how to be cheap. That being said, she grew up with a copy of *The Protocols of the Elders of Zion* tucked away in her house. Lior wasn't the easiest of sells to make to her, as she abhors militarism, machismo, and any form of organized religion.

"Men are idiots and religion is horseshit" is the sort of conventional wisdom she dispenses.

When she came to visit Israel in 1999, she insisted we avoid visiting any religious sites. In Israel, for goodness' sake! I managed to sneak her toward the Wailing Wall through the Arab quarter—a more circuitous route, with less signs to tip her off—and still the moment it came into view she snapped, "Oh, no! This isn't for me. You can do what you want . . . I'll be sitting by the exit," which was what she did until I was ready to go. I said a quick prayer (that included her) and we left. The Church of the Holy Sepulcher went even less well than that, owing to her being a lapsed Catholic.

The only thing Lior had going in his favor was Helen's rather recent conversion to Zionism, which was owed to her having read *Exodus*. The book (on which the 1960 movie with Sal Mineo was based) had persuaded her that the whole thing was a good idea. I owe a lot to that franchise.

"They made the desert bloom!" she asserted brightly.

I steered clear of bringing up the Eco-Zionism movement's repentant feelings about early agricultural policy as it related to the desert and Israel's ecosystem as a whole. People had since taken issue with a lot of what went on in "making the desert bloom" in terms of its environmental impact. I figured whatever kept Helen in support of the state as a concept worked for me.

Helen's had a rocky history with Jews, owing to her upbringing. She once asked the rabbi at my Hebrew school why none of the women worked, and then reframed it, "Oh, right, no, with you guys the women do all the work and the men all sit around, right? And study, huh? That how it works?" All this in the process of chit-chatting while kids got picked up after class. It was funny to find that Lior and she had common ground.

In the mornings, after packing quick breakfasts for the road, we kissed at the door—him in a suit, me dressed business casual—and I wondered, would we keep doing this until at some point it felt right? Keep going through the motions until being adult was actual and taken for granted and not half charade? Did older folks marvel each day at what artifice their bodies portray, with them still children on the inside?

I had begun to work as a hostess at a downtown restaurant, aka my "Should I just give up on acting now?" job. My main qualification was looking good in a skirt. The skill I actually needed to do the job well was deafness. So there was some acting involved. I should have been tipped off when the sports bar next door said they were always hiring.

The owner, whose main pleasure in life was torturing hostesses—according to the bartender—had formerly served in the French Foreign Legion. He was fat and stinky, and existed exclusively in a set of crumbling overalls, pressed daily into the end of the bar. From there he yelled at me as I walked back and forth from the kitchen.

"Hey, are you an idiot? Look what you're doing!" His teeth crushed bits of sandwich around the words as crumbs flew from the corners of his mouth. Tiny critters might well have scattered from the hems of his decaying pants. Sometimes he was joined in chorus by Carlos, the older Mexican busboy who also served as my supervisor. Neither of them thought very highly of me, according to their own commentary.

———

To supplement the meager income from my hostessing job, I began teaching Sunday school at a Reform temple across the bay in Alameda. The director had known me as a child and proudly gave me the job. *This must mean I am Jewish, right?* I thought *If I can teach it to others? Am I finally passing the test?*

Given absolutely no training or syllabus other than a holiday calendar, I was responsible for delivering religion to a dozen preschool-age children. I brought out Star of David coloring books and menorahs made out of Play-Doh. I attempted to teach them the Sabbath rituals by having them pretend to be a family of bears.

"Mama Bear lights the candles and covers her eyes with her paws ... Can you cover your eyes with your paws like Mama Bear?" I sing-songed while swaying and gesturing. None of the children obeyed.

Maybe the exercise was too abstract.

One Sunday morning, in a lame approximation of circle time, I tried to tackle the story of Jacob wrestling an angel.

"Does anyone here know what an angel is?" I asked an assortment of small dirty grinning faces.

"A made-up creature?" one well-dressed hipster tot offered.

"Yeah, maybe . . . or a messenger of God, perhaps?" I meekly responded.

Another child commenced picking his nose. His father, cross-legged, sat right behind him. The parents of my tiny charges seemed not to trust me; many of them stayed to spy on my lessons. Either that or they didn't know the stuff themselves.

Most of the kids came from houses with no religious practice. A couple of them were Russian Jews with parents who'd been prevented from learning about religion by the old Soviet regime.

Generally, the parents didn't believe in God but did want their children to have some religious heritage, so they carted them off to me once a week. It didn't hurt that it also gave them a scheduled activity on Sundays from 10 a.m. to noon. Part of parenting, as I understand it, is just filling up the day, trying to keep the young ones busy for twelve hours.

Because I understood the parents' motives and backgrounds and wasn't trying to rock the boat, when I taught things like the Sabbath, each mandated ritual came with the caveat, "Some of you may do this at home (light candles, say prayers, whatever), some of you may not. Both options are okay." I'm not sure it really made a difference to the toddlers, that conscious suspension of judgment, but I didn't want complaints from the parents.

18

Domestic Smorgasbord

etween going to work and catching up with family who weren't used to us living nearby, we got entangled in the details of daily life very quickly.

The best way to describe our relationship's transition is that we went from existing in an epic opera, replete with wars and global-sized adventure, to a sudden intimate theater piece, two lovers arguing over a dinner table. Our domestic fantasies had come to life, all that reaching for scraps of normality—dishwashing and laundry folding, sweeping and bed making—all of it bearing fruit at once.

It was the kind of harvest you become sick from eating. Suddenly we had all this family in immediate proximity. A smorgasbord of forbearers. We could have dinner with a different parent every night if we wanted to and still only see each of them once a week.

Since Lior's parents, like mine, were divorced, we now had the chance to see who they had become without each other—how the breakup of each relationship had shaped them. This was what I could tell about his parents from our visits: His dad had begun collecting art deco design pieces and had kept the family dog. His mom worked a lot. They didn't talk about each other at all. Nyna and Kyree on the other hand, loved to discuss what the other was up to. Visiting one meant updating her on the other. Folks handle heartbreak in a variety of ways.

My parents each experienced a sort of midlife crisis. Kyree went the spiritual route. She got into medicine animals, wolves in particular. Her vacations involved retreats to remote wolf rescue sites where she did visitor education and fed the pack scraps of horse meat. Always one for crafts, she began to slowly cover her walls with self-produced leatherwork featuring animals and nature symbols. A shaman had told her that it was necessary to collect the pieces of her soul that were still in Nyna's possession; only then would she feel whole again.

Along with the "soul retrieval" came a name change. Her given legal name had been Nora, but she associated it with the depression and rage of her former life. To be fair, "Nora" in Hebrew basically translates to "calamity;" a common phrase is *zeh lo Nora* (it's not the end of the world). When she asked us to go along with the change, my brother said, "Sissy, are you really going to start calling her by whatever name she chooses?"

"I sure am going to try," I said.

She chose "Kyree" as her new moniker, which was the name of a wolf in a fantasy novel she'd read. It's a name she shares with few people, and interestingly, most of them are young African-American boys. More than once she has heard her name called out—perhaps with a different syllable accented—only to find a mother sternly calling her son: "Kyyyrrreeee! Get over here!"

Nyna went in a different direction. During the time when the former family home seemed the emptiest, her old life the most gone, she threw herself into the flurry of activity that is the A.C.

Leather Corps—an organization within the leather community that raises money by putting on events like motorcycle runs and beer busts. Or so I was about to find out.

Dumb high school acquaintances had often inquired about my parents' sex life.

"Do you know if your dad likes a thumb up his butt?" I'd ask in reply.

"Excuse me, no . . . I don't," they would invariably say with a look of shock.

"Well, I don't really check into my parents' sexual habits either. Maybe you could figure it out on the Internet." That was usually the extent of the conversation.

But because everyone else was so interested, I was intrigued too. I wasn't clueless, of course—I was well educated, and my parents answered any question I asked. Unfortunately, their answers were limited to the questions I was willing to say aloud.

So, like everybody else, I got most of my hypotheses about their sex life from lesbian porn on the Internet. All the women in the movies were thin and surgically enhanced, whereas the lesbians I knew looked like real people, but I figured the menu of activities was generally the same. So I thought I knew what my folks were into—until I searched the house for their porn and the first video I found was of a fat, hairy gay dude giving it to another bearish man. My parents didn't even socialize with men. Why would they want to watch them fuck?

What had collected in my mind were a bunch of incongruent and unappealing details that I had little motivation to try and fit together. And it was from this place of scant education that I tried to understand Nyna becoming a public figure in a "leather corps," whatever that was.

Again with the hairy, gay dudes, apparently. I was to learn that the leather community has a similar history to that of motorcycle gangs in general. Both arose from guys serving in World War II, where they ran around in leather outfits on motorcycles with other guys and liked it. And some guys liked it even more than others. A lot more. So they formed organizations in big cities—a community was born.

Leather included a variety of outfit options. Some guys put their uniforms back on and partied in them. Many facets of masculinity were fetishized. The more I checked out the porn these guys were into, the more I felt I could get behind it. The guys in the pictures had big muscles but were not hairless and oiled like bodybuilders. They looked more like lumberjacks. I wasn't real clear on why my mom would ally herself with these guys, but I thought the fellow in the flight suit on page eighteen of *Drummer* magazine was hot.

I decided to talk to my mom about it. We were out at a divey Pakistani restaurant, eating with our hands and drinking steaming cups of milky tea, when I brought it up.

"Well, I got tired of the lesbian drama, so I decided to hang out with gay men instead," Nyna quipped, as though this were routine. She helped herself to more garlic naan.

"What do you do with them?" I asked. The spicy curry was not what was knitting my brow.

"We put on events and the proceeds go to charity. That's all."

"You and the leather guys?"

"Yup."

It seemed at once very simple and yet incredibly complicated. She had somehow become a part of the large but vaguely underground charity circuit of the gay community—a sort of leather Junior League. It's a great idea: they throw themed parties in which money is raised for a cause, and to their credit, the profits are spread out beyond just the most obvious choices of AIDS survivors and aging queens. My mother's leather corps gives their collected cash to veterans, animal shelters, and new immigrants as well. If the organization can stand to publicly accept a check that may be delivered by a man fully clad in leather, then they're willing to give it to them.

Between bites of channa masala, my mother enthused, "You should come to an event. Help out. Invite Jenny and Lior to come work."

And just like that, my best friend, my boyfriend, and I were signed up to work at the A.C. Leather Corps' yearly anniversary and awards ceremony. We would be manning the buffet table like cafeteria ladies, only fancier.

"You are going to have to wear a tux shirt and bow tie," Nyna told me later over the phone. "You have black pants, right?" she continued.

I breathed a sigh of relief that we were going to look like regular caterers at least. "Yeah, I'm sure we all have black pants."

"I'll provide the rest. Thanks for helping, honey. It's going to be tons of fun."

The two straight kids I'd signed up to work with me at an event full of carousing leather folk took the news admirably well. Together, we trotted down to a rented municipal building in downtown Hayward a few weeks later and set post by the buffet.

The place was decorated prom style, with balloons and ribbons hanging over the doors and round tables swathed in rented tablecloths with festive centerpieces and strewn confetti.

As the crowd filed past us and piled food on their plates, I surveyed who these people were. They tended to be older; lots of them were sporting crew cuts. It was practically all men, maybe 98 percent. And it was a black-tie event, so there were leather accents, like bowties, but mostly it was tuxedos and suits. I saw a leather kilt, but that was about as wild as it got, fashion wise.

With the lights dimmed, my mom got on the microphone and held court in an Oscars-style ceremony that honored members of the club who'd stood out in the past year. As their devotion and hard work became plain in the telling of the energy they'd put into raising money for good causes, I had to give it to them: regardless of whatever they did in bed, they were virtuous people. I couldn't be entirely sure I fit in that category.

Next to me, Jenny piled mashed potatoes on plates and pointed out the fellows she found attractive. "He's old now, but I bet back in the day he was a looker," she said after a barrel-chested muscleman passed by.

Many of the men thanked us profusely for showing up to help. "Mistress Nyna has clearly raised you right," said one brawny fellow. No one would have probably known our connection to the event except my mom had taken her chance on the stage to announce that I was the most beautiful girl on earth. That's my mom all right . . .

When the ceremony part of the evening ended, people started dancing and talking in groups, drinks in hand. Having thrown back a few vodka tonics myself, I was badgering my mom, playing the part of the kids that had driven me crazy with questions about her sex life growing up.

"So, like . . . what do they do in bed?" I couldn't help but try to imagine them all naked.

Jenny leaned over to listen, squeamish but alert. She'd always made a much bigger deal about not wanting to hear about my parents' sex life than I did. I thought maybe she was waiting to shush us if it got too gross.

"The same things as everyone else," my mom said patiently. "You know what gay guys do in bed, Kellen. Maybe these ones spank each other and stuff. Maybe they like to dress up. You like guys who wear uniforms, right?"

I looked over at Lior and grinned. He looked good in a bowtie, too, now that I checked.

"Well, some guys are into that too. Or they might like to dress up in leather. Whatever. If you're really curious, I'm sure you can look it up." She was very matter of fact in her pronouncements for someone who was dressed like a pirate—gauzy white blouse, black leather waist cincher, and long velvet skirt.

"Mistress Nyna," a younger man with a leather vest over his tux shirt interrupted. He had soft, sad brown eyes but wore a smile. "Do you know what needs to happen with the leftover alcohol at the end of the event? Because I would take care of it but I'm taking public transportation home."

My mom smiled and assured him that she'd take care of it. As the man walked away, I again thought to myself how very friendly and happy to pitch in and help everyone was.

The leather community, I mused. *Who knew?*

I learned a few things that night: (1) Drag queens serve the stiffest drinks, hands down; (2)Leather men are ridiculously polite; and (3) My man could handle any situation I threw him into. Not that he got harassed or anything—but my mom did get asked all night who the "hottie" with the cute butt was.

"Tell them they can look but not touch," I'd demanded of her before the event.

Lior was more relaxed about it. "Do these pants really make my butt look cute, baby?" he asked me in a private moment toward the end of the evening.

"Oh yeah, I can totally see why those guys want you."

"If someone were to slap my ass, I'd understand," he said with a wink.

"Well you should watch out, because I might just do that." I pulled him to me, wrapped my arms around his waist, and looked up at his hazel eyes. "I can't believe I finally get to have you by my side. I mean, geez, I had to wait long enough."

———

A few days after the charity event, we found ourselves greeted by a big, fluffy Australian shepherd on the steps of Lior's father's house. Inside, while Lior finished up a phone call, I took a seat across from his father on a sofa covered with dog hair.

"Do you want tea?" Daniel asked.

He started to rise again, but my head shaking interrupted him. I smiled and thought of things I could possibly say to pass the time. I was not so comfortable with men of his age, mostly because I didn't know what to talk to them about. I tended to skew toward stereotypical topics, like sports, which was difficult, as I know nothing about them.

"So you're a Niners fan like Lior, right?" I asked Daniel, seeing that the television, while muted, played a football game.

"I was the one who taught Lior to be a Niners fan," he said proudly. "We used to watch the games and I showed him how the quarterback throws to the receiver . . ."

My forehead probably scrunched as I squinted in an attempt to follow what he was saying.

"We could talk about things other than football," he said.

I tried to remember headlines from that week's newspapers that we could discuss. Or things I'd successfully talked about with his mom or any interest of his that Lior might have mentioned that we shared. When I looked at him, I could tell he was doing the same.

"You know, years ago I had this very butch secretary who used to be a marine, and one day we . . ."

It was the usual "I-have-a-gay-friend" speech, but I appreciated the effort.

Since I seemed to be involved in the parent-exploring business now that I was back at home, I had dinner with my father one night as well.

I hadn't seen him since his somewhat unexpected appearance at my high school graduation, but he'd remained in Berkeley all these years, and he seemed attracted to the idea of playing family again now that Lior was around and I was done with college. *Maybe we'll forge some sort of passable dynamic in my early adulthood at last,* I thought. *Maybe I'll finally attain what everyone has always said is missing.*

Personally, it seemed to me that many people I knew would be just as well off without their dads. And for a period during adolescence, most of those friends had been inclined to agree. But a lot of them had gained some extra appreciation for their dads as we'd gotten older; maybe I would too.

Lior and I arrived at a house comfortably appointed with overflowing bookshelves and tasteful art prints. My father came across as witty and cosmopolitan from the start. There was wine selected for each course at dinner, good bread with salad and grilled vegetables. I tried to recall why we weren't good friends. Lior came away from the evening completely charmed, wondering why things between us had gone so roughly in the past.

After a few more dinner dates, a few clues began to emerge. Every conversation we had ended with my dad and me tangled in an argument. Perhaps we were too similar. Whatever the issue, it made me long for the awkward silences that plagued my evening with Lior's father.

At one point, my dad declared the greatest ill of the twentieth century to be feminism.

"Um, no," I countered, barely able to contain my ire. "I believe it's another word that begins with an *f* . . . *fascism.* Yeah, that's the one." Columns of smoke might have been shooting out of my ears.

Elliot, on the other hand, was stifling a smirk. He liked to argue, just for fun. It took all my effort not to crawl over the table and throttle him. He couldn't actually believe his own points, so why was he saying them?

"You sound like a dinosaur," I sputtered. I'd never had blood pressure issues before then, but I could feel them developing. He seemed so antiquated in perspective, but he could argue like the attorney he was. I wasn't used to such a well-trained adversary; I was more used to adults pulling their punches, outside of the rare conservative demagogue.

I ceased to enjoy myself, unable to make any real headway. It reminded me of a phone call we'd had when I was a teenager: I'd tried to make a joke about the tribe in Africa with the clicking language—in passing, as part of a larger story—and he'd interrupted, "Oh you mean the Xhosa," and proceeded to give me a short anthropological history of the tribe. The man knew everything.

I quickly took to bringing more people to dinner—preferably new people who were susceptible to his initial charm—hoping doing so would defuse any potential conflicts between us. It buoyed my tolerance for him when my friends were duly impressed. Lior's best friend Josh said he'd never met someone so well read and interesting. I reminded myself of this when I next found myself wanting to strangle my father.

On top of this, he took to giving me household items of his on each visit. It made me uncomfortable, all the gift giving—one, I wasn't sure if he was doing it out of some suicidal impulse, and two, I wasn't sure how to accept all these things from someone with whom I'd had such an otherwise truncated relationship. I didn't want to be indebted. On one visit he gave me a dozen used world music CDs from areas as far-flung as Laos and the Silk Road, a large kitchen knife, a pasta maker with a ravioli mold, and a bamboo cutting board.

"I never use these things," he said, maniacally piling them into my arms as Lior and I got ready to go. He threw an electric toothbrush on top. "Better that everything should go to someone who'll appreciate it. Next time you come over I'll have so much more stuff to give you."

As I edged out the door I felt relieved to be headed to my car and away. I found myself looking forward to living elsewhere and only feeling obligated to see him on visits home.

19

Cascades

ior only applied to large schools in big cities. He was not looking for the typical college experience, and thankfully didn't want to strand me in some random college cow town. "Besides, I don't want to be stuck socializing only with eighteen-year-olds either," he explained. In the end he went for the University of Texas in Austin, the University of California in Los Angeles, and the University of Washington in Seattle.

"I think UCLA would be perfect," I said. "I could pursue acting again. We'd be close to home and family, along with the great weather. That's my top choice."

Only he didn't get in.

"I can't believe they didn't accept you," I said. "What were they thinking? You wrote your effin' essay about having been in combat—I mean, how many college freshmen can do that?"

Maybe then, with the wars in Iraq and Afghanistan gearing up, there were more than I thought. I'd expected Lior's experience in the Israeli Defense Forces would get him in wherever he wanted. Universities are full of people who have no comparable knowledge. You'd think those stuffy academics would eat it up. But that didn't seem to be the case at UCLA. So it would be the "San Francisco of Texas"-Austin- or Seattle, both places I'd never been. I didn't care which panned out. I was, however, surprised when the University of Washington became our only option.

"Are you flipping kidding me?" I said to Lior while rubbing his back. He was silently reading a letter of rejection. "Those losers don't know what they're missing. Besides, I didn't want to live in Texas anyway." My mom hadn't worked that hard to leave there just for me to go running back.

There was no discussion over whether I would go with him. I hadn't much prioritized my acting career during school or in the time since we'd been living in San Francisco. I could make no claim to acting's hold on me that would make it worth leaving the man I loved. He had moved back from Israel for me, I reasoned. I could move to Seattle for him. The memory of endless anticipation and delayed gratification was still fresh.

When Lior went to Washington for freshman orientation, he picked out a place for us to live.

"I trust you to find something nice," I told him before he left. "After all, I clearly will live anywhere."

He picked out an apartment in a neighborhood that was somewhat "whiter" and "cuter" than I would have chosen, but I let it slide.

"It's close to the university, in a neighborhood historically known for artists, and has a farmer's market on the weekends," he told me in consolation.

"Moving on up . . ." I joked.

Shortly before Lior and I left town, my father and I had our inevitable falling out. Our relationship had always been cyclical and disappointing, and this round proved to be no different. He claimed that I didn't pay him enough attention, that I had neglected our relationship, and that he wanted to end "this charade." By e-mail, he told me that there was no need for us to speak further, ever.

"Well, that was kind of harsh," I told Lior. "None of the people who actually raised me complain about the amount of time they get."

"Want a hug?" he offered, noticing my eyes welling up.

I'll readily admit that as soon as my dad cut me off I began to miss him, both as a figure and a concept. I wished that my mother had chosen some Frenchman, known only in old pictures and lost to time; then I could have built fantasies and pined, instead of trying again every few years with the man I had.

I didn't know him well enough to understand fully the ways in which we were similar. So much of my personality was clearly traceable to my mother that the rest was left in shadow. I drew him into the negative spaces.

I do know that my dad managed to win on Jeopardy for three days in a row, and I therefore credit my ability to remember minutiae to him. It's the sort of shallow intellect that I rely on daily and yet am ashamed of. My bad moods, anxiety, and moribund dramatic sensibility so differs from my mother's fierce optimism that I am sure he is also afflicted.

I knew that I owed part of my identity to him, and yet his entitlement to me seemed always to get in the way of our relationship. He got too caught up in the office of "FATHER," and then demanded things. This is what was preoccupying my mind during our move to the Northwest.

I drove most of the way up to Seattle because my name was the one on the U-Haul contract and Lior and I were rule-following folks—

to a point, anyway. Our friend had given us a Tupperware container full of weed cookies, so Lior slept through most of the ride, rising only to eat another cookie and fall back into a hazy sleep; I ate just one and ruminated on the father disaster and our future. In Weed, California, we pulled off the highway to snap photos, thanks to its silly name, only to see a grown man in a moose suit riding a child's tricycle around the parking lot of a roadside motel. He waved at us as we drove by.

When we finally arrived at our new front door in the middle of the night, we couldn't get in—apparently, there had been some confusion with the landlord. My anxious bladder took it personally that I had to pee in the cute public park next to our new abode.

"I can't believe we are going to sleep in the stupid moving van after driving this far," I said to Lior upon returning from the park with slightly damp panties. A middle-of-the-night call was made to our new landlord and we got inside.

Empty apartments are always so depressing. In the morning, when we rolled up the sleeping bags we'd thrown on the floor, I was disgruntled by the white walls and bland tan carpeting. *I'd rather live in a studio with Casbah doorways, like I did with Cody,* I thought. *Somewhere with some pizzazz!* I told Lior that I hated the whole place—everything but the pink tiling in the bathroom. I couldn't get away with claiming to dislike that, and I knew it.

"That was part of the reason I took the place, baby, I know you love pink . . ."

I stared at him, thinking, *This had better get better, quick.*

We began setting up our newborn household with the blend of our things but got stuck on the tapestry of the Virgin Mary I pulled from a box.

"We're Jewish and she is the mother of Jesus; there is no way she's going up on our walls," Lior said. "What's next, are you going to bring in a Christmas tree in December?"

"I don't know why not," I said. "It's just another misappropriated pagan symbol. We could call it a winter solstice tree. "

Santa never came to my house, but it wasn't because we were Jewish. We still had the tree and presents thanks to three out of four moms having grown up with Christmas. Santa didn't come because, in Nyna's words, "Why would I let some strange man into my house under the pretense of giving my child presents?" Mrs. Claus could come in through the window if she wanted to, my mother said. We didn't have a chimney, so the window part was reasonable at least. The thing is, none of my family's wacky sensibilities ever fazed me. I knew other kids weren't hearing the same version of things, but I also took for granted that we had a special relationship with the North Pole that allowed us this exception.

Lior, raised far more traditionally Jewish, dismissed Christmas and any assimilated compromises with it. My claims that our tree served to commemorate the solstice more than it did Christ's birth did nothing to convince him, even once he was made aware of our pagan traditions. I think he saw any celebration of the Christmas holiday as akin to bowing to the Romans or whatever.

"I'm not having Jesus stuff up in my house," he said.

"But the Virgin's the depiction of the goddess in Christian culture is all. It's the sublimation of her into the patriarchal paradigm."

"Whatever. I don't want it on the walls."

I suggested we wrestle over it, knowing who would win. While he pinned me, he said he didn't want a Christmas stocking either. I had to acquiesce. In exchange for my putting the Virgin back in the box, he promised to worship my own "heavenly" body.

Once all the stuff had been packed into cabinets and closets, books put on the shelves, and the TV set up and turned on, we sat down on a couch we'd salvaged from the street corner and admired our new life. It was a little depressing that it all went up so quickly, but it looked pretty good. We'd repurposed a marigold colored sari and tacked it up on the wall next to a table covered in a Provençal-printed cloth; the layered yellows gave that corner an especially cheery feel.

In terms of interior decorating, I could do anything I wanted with the space—Lior had no real investment in the decor. "Maybe I'll find a print to hang over by the bathroom," I suggested, but the idea sparked no response from him.

I'm going to have to find some girlfriends up here ASAP, I realized.

Within the first few weeks in Seattle, I found a job playing mother to a room of nine babies, ages three to seventeen months, in the infant room of a Montessori school associated with the university. The room was bright, with windows on two sides and blue mats on the floor as a complement to the low shelves that held wooden, not plastic, toys. Child-sized chairs and a wooden table sat next to a mini fridge that held bountiful organic snacks.

The concept in Montessori is all about self-propelled learning. In accordance with Mama Montessori's teachings, from the moment kids can do something by themselves, we should refuse to do it for them. As a philosophy it jives well with the American emphasis on independence and self-sufficiency.

I began to understand from my first day at the school that if they could walk, we weren't carrying them. Likewise we didn't tie shoes, wash dishes, or put on coats once the kids showed they had the capacity. There was no praise. When Bobby or Sue painted a pretty picture, we didn't judge it but rather picked out salient details. "I see that you used red and blue." This was so they could decide for themselves the quality of their own work and find self-fulfillment in a job well done. In a corner of the room, an alcove had mats on the floor so that when the babies got tired they could crawl to their beds and, upon waking, choose on their own to rejoin the group.

My co-employee clarified these ideas to me while we bleached toys—how the relationship between the teacher and student in Montessori was intentionally unobtrusive. We were observers in the classroom, watching over our petite charges to facilitate their safe exploration of the prepared world.

"They gotta be on the floor so they can crawl around and stuff things in their yammers. That's their 'work.'" She used finger quotes on the last word of the sentence. They loved that word there. Toys were called "works," the children's play was called "work." They sure thought work was great. I couldn't help but think of the words written on the gates of Auschwitz: *Work Makes You Free.*

Anyhow, as long as no one was crying, needing to be changed, or in danger of being hurt, the babies interacted entirely with each other. My supervisor, a calm woman who claimed to have been more boisterous in the past, said I wasn't there to entertain the infants. "I know you're an actress," she said, "but this isn't about you and your needs." I kept getting in trouble for kissing the babies. I'd been passed from arm to arm as a child, cuddled to sleep, awoken with kisses, endlessly attended to. The philosophical change was hard to adjust to.

There were two other girls who remained consistent presences while I was there. One was a Polish rocker with an interest in existentialism and a pixie haircut, and the other was a white girl from the West Seattle hood named Tiffany, or Taffy if you were close to her. There was also a third employee, but "she" was a wild card who changed with the season. The low pay resulted in high turnover.

The main two girls ruled the roost. They paid me no attention until I slipped up, partway through my second week, and mentioned to one of them that I'd done a bunch of drugs in high school, and she told the other.

"Sorry, but we totally thought you were some kind of Christian goody-goody," the rocker said. "Now that we've gotten that misconception out of the way, we can be friends. I'm Agnes." She extended a limp-wristed and fine-boned hand for shaking. She reintroduced herself like we were meeting anew, this time as peers.

Agnes was fond of talking about her recent triumph over methamphetamines and her penchant for older men—preferably in bands. Tiffany, the other girl, talked a lot about bar fights.

We weren't supposed to talk among ourselves but rather quietly observe the infants' activities and offer them appropriate stimulus when necessary, but that was a lot to ask of four girls in their early twenties. So in the time between tasks, such as changing diapers and setting up for snack, all manner of conversation arose.

Tiffany often, when swearing, would tilt her head down toward her chest and slip into a stage whisper—"Like I told the *bitch*, I needed to pee." The only issue with this was she generally had a baby in her lap when she did it, despite the philosophy of keeping them on the ground, so when she tilted her head it directed her whisper onto the top of the child's head, like a funnel right into the kid's ear, practically. It was almost as if she was swearing especially for the infants.

Tiffany was the first girl I'd met who regularly got into bar brawls, and she was always incredulous at our shocked responses to her stories.

"Don't you ever get bothered by these (whisper) *bitches* who want to start trouble?"

I wasn't sure if it was the difference in where we were hanging out that did it but I had to say no, that I didn't.

We all got along pretty well on the whole, and it seemed like we might be able to hang out outside of work, if not, perhaps, in

Tiffany's regular dives. So it was a great job outside of the fact that I made only a couple dollars above minimum wage and the day often ended with three babies in my lap and two more clinging to my knees, wailing. Okay, I was drowning in other people's children.

At those moments I was inspired to furtively observe where I had put myself in life. I moved here for him? To the Pacific Northwest? I'd never even been inclined to visit the region. How had I ended up living there? I was dismayed to be playing an adult full-time on the weekdays but still babysitting for extra cash on the weekends. There's only so mature you can feel when you are spending your Friday night sitting on someone else's couch and watching their TV with a baby monitor beside you.

One particular house in which I found myself on a weekend evening, after a short search of their bedroom drawers, seemed to have nothing naughty in it at all. Was it possible? Did they exist in a totally non-transgressive space? Would I someday do that— cease to crave exhilaration, a sense of wild? It made me want to cry. There weren't even photos from before the baby that suggested that they'd changed. Did they ever have mischief in their lives? I hoped not, since that would indicate consistent staidness, but still I wondered, would I shrivel into boring one day too?

I told Lior about my concerns the next night. We were involved with very different demographics. He got to go to college parties while I discussed which brand of breast pump was better. Maybe I was jealous that Lior got a chance to be young again.

"Baby, you wouldn't believe the kind of things that come out of these kids' mouths," Lior said to me over a dinner of tofu stir-fry. In a class for freshman about the temptations of freedom, he stood out like a sore thumb. The class was being taught by a junior two years younger than him. At one point she suggested the other students direct their questions at him instead—"You know, since you probably know more about this stuff than I do."

He mentioned living with me and another student asked, "Are your parents okay with that?"

He told me that he struggled not to laugh before explaining that it had been almost five years since he had lived with them and he'd been at war in the Middle East in the years since. He felt older than them by lifetimes and envious of their naive bliss; having decided that the army demanded he be plenty mature for long enough, he was ready to regress.

I couldn't blame him. Now twenty-two, I was vacillating around this whole adulthood thing. Like someone poised above a swimming pool, I couldn't decide whether to dip my toes or jump all the way in—I was tempted to wrap my towel back around me and go back inside.

20

2004

Seattle's gray and cold weather created preferences for indoor activities. Why take the time to bundle up and brave the elements if you can just get laid at home? We had made it into the second semester of Lior's first year in school and were slogging our way through winter together.

On a Friday night we were doing the classic couple "movie-and-popcorn-on-the-couch" thing, with a selection picked out from our local video store, titled *An Unnatural History of the Cane Toad*. A scene featured a young girl carousing in her backyard in a pinafore, a massive pet toad in her hands.

"I want a toad you need two hands for," I said emphatically to Lior. I could see myself in a pinafore and pigtails, with my new pet as an accessory.

We both liked toads and frogs. This mutual interest had already led to family members buying endless frog and toad tchotchkes on our behalf. Our little apartment featured quite a few amphibious collectibles and we'd already declared a moratorium.

"Do you think we're ready for a pet?" he replied with a grin.

"I think we might be ready for the responsibility of pet owner-ship," I wagered. Neither of us was fazed by the less-than-flattering portrait of the species contained in the film. Outside of the cute girl there had been no indication they made good companions.

"My dad has been trying to figure out what to get us as a shared gift for the holidays. I bet he'd be glad to pay for it," Lior said.

We looked up cane toads online and found that, thanks to the blessings of modern technology, we could order them then and there, have them shipped right to us. It would only take three days.

The company that provided them otherwise specialized in school supplies of the inanimate variety, leading me to believe that perhaps our buying the toads might be a rescue from a more nefar-ious conclusion.

"We'll be saving it from being a science experiment!" I exclaimed. I felt vaguely like Mother Teresa.

"It says they come in sets of three," he said, reading the website.

"Well, we only want one, right? Put it in the comments section."

And just like that, we were pet owners.

But when they arrived in the mail, I instantly felt rather guilty for having sent for them. The cardboard box contained two toads, even though we had asked them to send us only one—and even if two was a compromise, the box did not seem meant for both. Then again, I didn't think the idea of one toad, sliding back and forth in the space of the box, seemed much preferable, even if bet-ter aerated.

I wondered if they'd bumped together while traveling and if a particular relationship between them had already been forged in the confines of their cattle car–like experience. (You can project a lot onto toads; they don't provide much counterevidence for any opposing hypothesis.)

We called the school supply company from which they'd come.

"Where do you-all source these from, anyway?" I inquired.

"The swamp," answered a woman with a strong coastal Southern accent.

Learning that the toads were wild caught, I imagined that they hated us and blamed us for their incarceration. Had it been on our order that they were attained? If we'd never called would they still be wallowing happily in the bayou? I stared into the aquarium we'd moved them into. They sat on top of the coconut hull bedding that we'd bought earlier in the day along with a piece of bark for them to nestle under.

"Do you feel like they are staring at you with resentment?" I asked Lior.

"I don't think they have high enough functioning for that feeling. If anything, they probably just want to eat you," he said.

The species itself is considered a big pest in Australia, where it was introduced to combat some other scourge and then spread like wildfire. Because of this, it is regularly disposed of in a myriad of callous manners. A search online showed toads splashed with acid and squashed by the hundreds on the road. This did not abate my guilt, even though our misdeeds unto the toad population paled in comparison. I felt like a bad toad mother.

This was another level of commitment for our relationship. First the toad, then a puppy, then kids—that's how it goes, right? I wished we were doing a better job with our first attempt at co-parenting.

It took me past the end of winter, through spring, and part of the way into June before I came to terms with how one day bled into another at work in the baby room. Changing diapers, feeding snacks, getting ready to go outside, and taking a walk— a succession of daily routine. Every day was a variation on the one before, with me searching out tiny milestones to mark the passage of time. On long walks, when I pulled a wooden wagon piled with six infants, I noticed the flowers on the blackberry bushes becoming berries. The ducklings that swam behind their mother on Lake Washington lost their downy fuzz. One day, finally, I stripped off my sweater because it was so hot. My brow burst into sweat and I brushed the salty droplets back into my hair, squinted into the bright sun. Seattle on a nice summer day is incomparable. Everything is green; the water shimmers. People run out of office buildings to rent kayaks impromptu.

I took to carrying a pail with me on our alfresco jaunts and used infant/toddler labor to collect a dozen cobblers' worth of sweet blackberries. I let my workers eat their fill—resulting later in parent's questions about their kids' diapers full of seeds. Their purple faces all wore grins on those afternoons. Pushing the wagon through the brambles, I wouldn't have been surprised to find a bear following us, like in the children's book *Blueberries for Sal*. I made contingency plans in case of that, and also in case we rolled over a beehive. But even as I contentedly strategized in the sunshine, I wanted the old summer vacation of my youth—the change of venue, school break, camp, traveling. I felt old even though I had no right to. Was it part of aging, this holding on with one's fingernails to each season and passing day?

On one of those long summer walks, maybe in August or September, a newly striding toddler intently examined something long ago squashed on the road. Another teacher tried vainly to pull him by the arm away and forward. Ahead of us, a murder of crows sat on the telephone line. I studied them instead of paying attention to the squabbles between the kids in the wagon. Two fat black birds sidled up above us to watch our tiny drama as in the distance. One crow cawed and set off a crescendo of response. I smiled and thought of the name for crow in Hebrew, *orev*, and of Lior's army unit, Orev Golani.

That night at home, over grilled salmon eaten in the living room, I said, "Remember when we were involved in world politics?"

When Israel was in the news, we watched it from the couch, eyes laminated to the television. Lior followed any news about the Middle East intently but showed no interest in campus politics.

"I don't think any of those kids know what they're talking about, anyway," he said, "and it's not like any real change is going to come from college kids in the States hollering at each other."

"Did you feel that way when I was active in Israeli politics at NYU? That nothing I did makes a difference? Because that dialogue group is still going . . ."

If I was honest with myself, the concern that nothing I'd done truly mattered ate at me and burrowed like some prehistoric worm. Outside was a city, Seattle, far removed from war, united by an appreciation of nature and technology in equal parts, and most of the time it seemed like our lives were a drop in the bucket of humanity. I thought about how someone like the DC Sniper or the guy that married Britney Spears for fifty-five hours goes from being an unknown to center stage, in an instant, by way of a few decisions made in a day or two. We are all a part of history; sometimes it's just clearer how you're connected to it.

"But doesn't it bother you to feel so peripheral?" I pressed.

"It bothers me to be so far away from my boys and know that they are in danger," he said.

It had already been over a year since we'd been back. Lior's Hebrew had rusted slightly; mine had disappeared. Our lives seemed sculpted from a different material than before.

Sometimes the dream took place at Helen's ranch, other times on a cruise ship filled with kids from my high school. In the way of dreams, settings morphed at will, as did the people, but the core idea was the same: Lior had cheated or was leaving me for another woman. In response, I was distraught, but he didn't care, and no amount of caterwauling on my part would change his mind. I tore my hair. I screamed till my throat was raw and useless. I threatened my own life, and his, to no effect. I attacked him physically. I shrieked, moaned and eventually collapsed. I had no control.

When I woke in our bed after one of these dreams, tangled in the sheets, Lior was flat on his back. His face belied no anxiety when I went to rouse him. I wanted reassurance that it was just a dream, that in real life he cared about how I felt. I wanted him to hold me and quiet my mind. He seemed to be sleeping peacefully, but when I lightly placed my palm on his shoulder, he jolted awake. His body arched to sitting up, his eyes blinked instantly open and awake, sweeping the room. His hand grabbed my wrist. He dropped it a second later, when he realized where he was.

"What is it?" he said, the briefest bit of worry creasing his brow, his stoic veneer momentarily ruffled.

"I had a bad dream is all," I told him. "I didn't mean for it to be quite such a production. Are you okay?" He only vaguely seemed to be with me in the room; part of him still seemed in his dream, caught the same way I was.

"I'm fine," he said. The rest of him returned. His eyes met mine in the dark.

"A little leftover army training?" I joked.

The air around us was warm and stuffy.

"Probably," he conceded.

I felt bad for waking him up but the dream sat heavily on me, and before he went back to sleep he asked me if I was still upset.

"You know it's just a dream, right?"

"Yeah," I said. "I guess it hasn't worn off."

He settled back down and I cuddled my head on his chest, listening to his breath and the slowing rate of his heart, angry and sympathetic.

21

Longevity Breeds Stability?

We were barely twenty miles from our goal when the midnight hour approached: 11:58 on New Year's Eve.

"I think we should pull over," Lior determined.

At the last minute, a bottle of champagne was dug out from the duffel in the backseat and the cork popped. Bubbles poured over car upholstery. Perhaps deer watched us from the darkness. The air smelled like sweet grass and rain as the year changed to 2005. When we took a breather from our celebratory make-out session I said, "We didn't make it in time." The idea had been to spend New Year's at the ranch.

"But at least we're together, and that's what counts," he consoled me.

"I wouldn't rather be with anyone else," I said. "It's very nice of you to spend New Year's with me and my aging lesbians instead of out partying."

Not only were we driving up to the ranch to share the midnight toast with Helen, but Margery, who was eating only steamed vegetables with some plain yogurt as dressing because of her high blood pressure, had been our host for dinner back in the Bay Area.

"You're the party animal between the two of us, and I am perfectly happy to spend the night anywhere you are. Cheers, baby!" he toasted me, and took a swig from the bottle before passing it my way.

"You're perfect," I said to him. I observed the way the stubble edged his face, the sincere and direct look in his eyes that I could see even in the semi-dark. He was staring back at me.

"It's been awhile since you've said that. You used to say it all the time," he reminded me.

"If I've stopped it's only because you protest each time I say it . . . but it's true, you are perfect." I adjusted. "Perfect for me, at least."

"Okay—that, maybe."

We sat in the pitch dark of the country. Now that the magic midnight moment had passed, there was less of a rush to get to the ranch at any particular time. It wasn't so safe sitting partially blocking the tiny, twisting road, but we were ignoring that, along with the emergency brake that stuck in my back, as we attempted to cuddle across the front seat. For the first time, I had the sensation that I'd always been running from man to man, from class to class. Always on the move. But Lior was solid. Immovable. A rock. An island, like Simon and Garfunkel said. I breathed in the field-scented country air. The new year stretched out ahead of us like the road, bathed in the dark.

Time passed, and the more that went by, the more it seemed like this was really going to happen. This "us" thing. We'd been together for a few years; they'd begun to stack up in a promising way. We had survived war, moral arguments, moving in together, traveling, moving to a new city, him being in school, and me being in school.

At that point, if you were me, you would have thought it was going to work out too . . . right?

It turned out that 2005 was the year our friends began to get married. We were entering that middle-class American marrying age, the mid to late twenties. It seemed reasonable for us to consider marriage in our future.

We weren't in much of a rush. We'd always planned that after he graduated from college, we would get engaged, and then at some time, once some money showed, we'd actually get married. I was planning to be a movie star eventually, so maybe I could pay for the wedding.

The details coalesced in my mind rather quickly, though, during Seattle's interminable gray winter that year. The ceremony would be on the ranch, on some perfect little hilltop knoll, and then the reception could be down in the valley. We could use river rocks and the moss that hung dense from the oaks as centerpieces, with some fuchsia orchids added for color. If I could learn to hand-mill wood, we could use some of those giant, looming oak trees to make Tuscan-style tables. Between my days spent in the baby room and the time at home spent entertaining myself while Lior did homework, I had a lot of hours to fill with whimsy. I went so far as to draw up a preliminary guest list.

"We're looking at two hundred minimum. I mean, unless you're willing to start sacrificing, because I for sure have a hundred on my side," I told him.

There was no discernible reply. A paper or two might have shuffled from one end of the couch to the other, but that was the only sound.

A week later, while the streets were still covered in snow, I tried again.

"Baby, if we do wedding favors can those be the homemade aspect that I keep talking about?"

Still no real feedback, but maybe like fashion this was an arena I should expect him to avoid.

Some stuff I had already thought out long beforehand. I had been planning my wedding for as long as I could remember, since my parents' ceremony when I was five. Marriage as a concept was not all that appealing to me, but weddings are the ultimate excuse for feminine excess.

Planning one is difficult, though, because it's all these dreams wrapped around a myriad of details—all these hopes woven into invitations, flatware, flowers, and white versus chocolate buttercream. I, who had never realized anything perfectly or even in an orderly fashion, I of the never straight line—of the little bits sticking out—was anxious about the many ways in which my wedding day would be wrong and messy. Fraught with anxiety, I called Jenny on a lunch break one day.

"If I can't gift wrap a box for a friend's wedding, how ramshackle is my own going to be?" I whined. I knew my family wouldn't help; they embraced imperfection like a long lost relative come home. "And on top of that there is the culture clash that will occur as all the many facets of our lives—mine and Lior's, I mean—collide in full. What are all these people going to think of each other?"

I was breaking into a cold sweat. I tried to play out in my mind the leather boys meeting the religious Special Ops soldiers and then Lior's old Jewish relatives trying to make conversation with Helen. It was unwieldy even in fantasy; safer to obsess over details like flowers and favors.

"It'll be fine, Kellen," Jenny counseled. "Just get him to ask you, already."

At some point—somewhere between the frigid winter and the drippy spring thaw, before Lior had a chance to ask me—the wedding planning got to him. I was midreverie when it happened.

"Do you think buffet or sit-down plating is better? Since the wedding's going to be kosher, if we have salmon, so we can have dairy, will it be hard to get all the plates out at the same time? " I asked him while he tried to do homework in the evening.

"There isn't going to be a wedding if you keep this up," he snapped.

I quickly backtracked. "But it's not serious—my fantasies are too overblown to take seriously. I mean, come on, do you have the ninety grand that I've estimated the tenting will cost? Do my parents? I don't expect it to happen . . . anytime soon."

He had nothing to worry about, but there was a twinkle in my eye. I couldn't help but grin as I said the last two words. He didn't seem to appreciate my pop-in-the-groom-at-the-end, this-is-my-big-day, narcissistic, Bridezilla wedding philosophy.

"Kellen, I mean it."

"It's not about you, so you can chill out. Besides, you were the one who used to be all about getting married."

That seemed so long ago. What relation did the man standing before me have to the young soldier I'd fallen in love with? He used to be fearless; now commitment terrified him. Was the idea of spending the rest of his life with me so much scarier than war?

"Just, if you want it to happen, ever, you have to let it be for awhile," he said sternly. "No more engagement ring style tips. You have to destroy your profile on TheKnot.com. Can we try not focusing on the future so much?" He was wearing his serious soldier face.

If I had to give up the wedding to save the relationship, so be it, but this moratorium on talking about the future was tough to maintain. I worked with babies; it was hard to keep myself from asking about important related issues, like were we going to make our own baby food? I had a strong opinion and I didn't know where he stood on the subject.

"I'm worried you're not even going to let me touch the thing, you're going to be such an expert," he snorted.

Even with the attitude, I thought, *at least he's entertaining the idea.*

"Well, you can definitely have babytime in the mornings and during the middle of the night. That's what all that army training was for, right? Preparing you to be awake at all hours of the day."

I just couldn't help myself.

I had to admit, though, the thought of commitment (as opposed to the thought of wedding cake) was no less scary for me. There are only so many movie nights one can take.

In protest, I got drunk on a Thursday night, like back in my college days, and puked red wine all over our apartment—a consequence of playing hostess and out drinking the guests before smoking *nargilah* and finally trying to make sangria out of turned red wine. That's what always did it—that or making sangria out of cheap red wine and Mountain Dew. Either way, it was bad news.

The next morning, while I felt really stupid, I also felt like, *Finally, a little action around here.* I wished I'd gotten drunker, felt drunker beforehand. *There goes our security deposit*—that's what I bet Lior thought when he saw the crimson stains on our carpets in the filtered morning light.

When I got home from work that night I got a lecture from him. "It doesn't tell you something that you keep puking? That doesn't tell you you're out of control?"

"What are you, my dad? How about I won't condescend to you and you can try to do the same for me. It's not like I drink all the time. I'm not even twenty-five! I fuck up sometimes." *He treats me like a teenage daughter. Why do I inspire such paternalism?* "I took care of myself well enough before you and I could do it again," I told him. "If I want to puke all over my house, that's my prerogative."

Drinking and distraction was what had kept me afloat during the nail-biting months of Lior's army service, but apparently at twenty-four that method's scale of cute was diminishing. I wanted to run out from the house and start a whole new life somewhere exotic. If only I didn't have such a pounding headache.

I was going to be a terrible married person.

The lyrics of The Walkmen's song "Rat Bastard" were stuck in my head. Like them, I felt like I used to go out and know people everywhere I went—and now, if I even went out, it was by myself.

Now that wasn't quite true, of course; back in New York, there was no way to know everybody, and these days I usually went out with Agnes from work. But I was down with the sentiment.

Agnes and I made a real go at making glamorous lives for ourselves in Seattle. In that city of plaid flannel, kayaks, and sandals worn with socks, we tried on wigs, drank bottles of dry rosé wine, dressed up in vintage, and took tons of pictures. In short, we acted like eccentric old biddies together.

"You look mahvalous, dahling," she said, swooning and snapping photos as I played model. "You are the Georgia O'Keeffe to my Stieglitz!"

I was more than happy to have my picture taken and see that I looked good. My dark, cropped bangs and bob had grown out into beachy waves that twisted and looked golden in the sun. The photos confirmed my confidence in a way Lior could not anymore. I felt like the consistency with which we slept together had disqualified him as an objective observer of my looks.

"Let's get all gussied up and go see Mars Volta," Agnes suggested once we were both festooned in miniskirts and boots. "They're playing at The Sunset. We can flirt with hipster boys in glasses!"

I had grown up on country, reggae, and lesbian favorites (read: Tracy Chapman, Joni Mitchell). I'd had a punk rock phase in my adolescence and had picked up hip-hop with blunt smoking; now I was sidling up to rock and roll.

In Seattle, what you listen to is paramount. It's a music city—and not just because it birthed grunge in the early nineties. (Disclaimer: Nirvana *is* my favorite band and always will be.) Head to a house party, and it is likely to have live entertainment; and even if there aren't a couple of long hairs pounding out rock and roll in a corner, music will be the subject of most conversations.

"Did you hear that The Hold Steady are coming out with a new album?"

"Have you heard Thom Yorke is working on a solo project?"

There was no end to the details and speculation.

Keeping up meant learning about a slew of new bands all the time, but it also meant that you could impress your friends with how hip you were, even back in the Bay Area. Between the coffeehouse lit scene, the fresh veggies down by Pike Place, and the quality shows, I felt like I could make a go of my usual snobbery.

Even though Lior showed no interest in accompanying us on our social adventures, with him being so busy I was reluctant to give up the time with him that I had. It meant that my weekends were a tug of war.

"Lemme see if Lior wants to come out with us," I'd tell Agnes. But he'd inevitably say he'd rather watch a movie at home, and I couldn't stand the thought of another night spent on the couch, or the excruciating co-deliberation of what to see. I hated the decision making involved with a Friday night. *What do you want to do for dinner? What do you want to do after? Any ideas?* I felt like the entertainment captain on a cruise ship, responsible for all the fun.

"Okay, well, I'm going out without you then. Call me before you go to bed," I told him before Agnes and I wrapped scarves around our necks, instead of layering on more appropriately protective clothing, and rushed out, arm in arm, into the cold.

"I'm twenty-four . . . why do I feel so damn old?" I whined to

Agnes. "I don't want to stay home and behave. I mean, am I supposed give in on this one?"

With me and Lior this far in, when something bothered one of us about the other we had to consider, "Am I willing to put up with this for the rest of my life?" Forever hung between us.

"Honey," Agnes said, "let's go see how many drinks it takes till you feel young again. I bet it's under three."

She was right, because within two margaritas I was dancing like a rocker chick in an eighties video, and kept at it until my feet hurt so badly I could barely walk.

The drinks and dancing made me friendly. While out at The George and Dragon, an English pub, we met a pair of British tourists who bought us drinks and regaled us with tales of the old country told in funny accents, though through my buzz I could barely understand them. When the bar closed and we still had the energy to party on, I suggested stumbling over to my place and crowding into the living room. We were talking in the super loud tones of drunkards and smoking a joint when Lior shuffled out of our bedroom in his boxers, fists rubbing at sleep-crusted eyes. He looked like a father awakened by children jumping on the bed.

"Hello," he said to the two British fellows, who, based on their looks of surprise, were unaware there was a man at home. "Hello, Agnes," he said, nodding in her direction. "Kellen, may I speak to you in our bedroom for a moment?"

The party was over. As I stepped into the darkened room, everyone slipped out the front door. I couldn't quite explain that in my drunkenness I'd momentarily forgotten that he existed. He stared back with bleary eyes that sought response, a question waiting to be answered. Everyone had to go home, but I, in theory, was already supposed to be there.

I looked at him, closing one eye at a time, trying to focus on him through my stupor. I waited to see what he would say, but now that everyone had gone we found our tongues tied. He climbed back into bed as I stripped down, stumbling slightly when I tried to balance on one foot. He let me crawl in next to him, even though we both knew he was mad. The way he trusted me was scary—it was like bestowing trust on a wild animal in a cage. Like Siegfried and Roy with those tigers.

It would have been nice to be less aware of my slow self-destruction, but I was getting good at self-analysis thanks to my diet of pop psychology books as administered by the library. (I had to do something while Lior was doing homework.) Upon reflection, I decided that part of what was troubling us was that we'd begun to bore each other. It was not one-sided, this malaise; he was no more intrigued by me than I was by him.

We had heard all each other's stories. I was failing as Scheherazade. We were the people who could take for granted all those things we'd dreamed of when he was at war and I was more certain of our love.

During an army buddy's visit to town, I became even more aware of how novelty feeds attraction. Lior was super busy that week so I was left to show his friend around Seattle—his very handsome army buddy, the one with the sexy Mizrachi accent and male model potential. With his black, curly hair and dense, long lashes he reminded me of a particularly good-looking sheep. Despite our having met many times before in Israel, he was still comparatively unknown to me.

You know that phrase "look but don't touch"? I brought along a camera when we went sightseeing, my boyfriend's buddy and I, to Pike Place, Lake Washington, and the locks to see the salmon jump. When we developed the film Lior wondered aloud, "Why are there so many pictures of Omer?"

I blushed and got defensive.

In an attempt to revitalize our love life, I suggested that maybe a little role-playing was the answer.

"You could always dress up in your uniform, for old times' sake," I suggested, trailing a finger over his still-clothed chest flirtatiously. "We could fool around . . ."

I'd gotten gussied up to retrieve him from the Hebrew school where he'd begun teaching. On the drive home, I'd enjoyed the world music program that played Tuesdays on KEXP, the public radio station, and had taken inspiration.

"If I never wear that thing again it'll be too soon," he said. "Besides, I don't think any of what I did over there was sexy. Thoughts of the army don't turn me on," he answered before turning his attention to the homework that sat on the kitchen table.

"Yeah, I guess playing a Palestinian at a roadblock would be wrong," I conceded.

It was my ninth hour of boredom that day. My job with the babies, while emotionally fulfilling and fun, wasn't exactly stimulating for my mind. Now I was alone in the laundromat two blocks from our home, since Lior was studying for finals. I resented doing the majority of the household work, but on some level I must have thought that was how it should be, because I did it anyway. *Fucking patriarchy and its wily little tentacles*, I fumed. Why did I feel so pressed to please him and so dissatisfied at the same time?

There were moments when I was able to turn routine into ritual, but the predictability and intellectual coma I could have done without. By the end of the day, I desperately wanted some adult interaction. Instead, I came home to a man who was impenetrable. A deep, dark pool. A lockbox. A cloudy sky. Which way would the weather go? Was the war to blame for his moods, or was the human condition?

I was trying to reclaim a sense of loving purpose by washing clothes while a hobo dozed in the corner. I sighed loudly and dramatically—the one other person in the laundromat stared at me like I was the crazy one. No one else seemed to be doing laundry quite so emotionally. Could I blame my parents for giving me too much praise as a child? For making me feel like I deserved this huge, exciting life? I was scared my life would turn out to be like everyone else's. My obituary would read: "Routine kills romantic."

When the dryer buzzed, it was time to go home and try to appreciate each other. I focused on all our recent successes: lazy Sundays spent in bed together, my twenty fourth birthday celebrated with a picnic held on blankets laid gently in the grass, with chilled apricot soup and plastic cups of sparkling wine. I used the images, mantra-like, to will myself toward gratitude as I bundled the wash into the backseat of my car and drove the couple of blocks home.

"I'm going to write a book about us," I said to Lior when I waltzed through the front door with our laundry in hand. "I had an epiphany on the way home from the laundromat. I'm going to call it *How to Plan a Gay Kosher Wedding for 250*."

"People are always telling you to write a book about your life," he admitted, looking up.

"And this is a love story for the ages. I mean, if we can make it then anyone can, right?" I said.

He nodded his head.

"You know, usually I feel all blah about our relationship, but then occasionally I have these moments of happy revelation," I continued, not thinking before I spoke.

This seemed to ruin the nice moment we were having, though his retreat back into study didn't really show me one way or the other how he was feeling. It's weird how you can both feel like you never see somebody and be bored by them at the same time, or fight when you really want to make love.

Once I put our clothes away I approached Lior again, this time like a lion might a wildebeest: strategic, trying to play it cool. I had hope that he could be convinced to put me before study, the way I'd dropped everything for the chance to talk to him on the phone when I was in school.

"Hey, baby. How's studying going?" I shifted on my heels, impatient for response.

"Fine."

I watched him work, watched the intensity with which he engaged in his studies. What did I care that much about? Outside of him?

"Are you hungry? I could make you some dinner." Cooking would at least give me something to do.

"No, I'll make myself something if I need to. If you're going to watch television, I'll move to the bedroom, but can you close the door to this room?"

"Yeah, no problem," I said as he gathered his books and went toward our bed without me, closed the door with me on the other side.

"I love you," I said loudly toward the door. *Stupid enigmatic fool! Screw you, your studying, and your dinner!* I stalked off feeling rejected and tempted to hit the town without him. I'd show him who could keep herself entertained. I'd show him that I didn't need him at all . . . but was that the point? Turning to research, I flopped down on the couch, turned the TV on, and launched into reading a relationship book my mom had sent me the week prior. My lesbians love a self-help book.

Though I admired the fact that Lior was putting himself though school, it meant his schedule was hectic. He was at class; then he was at work. He was studying, or he was checking his e-mail. I felt like I didn't ever know what was going on with him outside of physical location, if that. My book suggested that this was an issue.

Since I wanted him to ask me what I was thinking (so I could share it all with him), I thought I'd lead by example.

"What are you thinking about?" I pried, having snuck into the bedroom to bother him.

"You always ask me that."

He tilted his head to stretch his neck. Across the room our toads sat in their aquarium, watching our exchange silently.

Perhaps with a hint of reproach.

"It seems like there's something wrong. I'm getting that stressed-out vibe."

His moods were like a summer Southern night—humid, fetid, tinged with mysterious grief. Although maybe I was being sensitive.

"No. I just have a lot of studying to do." He rubbed at his neck with his broad palm.

"I could give you a massage?" I offered with a wink.

"No. I better stick to this." He wanted me to leave him alone.

I didn't want to.

"Give me an emotion. Are you happy, sad, angry? Do you want to rip my face off? Something, anything? Give me a sense of what's going on with you. Lemme in a little."

Silence greeted my inquiry; there was so much of it. We didn't fight as much as I pestered a wall. It felt like throwing rocks at a tank.

"I'm fine," he said. "I don't have anything else to say. I'm doing my homework is all."

It was clear that for him this was the end of the conversation. Fine. *I can be silent too*, I thought. *I'll sit here and sulk also.* I was learning to be quiet and entertain myself at long last.

It reminded me of being a child, before Ethan was born, and wanting someone to play with. There were days when no one felt up to a round of Barbie, even though there were four of them, and I had to play alone. I never liked that and wasn't adept at containing my ire; usually one of them finally caved. Unfortunately, the lessons we don't learn in childhood, we have to learn as adults.

This time I barely made it through the third minute of silence exiled in the living room before my impulses overrode my prudence. I don't claim to be psychic, but I felt a certain upset in the air!

"Did I do something wrong? It really seems like something is wrong beyond study stress. Are you sure you don't want to talk about it?"

He did not. Lior had feelings but didn't want to admit to them. I was used to a much higher level of emotional expressiveness. Think constant processing. Total sharing. Think raised by lesbians.

22

Mostly We Were Happy

'm acting like this because I'm trying to get a rise out of you," I howled. "You don't love me anymore. You never do anything romantic unless I ask for it. You have no passion."

Lior and I had spent the week fighting, starting Wednesday night with me feeling despondent about life and him not caring about my despondency, and continuing on Thursday, when we'd agreed our relationship was a 2.8 on a scale of 10—mostly owing, I thought, to his lack of effort and refusal to prioritize me. Or at least that was what I had concluded through my tears.

He disagreed.

"I've got a lot on my plate these days," he said, his voice a calm monotone. "I just made it through finals a couple of weeks ago."

"You're on the quarter system, though. You have finals like every three weeks. You had a lot on your plate when you were in the army and that never stopped you."

"I'm tired. I don't feel much passion for anything right now. Maybe I'm depressed," he offered.

His depression didn't concern me; instead, I wished he would do something spectacularly romantic to recapture my heart and distract me. But how could I prod him into action? How to inspire something uninstinctual and unlike him, to be brought forth?

"I don't know how to read your mind," he said with resignation. "I just want to make you happy." He said it like a demand.

"I want you to bring me flowers but I don't want to have to ask you to do it. I want you to do it spontaneously," I declared. "You don't know how to change my mood when I'm upset, but if you were to just pop a bottle of champagne and say we were going to go do something fun that would be a start!"

I was guessing at what might work to make me happy; I didn't really know. This made me burst again into tears. I let them run silently down my cheeks.

You want me to be happy? You and the rest of the world, I thought. If happiness were at my disposal, what was keeping me from grabbing the brass ring? What did happy people have that I did not? I could hear my moms saying it a million times through my childhood, like a Greek chorus on repeat: "All we want is for you to be happy." Being happy was about their only expectation, the only thing they wanted of and for me. Consequently, it was all I wanted from everyone around me. Lior's bad moods and my own were a direct violation of that rule. We should be happy. Life was working out great. Only we couldn't seem to feel the happiness we should, so we fought instead.

Two nights in a row I cried alone in the living room while Lior went to sleep early. The second night I slept on the floor and woke at seven in the morning, when he did, even though I didn't work until ten, to continue fighting. I was of the mind that commitment meant staying up till things got worked out, or else waking up the next morning and continuing to deal with it.

He was always trying to slip away.

"I need some space. I can't take this anymore" was his refrain.

He needed space? I'd grown up in a household of women. I didn't know what that meant.

As the sun crept into the skyline, I stood in our living room, nude, and screamed at him, feeling totally crazy, doing my best banshee impression. He remained totally calm, passive, nonplussed. A parent watching a toddler's tantrum. The more I screamed, the more . . . nothing. It was my nightmare come true. I made long-winded arguments. He acquiesced but didn't change his mind.

"See," I screamed, "you don't care. Look at you—here I am, hysterical, and you're fine, you're barely upset." Hysterical, that's what I had become—a raving, sobbing pile. He was standing across the room from me with his arms crossed. He looked tired, mostly. I wanted to make him so angry he would hit me or scream or something. The best I could get was a stern tone and a slightly raised voice. That could turn a normal woman crazy.

"I'm going to school and then to work. We can talk about this again when I get home," he said hoarsely.

"No. If you cared, you'd stay and argue until we figured something out. You prioritize everything else," I sobbed from the floor.

In theory I could have gone back to sleep, since work didn't start for another two hours, but instead I stayed up and, once he left, called my mama Nyna.

"Hey, Princess," she answered, still sleepy herself.

"I want to leave him. He doesn't care about me or my feelings," I said dramatically. "I scream at him and he doesn't care!" I broke down again into tears.

My mother's voice swept in. "It's his coping mechanism; he's dealt with people yelling at him before, getting in his face. He was in the army, right? He had to stay calm then too." She told me relationships are all about accepting other people for who they are.

"He can't react differently to your hysterics—he doesn't know how."

She wanted me in therapy, or at least in Al-Anon meetings. "They're free," she said, "and it would provide you with someone other than him to deal with some of your feelings. You've got a lot of them; maybe you should spread them around a little."

A surfeit of feeling. High-strung, with a penchant for hysteria. Genetics? Maybe I'm just a brat.

Maybe my mom was right, and our isolation had forced me to rely on him too heavily for emotional contentment. *How do marriages ever work out?* I wondered. *Is it attached to a gradual lowering of expectations? How do I know if what I am asking for is reasonable, or possible, even?*

The next time we fought he said, "I think you're right—I haven't been treating you right. I think that while I love you, I'm not in love with you."

The words were like a slap across the face. I thought to myself, *It's because you've never had a long-term relationship before this and so you doesn't realize this is natural. The honeymoon phase is over; feelings of love between partners ebb and flow.* I had to stop him. He was still talking.

"I feel like I've never been on my own. I was with my parents and then the army and then you. You are all I've known of an adult relationship."

I was stuck in some other movie, not my life, some other's person's reel. He was still talking.

"I need to be by myself for a while. I have growth to do as a person and I don't think I can do it within our relationship."

We'd trapped each other in archetypes: He was boring, antisocial, judgmental, and controlling. He thought I drank too much, was irresponsible, flirted too often, didn't work hard enough. Our lists of each other's flaws were almost as long winded as the litany of praise we'd once exchanged. It was all a creation of our relationship. It wasn't who we were.

"Our relationship seems like a burden. It overwhelms the positives," he said.

I wondered if he'd made a pros and cons list. I wondered if I'd like to see it.

"I want to be selfish and not have to accommodate anyone," he said. "Maybe we should take a break."

At work Friday morning, with tears in my eyes, I held a baby in my arms and studied the tiny curled fingers groping for a mouth, the button nose, and little legs kicking in the air; listened to the sweet grunts and exhalations coming from their precious lips. Babies are the best salve for heartache. I thought about how Lior and I could have had a baby this age by now if we'd been less careful, a baby with beautiful eyes, thick hair, and a cute, plump behind. It made my chest ache to think about how much I loved him and yet how unhappy I was. What's the point of sacrifice and being miserable and moving hundreds of miles from home if it goes unappreciated?

I'd been so busy concentrating on why he didn't appreciate me that I hadn't put a lot of thought into how unhappy I was. It wasn't black and white, it wasn't me 100 percent committed in love and him walking out—we were, in all likelihood, equally unhappy. He was just ready to do something about it. And if neither of us was all that happy, it was the right choice. Just because we'd been so incredibly in love at one point didn't mean that we were working now. I sat down at my lunch break and I wrote him a letter:

Where to start? If anything should be familiar it is this—writing to one another. So many things to say: I think you are a selfish prick and that if I had any backbone I'd leave you or not coddle you as you break my heart, and I think it's totally unfair the way you shut me out about your feelings—what about the team, man? I don't understand what makes me not good enough or if that's not what this is about. Sometimes I think I should get something—commitment? security?—for all that I've put in, but now I think obligation is the worst of reasons to be with someone. I want you to be happy. I don't want to be married someday with you thinking "what if."

What do you do after both parties have acknowledged the inadequacies of the relationship?

Nearby the school where I worked, there was a small Orthodox congregation, and during my relationship crisis I started to go watch the Jews on my lunch break. I cried while black-hatted men weaved in and out of the shul—then I called Jenny, frustrated that I was never in the same place with all the people I loved. My life switched from phone calls with one person to calls with another.

"Life really punishes me for becoming too settled in with trust, you know. It always sends a sharp reminder not to get too cozy," I said to her. I heard my mom in my head insisting that as long as I loved Lior, I shouldn't give up.

"How long do I hold out for the ring if it might not ever come? I hate that thanks to patriarchy, it's up to him to decide," I complained. "He decides when to pop the question, if at all."

I felt like I should get to know what was in store for me so I could make some decisions.

"I mean, give me a probability at least, right? Is it likely? Is there a percentage of likelihood? Give a girl a bone, jeez," I said to Jenny instead of to my boyfriend.

"All you can do is make the decision to stay or go," she said in a patient but resolved tone. "Right now it's not looking so favorable, I would say. It's a bitch not being able to control people, huh? I try all the time," she sympathized.

"This is just part of being together long term . . ." I whined, interrupting.

"But he doesn't know that," she said. "He just has to figure out that he still wants to be in a relationship with you. What keeps folks together is whatever they can give each other that nobody else can."

I thought about the way he made me feel safe and sane. What was I giving Lior compared with what I expected? What about me was worth keeping?

We took a month off to consider things. It lasted quite a bit less than that. Whatever it was that was so great about me, he couldn't stand to be without it. The night we got back together, he was apologetic, taking the blame and promising to make me more of a priority. When we finished the vegetarian dinner he had cooked us, he led me to where he had put rose petals on our bed and set out a bottle of my favorite champagne, Veuve Clicquot. Two glasses sat on our bedside table. He popped the cork and poured us each a glass.

"I love you, baby," we both said. We went back to doing some of the romantic things that had filled our relationship's first few years: notes left for each other in the pockets of our clothing and on surfaces around the house, meet-ups for quickies during lunch. Another year passed.

———

We came to an easy consensus that we should stay at the bed-and-breakfast that advertised llamas as an added attraction when, for our fifth anniversary, we took a vacation to Washington's wine country. Winding through dark green hollows and then orchards, we found the place at dusk, the animals raising their long, slender necks as we pulled in. The bed-and-breakfast stood in a wide-open plain, with rows of story-high green vines on one side. At night we took a walk in the spaces between rows of what we discovered were hops. He held my hand and I thought the eerie surroundings would be scary except that he was beside me.

"What was your favorite wine today?" I asked him.

We compared notes, talked about the funny people who'd tried to sell us on their old grape juice.

"It's not quite Napa," he said.

"It's nice, actually, that it's so much less developed," I said. "Less obnoxious wine snobs everywhere." I smiled at a memory from earlier in the day. "Good job ghost-riding the whip, by the way." In a tipsier moment that afternoon, we had decided to try out a recent hip-hop convention popular in the Bay Area, the deal being you put the car into neutral so that it rolls very slowly and then dance beside or on top of it—or, even less adventurously, hang out the side.

"Oh yeah? You were quite the rock star today yourself—remember when you rolled down the hill at that winery?" He chuckled.

My being in a skirt and kitten heels hadn't stopped me from asking the people who worked there whether anyone had ever rolled down the perfectly manicured and precariously steep grassy embankment that stretched in front of the pseudochateau and, upon hearing not, asking whether it was allowed.

"Well, if it wasn't against the rules..." I said, grinning.

"I just don't think they expected you to go and do it." He looked over at me proudly.

"We were on our way out anyway, and I thought, well, I'm never going to see these people again."

We amused each other. More than anyone else I'd ever met we seemed to have an inexhaustible flow of conversation. Wasn't that what compatibility ultimately was?

"Don't the hops look like a big green blanket laid over a giant clothesline?" I suggested in near whisper. The leafy vines rustled in the wind. The moon rose slowly over them.

He pulled me close and kissed me until I was shivering with something other than cold. I said, "We could lie down here in the rows but I bet there's bugs in them."

Our room had an antique bed with a quilt and a parlor with a tea set spread out on the spindly wood table. The next morning I raised the pot as though to pour tea into one of the intricately decorated teacups so that Lior could take a commemorative photo. Looking at it, you can tell that I was really happy.

2006

Working as a daycare wage-slave had dialed up my debt. We only got paid once a month, so after funds ran out on week two the rest had to be put on credit. Month by month it added up, until finally, after being refused a fifty-cent raise two years into the job—a raise that would have brought my salary up to a massive ten dollars an hour—I'd had enough. I marched into the front office and I told the day care director I thought I could do better for myself.

"Is that a threat? Because I don't take kindly to ultimatums," she bellowed. Her personality could best be described with the phrase "a bull in a china shop."

"I have an NYU degree—I think I can find other work," I said with an admittedly self-satisfied tone.

"Well, I bet you can't even get hired at McDonald's," she said as a sort of good-bye.

Thank the sweet Lord I was right and my former boss was wrong. I did get hired for a good position, although one much better suited to someone with more extensive experience in the childcare field than I had. I went from underestimated to overestimated real quick. Answering one ad off Craigslist and dazzling them in a brief interview with big words like "developmentally appropriate" and "child-led pedagogy," I was hired.

Suddenly I was in charge of "continuing education and quality improvement for childcare providers" for all of Snohomish County, the one due north of Seattle. I could barely pronounce the name of the place and was expected to tell twenty-year veterans of the industry in the area how to better do their jobs.

––––––––––––

The town in which my new job was located had a vaguely postindustrial apocalyptic feel, only it seemed the world had died from shooting meth, judging by the looks of the zombie resident survivors. They had dead eyes, acne-scarred faces, and a lurching shuffle instead of a walk. Downtown was full of them.

The office was one branch of a much larger organization, the twentieth largest charity in the United States, one that funded cradle-to-grave services, everything from childcare referrals to nursing homes. Our office was in a wing of a building holding multiple divisions. Because I was hired during the holiday season and it was a Christian business, it looked like Christmas had imploded inside, which, despite my discomfort with cultural hegemony, was a nice contrast to the world outside.

My first day on the job, the head of the department pulled me into the same office where I had been interviewed. Addressing me like a confidant, she said, "There's an office culture that's developed that I don't see as positive. It's an acceptance of the status quo—a sense of entitlement, a 'my job is hard enough' attitude. So I felt like we needed to bring in some fresh blood." Basically, I was supposed to show everyone how it was done both in the office and in the field. Lead by example. Revitalize morale. Meanwhile, I still didn't know where to get lunch.

Not fifteen minutes after I'd gone back to my work, a blonde with an early nineties feathered haircut came by my desk.

"I see you met the boss," she said. "Well, she's new too, barely been here a year, for the record. I've been working here for six years now, and I'll tell you what's really going on. I'm technically the receptionist, but you might as well say I'm in charge."

When I stared beyond her I could see alphabet cutouts like the ones in my kindergarten class push pinned into the wall. I wondered if I was meeting the interior designer of this locale. It turned out her older sister was my supervisor.

"They actually hired her after me, but since she has no power over my position they said it was okay," she said, putting extra emphasis on the last part and sticking out her tongue, since her sibling was passing by. I could tell these were the people I would have to keep happy.

Up until six months prior, the building I worked in had been a thrift store, so although there was a sign in the front window breaking the news of the change in business, people wandered in off the street all day. They breezed right in, assuming we were still a thrift store. And because thrift stores cater to those who need things cheap, the people who barged in tended to be an assortment from the underclass: the homeless, the elderly, the mentally ill, and the drug-addled. Along with an older gentleman picking up my stapler right off my desk and asking me how much I wanted for it, we had a homeless lady come in one day during my first month there and pee in front of the counter that served as a reception desk.

"I guess I'll clean that up," said the blonde with bad hair. "Since I do everything around here already."

Taking an administrative job in childcare policy quickly convinced me I wasn't made for an office environment. My first clue came

195

when my supervisor showed me a log in which I was to write the details of any call coming in or out through my line for funding purposes.

"We're on a grant, so they really want to make sure that we aren't wasting their money," she explained.

It seemed to me like the needless extra step was the waste. This focus on efficiency did not prevent them from spending the majority of every day holding meetings in which we discussed all sorts of inane minutiae that in theory helped large projects get accomplished, although I wasn't clear on how. The days full of meeting after meeting and the requirement of constant documentation overwhelmed my sense of whatever good I was doing for the community. Even if it directly kept people from being tortured, I wasn't sure I was willing to sit and do paperwork all day.

Site visits were my only respite from the meetings. The basic gist of those visits was that I came into people's places of business—often their homes, in the day care cases—and told them what to do to "improve the environment."

They gave me supplies to hand out in order to make it a slightly less bitter pill—coloring books, craft kits, and the like—but the adults weren't usually real happy to see me. I'd saunter into some woman's home, cluttered with the debris of childhood and the grubby youths that went along with it. I'd try to make conversation about the fact that her husband was a military man and I knew how that was, but no real trust would be built. So then I'd focus on the children.

They all just wanted attention and love. That's all most people want—that and not to go hungry, which, since my territory covered both urban and rural areas stuck in the mire of modern poverty, was sometimes an issue. I had never seen white kids that

196

poor before. I had thought that such destitution was confined to the third world, yet there I was only a quarter tank's drive from Seattle.

At a Boys & Girls Club, a boy with straw-colored hair and a missing front tooth came up to me. He had that "take attention wherever I can get it" desperation wafting off him. He didn't have a jacket and it was unseasonably cold out. I shot the director of the program a look.

"Sometimes they forget them at home and sometimes they just don't have them," he said, inferring my disapproval.

"I didn't get no lunch and I'm still hungry from snack," the kid said. His blond hair glinted in the fading sunshine. "My stepdad burnt down my mama's house," he said, all nonchalance.

I tried to think which of the books I'd brought might make his life more manageable but I knew neither the one about pirates nor the one about dinosaurs would make up for his lack of a decent home life. My site visit did little to make those kids' lives better, or to make their town less bleak.

Between the frustration of not being able to mediate the tragedy apparent in the childcare system and the drudgery of spending most of my time in meeting purgatory, acting began to regain its original appeal. My dreams began to form around that instead of weddings, my old fantasy of choice.

First I would become an indie movie star, like Chloë Sevigny or Parker Posey; then Lior and I would get married in my old dream wedding, move to the ranch, have some babies and foster some kids and maybe even open a lesbian retirement home. I could occasionally do films from my rural wonderland. *InStyle* magazine could come do a profile, since I already had the movie star–like property. I'd give away millions to charity. Lior just had to get on board.

"What do you think, baby, can you find something to do with your economics degree that allows you to work from the ranch?" I asked while giving him a shoulder rub one night after work. He didn't answer. In theory we would be moving to Los Angeles so I could properly pursue my acting career in the next year and a half. This was the trade-off for my having spent the last three years in the rainiest corner of the country.

It turned out I didn't have to make it down to Los Angeles for the press to come calling for me. My lesbian parents managed to get me some media attention not a month after my first conversation about returning to acting had occurred. The lesbian parents—they're good for that.

It had been awhile since I'd been called upon to represent my family in print, so I'd had to seek the limelight in other ways. I'd been a media star as a child, but interest waned the older I got. Past high school, media interviews about my lesbian moms were rare. It made sense, since people's parents presumably fade to the periphery of their lives around that time. But now someone was writing an article on adult children of gay parents—perfect for me, since I was getting good at pretending to be a grown-up.

On a predetermined afternoon, I spoke to a reporter from the *Seattle Times*. Actually, first she stood me up, which made me feel like I'd presumed a little too much self-importance. However, when she did arrive it was with extra reverence, so maybe it balanced out

Her journalistic strategy was tell the story through my voice, using my words. I pretty much summarized for her everything I've said in the last two hundred pages here. She struggled to keep up with me as she took notes on a yellow standard pad.

With barely a prompt, I launched into my family structure and

I talked about being a representative for my community and how being raised by lesbians had shaped my world view.

She asked how I felt I was different.

Growing up with gay parents, I told the reporter, was like being the child of celebrities. I gave her a list of things I shared in common with Jamie Lee Curtis: We both grew up with people's curiosity and the sense of living in a fishbowl; we both had to defend our parents in the media; we both probably felt like freaks sometimes; and we both had to prove ourselves as individually interesting when compared to our folks.

"But then again, we are sort of inevitably more interesting than average, thanks to our unconventional upbringing."

"Even if for the rest of my life I was a yuppie—a fine-wine, fancy-restaurant soccer mom—it only takes a trip home to give all that up, to stride right back into the counterculture." I carry that possibility like a turtle shell. That was part of what I tried to explain to her.

Since the interview took place at a coffee shop where my friend Agnes worked, she listened in. Agnes seemed surprised at my blabbering on for over two hours, and at some of what I admitted. She also thought too many of my jokes could be misconstrued.

"Come on Kellen, what if middle America reads this and takes you seriously? I can't believe you mentioned lesbians castrating cattle on the ranch, it's no good..."

"But we do castrate them, twice a year!"

Agnes wiped down countertops as she dispensed her retroactive advice. And much of what she said was valid; I'd forgotten to self-censor because I was out of practice. I'd worked the interview as vaudeville, almost, with "Did you hear the one about lesbians collecting their lovers?" interposed with my opinions on legislation about custody or my own reflections on American masculinity. I probably came across as both coached and obliviously inappropriate all at once.

The newspaper sent out a wonderful photographer to take pictures of Lior and me as a couple, a fellow who used his headlights as lighting to capture us on the street after dark. The photos made us look like coat models for London Fog. Our hair looked done though it wasn't, his dark, glossy ringlets complementing my smooth golden mane, the stairs out front of our house momentarily transformed into a film noir scene.

The article had funny effects in the more public spheres of our lives. People at our respective workplaces saw it and brought copies to meetings we attended. E-mails poured in from acquaintances—"I saw you in the paper." I was used to it and amenable. Lior was not. I tried to convince him that there were perks to balance out the invasion of our privacy, like the photoshoot. He was not persuaded.

I'm not sure he liked my description of him, either. He definitely bore the brunt of my sound bites. I cast him almost mythologically—"a soldier, yet remarkably homophobia-free."

He objected, noting the Israeli Special Forces is not a hotbed of homophobia to begin with. "Our cook was openly gay, remember? And all of us got along with him fine," he reminded me.

There is a much more relaxed and affectionate culture among men in the Israeli military—Lior's unit had paired off into cuddle buddies on cold desert nights without fuss.

He didn't appreciate being boiled down, summarized, sketched to the public in random details like "He's a man's man" and "He's sure got his fair share of mothers-in-law." He disliked the trite. He knew himself to be much more than the caricature he saw in my description.

"I can't help that you happened to have worked with my fantasy of men, garnered from Marlboro ads and the like," I responded. "You enable my projections."

It was another rainy day in Seattle. The mist hung off the boughs of trees, washed over my face anytime I left the house—not that I was headed anywhere. Generally speaking.

"I'm sad," I told Lior. "I don't know why. Make it better." I remembered a time when just the sound of his voice on the line could make the worst of days melt away—how I'd told Cody to call him and put the phone to my ear if I was ever really upset.

"It's probably the weather," he offered now, over five years later. Was he right? Was seasonal affective disorder the cause of our failure? Would a light box have saved us?

"No, it's not," I said."I feel like I have nothing going on in my life to make me happy."

"You should try and do a play or a movie, maybe."

He was trying to be helpful.

"Who's to say that acting will make me happy this time around? I hated it in school, and the business is set up against me," I snapped. I felt guilty for my bad mood, and my guilt made me angry at him, but I also felt like I should have built up credit for all the days I'd greeted him happily, cheerfully, then ignored him, gotten out of his way, as he liked me to when he was working.

"You need to at least give it a try," he said. "You have so much you want to do with your life, but none of it seems to be happening right now. You need to start with baby steps. I feel like you'd be happier if you were doing something, not just going to work and coming home to me."

"Why don't you work full time and see how much energy you have at the end of the day?" I said. "You tell me how it is once you're out of school."

"I do work all the time, Kellen."

It stung because I did feel unaccomplished and unproductive. It stung because it echoed the litany of flaws that ran through my own head: you're doing nothing, have done nothing, the only thing interesting about you are your parents. Mired in those insecurities, I was feeling jealous of those days when expectations for women were limited. Second-wave feminism had set me up to fail. If indeed I could do anything I wanted—why wasn't it happening? Why wasn't I an astronaut or president or at least famous? It had to be my fault. I felt stymied by my freedom. My shame made me defensive.

"You have no idea what you want to do with yourself either," I replied. "At least I have dreams." I had him on that one.

For the first time since he was seventeen, Lior would have to decide what to do next. During his last transition at least he'd known college was the right step, and it was just a matter of choosing one that would have him. He had expected the answers to come from the classes he took, but in the years of studying that had followed, he'd realized that none of the classroom abstractions had made the choice any easier or clearer. Neither of us really had any idea what we were doing with our lives, and as we stared at each other, our eyes relayed that fact back and forth.

23

Entropy

For her thirtieth birthday, Cody's older sister had decided to fly six of the people with whom she was closest to Puerto Rico (amazing, right?). Cody was one of the lucky halfdozen, and her sister was worried there wouldn't be anyone for her to hang out with, the rest being her sister's friends and boyfriend. Cody being legendarily antisocial, she sprang for me to come along. If at any point in life I can afford to be that magnanimous, I hope that I am.

We flew into San Juan and then took a boat to the island of Vieques, the former US Navy testing site and up and coming tourist destination. From the tiny harbor we drove in open Jeeps out to villas caught in the jungle foliage. With a week to relax and eat and wander, Cody took the opportunity to ignore me the whole time, preferring to read novels and eat saltines over exploring the local culture with me.

"You and Lior would get along great, really, he should have come along. He loves ignoring me too. Y'all could ignore each other," I said, fishing for any sort of interaction.

"Mmhmm," she said.

I hadn't seen Cody since she'd come to visit us while we were living at my mom's place in San Francisco three years prior.

"I can't believe your sister shelled out all this cash and you don't want to go check out the place where we're staying with me, go see what the island has to offer," I said. All around us teeming jungle wilderness beckoned. Monkeys screeched from the nearby trees. An iguana staked out turf on a branch.

"Do you bother Lior this much?" she said from behind the pages of her latest thriller.

Before I'd left for Puerto Rico, Lior's best army buddy had had a baby boy and Lior had gone out of town to attend the bris. When I got back from my vacation, he left for another trip of his own: the bachelor party of a good friend. Nothing worrisome. Men fishing on a lake. No strippers.

We arranged a perfect trade-off of the car at the airport. As I exited the terminal, he handed me the keys and put my suitcase in the backseat.

"I filled it up with gas and there's five bucks for parking in the front seat."

His hazel eyes twinkled at me. "How was your trip?"

"Lots of fun . . . You excited for yours? So much traveling, huh?" I said while rifling through my purse.

"I wish we got a little more time together in between."

"There's never enough time together," I said and smiled.

That was our old refrain from the days when we saw each other for only a week or two every couple of months. We hugged each other like old friends seeing one another after a long time, kissed without tongue, and said good-bye. I told him to have a safe flight. He'd be back in a few days. It was mid-June of 2007, and the summer stretched out before us. The twelve sunniest days of the year in Seattle were almost within our reach.

Entropy

We had been home together less than a week when the end began.

The specifics of breakups are in some ways irrelevant.

I do not mean the larger circumstances; there is a difference, clearly, between slowly becoming more like friends and being with someone who sleeps with your sister then kills your cat for effect. No, I'm referring to the facts of the disintegration itself: the conversations and arguments that compose a relationship's end. Few people will ever guess what words pass between you then, the thoughts and memories that, unbidden, spring to mind. Why *now* do you recall the last time you made love outdoors or the way the salmon with beurre blanc tasted earlier that night?

The reasons for the dissolution are crucial but private, totally understandable only to the two people trying to work themselves free. The heartbroken mind replays the particulars, as though in the constant rehashing details will suddenly become clear and some meaning will be deducible. Did he at the bris imagine us as parents, consider what it would be like to have me as a wife, hormonal and pregnant? Did he imagine me tired and red-eyed from long nights without sleep? Did he at the bachelor party consider that soon enough he would have to decide one way or the other about settling down? Did he put me on a giant theoretical scale and measure the weight of what was good about me with what was bad and find that the scale was in fact tilted one way?

When we both returned from our separate vacations, Lior had a friend, Beth, come and visit with a friend of her own in tow; the two were road tripping up the West Coast. We both had plenty friends of the opposite sex, and while occasionally there had been tension around my gaggle of guy friends, I had no objection to his long-standing relationship with her.

We made the requisite round of tourist spots when I met up with them after work. I was trying to shed my workday daze for genuine conviviality and was succeeding, I thought. We strolled through the fog of the wharf as I tried to brainstorm entertaining anecdotes to share.

I told them about the most recent site visits I'd been doing, "You would not believe some of the places they send me. Tiny meth-infested logging towns, like a northwestern set for *Deliverance.* I was up in one mountaintop holler, Darrington, and they started complaining about the slightly larger and lower-down-on-the-mountain town, Arlington, like they were big-city scum who'd lost all sense of values and . . ."

No one seemed to be listening. I tried to brainstorm some more anecdotal tidbits.

There is a very particular desperation that takes over the loquacious when their standby social skills seem to create an unpleasant affect. Instead of chilling out and trying to blend in, we go into a higher gear—more talkative, flirtatious, and eager to please, a manic clown.

I was halfway to stand-up comedian when I had a moment of clarity and stopped myself midsentence. These were his guests; they probably would rather entertain themselves.

Once at our place, I retired to the kitchen, where I did my best impression of a fifties dinner party hostess, completing the act with an ending flourish of doing the dishes. I came back out afterward—having left the conversation undisturbed for over an hour—and told a joke that fell flat.

I'm not sure at what point I realized that the man metaphorically booing in the audience was my lover—by which I mean his eyes were the ones leading the parade of disgust. It is as though at that very moment he gave up membership in my fan club and took up with the opposing team.

"What's up with you treating me like shit?" I asked him once we were alone.

I feel like I knew right then that it was over. But because I'd recently been feeling secure about how our relationship was going, I didn't recognize it for what it was. I assumed there was some unspecified but correctable cause to the disquiet between us, and that with explanation and compromise, perhaps, it could be righted. There was no reason another miracle might not appear.

———

Nyna suggested that Lior and I set up a time to talk, later in the week, so Lior could have some time to think things over.

"I don't even know what's wrong—why should we wait to talk?"

"Just give him some space, hon . . . like I'm always saying." For a lesbian, she seemed to know a lot about men.

"But we've just been away from each other for two weeks. How much more space can I give him?"

———

On the next Sunday, having both had a couple days to mull things over, we sat down on our couch to talk. I had a bad habit of interrupting him, so we had developed rules in which one person can talk uninterrupted until finished and then it's the other person's turn. I told him he could go first.

He said, "I've been thinking, and we need to break up."

This is why I didn't want to wait, I moaned on the inside. If only I hadn't listened to my mother, maybe I could have convinced him days earlier this was all a really bad idea. It was my mother's fault.

"What? What do you mean?" I whined.

"I need to figure out who I am on my own, like I've said before. I don't want to keep leading you on, and I won't be able to settle down until I know who I am. We got together when we were really young. We want different things. I'm a different person now. We've both changed." He was strong and calm, like always. He didn't seem all that different.

My eyelids felt heavy, leaden—and then they were full and overflowing. My limbs were devoid of feeling entirely. I felt myself being suspended, watching myself from the ceiling. I couldn't believe this day had come. I had dreaded it. My mouth began to move. The squeakiness of my voice surprised me.

"Please don't leave me. I love you. We can work it out. I'll stay in Seattle as long as you want. We don't have to move to LA. I love you," I said.

"No," he insisted, cutting me off from my chance to beg. He wanted to leave that night, had already arranged a place to stay. Panicked, I scrambled for reasons he should stay, do me the favor of remaining in our shared home.

I remembered that our relationship started with my trying to convince him to stay with me— a flashback of the kiss and him running away. I had to make him change his mind about leaving.

I hit upon a winner with "I can't stay in the same city as you, my heart can't take it, but I need a little while to quit my job and stuff, so maybe you could just stay in the apartment while I figure a few things out. I promise I'll leave after that."

He stayed the night. The first night we were no longer a couple.

We were in the same bed, like we had been for thousands of nights before, but now my head was full of new and unwelcome worries. Both of us were awake and quiet, pretending to sleep. His body lay next to mine, but within it was a person I no longer knew.

24

The Aftermath

I thought I was doing well as I drove my forty-five-minute commute to work two weeks later, crying profuse tears but maintaining a relatively unperturbed expression. I was listening to my favorite radio tune at the time—the one in which the R&B singer proclaims that he is so sick of love songs, so tired of tears. *My eyes are leaking is all*, I thought proudly to myself. I've always liked to cry in the car; it feels private regardless of where you are, and no one can hear if you're yelling. I maybe also liked the idea of strangers seeing me sobbing and wondering what possibly could have happened. This was a small comfort to me as I drove up I-5.

At work, my supervisor approached me during what I would have described as a period of above average productivity. I hadn't even stopped for lunch yet and it was 2:00 p.m.

"Kellen, maybe you should take a break and sit down in the break room for a minute, pull yourself together a little," she said. "I could get you some coffee."

"No. Why?" I asked. "I'm okay. Really. Is there a problem?"

"Well, your desk's next to the window, and it's kind of weird to have you up here crying on display."

Only then did I notice the splotches on the paper below me. *I guess I'm crying*, I realized. I had gotten used to crying all the time, to the point that I didn't notice myself doing it anymore.

I cried the forty-five minutes on the way home as well.

———

In front of our apartment, I tucked my hair behind my ears, wiped off the remaining snot and tears, and did the pulling together I couldn't manage anywhere else so that when I walked through the door I could play my part in the strange fantasy I was insisting on living out—one in which I tried to glean a last few days of happiness from our relationship.

Because he was willing, when I managed not to dissolve into tears and begging, to pretend that none of this was actually happening. We could spend the night in relative calm, watching a movie—the type of evening that just months ago would have bored me to death. And thanks to the heart squeeze of cinema, if a tear or two slid down my cheek during the film, well, for once there was an excuse.

———

In the final three weeks we lived together, we broke up more and more a little bit at a time, though largely Lior seemed relieved to have gotten the burden of officially breaking up with me out of the way. Without the future hanging over us, we could enjoy each other's company again. That is, until one of us decided we needed to bring up what was going on. It was a game we played: let's see who can go longer without mentioning the larger reality.

When we did fight, we said the things that would have enough gravity, enough weight, to cut through all the attachment—to help cleave us apart.

"At what point did you decide we weren't meant to be? You must have made that choice. When was that?"

I asked him this in a moment that could have stayed placid; the surface between us was, for the moment, calm.

"I'm not sure I ever loved you the way you loved me," he said.

Ouch.

"Well, all those love letters you sent me say otherwise," I stammered. I wasn't sure who out of the two of us needed convincing, but my tone suggested that at least one of us did. The world whirled around me in a nauseating way.

He didn't offer a response before heading out for the evening. "I'll see you later. I'm meeting up with some people for drinks," he told me as he went out the door.

When did he get all these friends? I hated him. I hated that he had a life without me that would continue when I was gone.

Another day, in revenge, I said to him from the safety of inside the shower, where I didn't have to look him in the eyes, "Just for the record: I'm not going to miss who you are now. I'm only going to miss the man you once were. That guy I really cared about."

These words strung together were a wave that crashed over the relationship. We were closing ourselves off from our future together, shutting the door to that world. I wanted to scream obscenities at him. Tell him I never cared and had cheated and would replace him as soon I could. But even when I wanted to throw things and curse, scratch his eyes out, I knew better. We were slowing pulling the Band-Aid off instead of yanking it. I wanted to push this man away, but he had the same body as my long lost lover. That knowledge made me softer.

In a fighting moment on yet another evening, one in which I begged him again to tell me why it wasn't fixable, why we couldn't work it out, he said, "Look, I don't want to live on the ranch. I don't want to have foster kids. I don't want to be married to a movie star, okay?"

He shot down my dreams. Just like that. I thought, *How dumb, I'm not a movie star yet, it's likely I'll never be one. What a stupid reason to dump me.* What if none of those things came to pass and we could have gone on loving each other? What if my dreams were big balloons, and once they popped I was going to end up alone?

"Well, what do I do then about all these years I wasted waiting around for you to figure that out, huh?" I said. "I wasted the best years of my life on you. Young, hot-in-Hollywood years . . . wasted!"

I wanted my youth back. I wanted my heart back.

"I'm sorry," he said. "I didn't plan any of this."

"What do we do with the toad?"

One had died the year before, leaving a solitary animal to be split between us. Neither of us wanted her—that was the truth of the matter. I liked her but worried excessively over her eating. When she refused her mealworms it really stressed me out.

We contacted the local herpetological society, discovered easily with a simple Google search, the same way our toads had originally been found. I told them we had a toad we weren't sure we wanted to keep and they adamantly insisted we hand her over.

"Toads can be tricky to care for. We recommend that owners recognize when it has become too much," said the lady on the line. I imagined she looked like a human version of Edna—plump, possibly warty.

"You'll find her a happy home?" I was giving up my toad for adoption. I could hear the hopeful desperation in my voice. Maybe there was someone else who could provide for her better.

The Aftermath

I met a fellow for the handoff in the parking lot of a strip mall. I'd struggled to fit her aquarium into the backseat of my car. Though I'd emptied out the water from the fake stone pool that was her favorite resting spot, she'd nestled back into it anyway. As I helped the guy wrestle the tank out, she looked up at me with the same expression as always. But this time I superimposed upon it all the ambivalence I felt over her leaving—a mixture of sadness and fear and regret, coupled with the small affection that sat in my heart.

26

Bunny Slope

One of the things I couldn't understand was that while I was talking to friends and family multiple times a day, strategizing on how I might best handle this crisis, Lior appeared to be going it alone. I recognized that I was an extreme—I consulted with all four moms about total minutiae—but it was still suspicious.

"What do your best friends think about all this? Do your folks think you're making the right decision?" I asked him over dinner.

He chewed thoughtfully before answering. "They trust me to know what I'm doing."

"But you don't . . . you have said yourself this could be a mistake. Don't you think you should get some outside input?"

Why was no one telling him what a terrible idea this was? Weren't relationships supposed to be supported by the community?

After the dishes were washed and he was ensconced in his homework like usual, I called my mama Nyna.

"Mama, why isn't anyone telling him he's making the biggest mistake of his life?"

I thought these people cared about me, but no one was protesting my disappearance; all of those relatives of his who I had spent so much time befriending—none of them were defending me.

"Do you want me to call his mother and talk to her about it?" Nyna said.

"No."

"Do you want me to tell him it's a giant mistake?"

"No."

"I will, if you want me to," she said. "I'll tell him what an idiot he's being."

I couldn't help but smile as I refused her offers. I was glad that even though I was being abandoned there were still people who loved me in the world.

Nyna and Jenny came on my last weekend to help me pack up and say good-bye. On the first of the two days, while I was across the street in the cute park I'd used as a restroom the night we moved in, having a going away party, she sat Lior down for a talking-to, even though I'd told her not to.

I had bought lots of picnic wine for the occasion and was drinking inappropriately in front of all of the people whose kids I'd been caring for. It was surprising, really, that people let me anywhere near their children considering the state I was in. Probably it was because they were there to supervise and we were on grass, so even if I dropped their babies it wouldn't have been the end of the world.

I was sloppily making conversation when my mom and Lior emerged an hour later with tear-stained cheeks, she with crossed arms and he walking behind her. In my drunken state, I thought, *Oh no, what if she convinced him to stay with me? Wouldn't that be worse? To have him stay based on guilt applied by a mom lecture?*

If I'd been more sober, I'd have known by the looks on their faces that nothing had changed.

"He thinks he knows what he is doing," my mom said. "He has no idea."

She later told me what she had said to him. "You'll never find someone better than her. No one will ever love you better. And she's not going to wait around for you to get your shit together unless you specifically ask her to. There's no going back. I won't let you mess with her heart. If this is it, then that's the end of things."

She said he started to cry but didn't change his mind.

It felt a little like someone else doing my dirty work, like in second grade when Kyree (then Nora) called the home of a classmate of mine. She had taken the crayons that I'd brought from home that day, so my mom called and asked to talk to her mother. When the little girl insisted that she wasn't home, my mom went into momma-bear mode and said, "Fine, I'll talk straight to you then. Did you take Kellen's crayons at school today?" The little girl began to stutter in response to my mother's strong tone. "Tomorrow, you'd better give them back." The next day, there the crayons were, lying on my desk. My mom had accomplished what I could not.

I didn't think my mom could save my relationship, but I was thankful that she had stood up for me—that she had made sure Lior had heard what I thought someone should say to him.

When Lior joined the crowd in the park, people didn't know how to treat him. They shuffled their paper plates between their hands and shifted their weight from side to side. They made excuses about needing to leave and how overdue their babies were for a nap. They all knew him from the past three years, but since it was my good-bye party and everyone knew I was leaving because he'd dumped me, it was awkward. They seemed surprised to see him, but it was his good-bye party too. They'd never see him again either.

It was my last day in our shared apartment, and Lior was using his natural talent to rearrange things to make sure the moving van was packed with economy and intention. The last thing he could do to help me out.

"In the army, I was known to be a great packer," he bragged.

I was watching our lives separate materially. The feeling paralyzed me until a steady hand descended upon my shoulder and I turned to look at Jenny, box in her hand, midway through a trip between the house and van. My mom had flown back to the Bay Area the day before but Jenny was still there to collect me and my things and bring me home—"Kind of like a dead soldier," I mused to her.

"Who's that guy?" she asked me, pointing to a bald guy—and that was how we finally met our downstairs neighbor.

This was a man with a giant reputation. He'd been known to me and Lior until now only through a relationship of sound, a chorus of clues sent from below. He was up twenty-four hours a day, it seemed, just as likely to send blips of video gaming our way at 3:00a.m. as at 8:00a.m., just as likely to be mysteriously drilling and hammering at 5:00p.m. as at 5:00a.m. In some ways this had proven a comfort to us, as it meant we'd never concerned ourselves with quieting at any particular hour, but it had remained a mystery I was curious to solve. Our houseguests had been the most put out, having only a thin futon between their attempts at slumber and the living room floor, which often reverberated late into the night with his lively machinations. Repeatedly, exhausted friends and relatives had wondered aloud in the morning, "What exactly is your neighbor up to down there?"

We'd had no answer to give them.

We had seen him occasionally, popping in and out of an open-framed Jeep, and we of course had theories, like: He's a drug dealer, meth or coke most likely; or, he's a very social gay man. Maybe both. The being awake at all hours and the constant coming and going of various men could have indicated either. Until that last day we had no conclusive proof for either hypothesis. But then Jenny introduced herself and I had all this extra gay porn that I'd collected on the last trip back home and had not adequately distributed—suddenly we were BFFs and invited into his apartment.

In the dim light of the entrance, I made out a gigantic pull-down screen across one wall—handy for the projection of all-hours video games—and a multitude of houseplants. His apartment was a replica of our own above, except his things were in his, and our place was now oddly half-empty, the negative space of my leaving. But where our couch still sat upstairs, down there he had a tiled wall that gleamed slightly even in the darkness. As I approached, its copper tiling glinted an aura-like sheen.

"I've been working on that pretty much since you guys moved in," he said. "You have to drill each tile with the necessary holes to fit, and then hammer them individually into place."

Years of unexplainable sounds became manifest before me.

"Hope it wasn't too much of a problem for you," he said.

I reached out and ran a finger over the place where the opaque color of the center of the tile bled into the watercolor-like edges. He would have this wall longer than I'd kept my man, and I'd spent at least as much time investing. Maybe material things have lasting appeal after all.

We were making love one last time in the apartment that was now bereft of my things. I was sitting on his lap, naked, facing him, gripping on like a tiny monkey—a drowning one, perhaps—holding onto a piece of driftwood. Downstairs, Jenny was gossiping with our newfound neighbor friend. I heard him suggest that they take the hose from the front yard and water down the windows as a hurry-it-up sign. Lior and I had been in there for an hour saying good-bye.

Jenny was impatient, ready to leave—"He dumped you, let's get out of here," she had said before I went upstairs. "You don't have to waste another minute on him."

Instead we were inside having great sex, the kind that obfuscates the torture of the situation and the tears that are to come. It was one of life's cruel ironies that we came together, as we had suddenly recently been doing, some kind of orgasmic contradictory evidence to our downfall. Because the moving truck was sitting outside we could once again declare our everlasting attachment.

"I love you," he told me. "This doesn't mean I won't love you for the rest of my life." Just like when he was in the army—now that I was leaving, love was far away enough to be safe and true.

"Ditto," I admitted.

We kissed each other with all the passion of one of our army-bred good-byes.

In the end, we had made it through the calamity and uncertainty of war. We had navigated the differences of our upbringings and perspectives. We had even come to enjoy each other's crazy families. What had destroyed our relationship had turned out to be the slow wearing down of routine, the building of resentments and unsatisfied expectations that plague each couple before their demise. It hadn't been the big things that did it at all.

27

Dirt

What is the meaning of this unraveling? Is this some harbinger of my inability to maintain a long-term relationship?" These questions circled my mind like goldfish in a cramped bowl.

"Is it a sign that Lior can't either, then?" Jenny asked. I was getting free therapy as administered by my best friend—eighteen hours of it—as we wound southward with my belongings. "Because if you can't, he shouldn't be able to. You can't be the only one blamed for it not working out. It's both of your responsibilities. And he doesn't have gay parents as an excuse."

"I miss him so much already," I said. Having him gone felt familiar to me; the heartache felt the same. Only he wasn't coming back and it wasn't war that had taken him away from me this time.

"Do you think I'm impossible to love?" I asked.

Ex-boyfriends had used words like "spoiled" and "high expectations" to describe me in the past. And here's the problem with having really good parents: it sets you up for disappointment. No one would ever match the sort of unconditional love they'd slathered upon me. She, and the rest of my family, loved me whether I called them or not, whether I behaved or not, even when I was on drugs, even if I was a slut. Every drawing of mine had been kept, every performance attended, with flowers in hand. I was the most overloved child in the world, and this was where it had gotten me.

"What did I do to deserve this? What did I do wrong?" I moaned to Jenny. "I tried my best, I swear. I thought that was supposed to count for something. I would have given it all up—the foster kids, the ranch—I mean, not the property, but living on it full time—my acting career. . .That's the fucked up part; I really would have."

"Then it's a good thing he dumped you," Jenny said decisively. "You're better off without him and still having your dreams. You're one big pity party now, but wait till you get pissed. You weren't happy either. You've been complaining for years that he doesn't treat you right."

"But I wasn't going to give up!" I had been so sure that we were going to get married that all the fighting had seemed like something to be endured. I imagined if we had gotten married and divorce weren't an option. If it were "for better or worse." I mean, comparatively, things weren't half-bad. Nothing is perfect.

"Why would you want to be in a relationship that doesn't make you happy?" Jenny asked me.

"That's what commitment's about."

Love and happiness were not one and the same. Some part of me knew this.

Jenny played clairvoyant, predicting the course of my emotions miles before I arrived at them.

"Sixteen minutes or twenty miles till angry," she said partway through Oregon.

"I really just think he freaked out and had some sort of quarter-life crisis and decided to fix it by dumping me. I mean, commitment is like bull riding, you just gotta hold on. It's basically the choice to tie your hand to the saddle. He just had to choose to stay, but he didn't. How come?" I whined.

"Cause he's an asshole, Kellen." She was egging me on. The wind from the window brushed back her dark curls. We were flying down the highway.

"Yeah, because he's a selfish asshole. It was time for him to move for my dreams like I'd moved for his and he flaked out!" An intense rage momentarily overtook me; righteous, indignant anger replaced my blood in my veins. *And whoever he dates, that next girl, I'm going to have to kill her.* Bile rose in my throat. This is why women hate men. If I were a lesbian this wouldn't have happened. Lesbians don't care about men. You have to love them and be hurt by them to be this hateful. Really it's straight women who've cornered the market on hating men. Women like me.

"I wish he'd died when he was in the army. If he had died then I could still love him." Even in my rage I knew this went too far. A lump formed in my throat as I said it, and I went back to being sad. I gave up bitching and stared out the window at the conifer-laden outdoors.

"Better that he do it now than when you're fifty-five," Jenny said by way of putting the matter temporarily to bed.

We passed Albany and Eugene, Oregon. The landscape was flirting with the occasional hint of civilization but mostly holding steady with trees. I told Jenny that I thought it would be strange to go home since I'd gotten used to a more mainstream routine. My life with Lior resembled that of a majority of my peers.

"I'm going back into wacky lesbian world," I said. "Who am I kidding? That must be where I'm meant to live." And with that, I deflated. I'd been visiting Kansas, and now I was headed back to Oz.

Dirt

Had I been conforming? Had I been living my very normal life (read: boyfriend, lame job, cakewalk right into suburbia) because I wanted to? Or had I been doing it out of fear, or maybe just out of some ineffectual character flaw that prevented me from being a wilder, more adventurous person? I could not outlive my mothers. Was I being boring in reaction? If so, why hadn't it worked out?

Boring shouldn't be so impossible to pull off.

My unconventional background tugged at me. *Are the most exciting years of your life going to be your childhood? Are those stories going to age into canon, and maybe myth, with no addenda, no big life lived after?*

I heard Helen in my head. "There are only twenty-four hours in every day, kiddo, but it's up to you what you want to do with them." My mothers all sit in my head, a perpetual chorus.

"Jenny, he was my one chance at having a normal life," I said. "I mean, I gave it a shot, the whole settle-down-marriage-style thing, and it blew up in my face. I'm over it. I'm bowing out of the game." The risk of ever again loving someone seemed too large.

"Only you would say that," she said. "Just cause it didn't work out this time doesn't mean you should abandon the whole proposition of marriage wholesale—that'd be like some other girl getting dumped and saying, 'Well, I guess I'll just become a nun.'"

"He was my harbor. I feel like a sailor going back out to sea," I told Jenny.

Between Grants Pass and Medford, the rain turned into a general mugginess and we spotted a roadside sign advertising PEACHES. We pulled the hulking moving van off the smooth highway and onto a gravel road, the van skittering over the stones. Down a long driveway sat an aging Victorian with a peach-selling operation, its epicenter located in a freestanding garage while the rest spilled into the front yard. Each peach was being set into its own private plastic cell for shipping.

When we came close to the table, the smell of ripe peaches caught on the light breeze ruffling the hairs on the back of my neck. I pulled my sweater closer around me despite the relative heat while Jenny picked out peaches.

"If I didn't think they'd rot in the van before we got home, I'd buy even more," she told the potbellied fellow who sold them to us.

Back in the van, she insisted I eat one even if I had no appetite. The juice burst out the moment my teeth punctured the skin and slid down my chin. It sang with sweetness in my mouth, every droplet sun light crystallized into sugar.

"It's really good," I admitted.

"You're still alive," she said.

───────

We went to bed for the evening tucked away in a dingy motel right off the highway in Yreka, having exhausted ourselves in an effort to make it to the California border before stopping. In the dark provided by the ancient polyester curtains, I curled up in fetal position while Jenny lay stretched out next to me on the bed. She, being an insomniac, would have had trouble sleeping no matter where we were, but my restlessness was because this was my first night without him.

The first night of the rest of my life.

Inside my chest it felt like all my organs were frozen and cracking apart, the way ice on a river creaks and groans. I felt my eyes leaking once again, my insides thawing into liquid and slowly dripping out.

"Will it hurt this bad forever?" I said into the blackness. I wanted to crawl out of my skin, it hurt so badly. My heart had been broken before, but similar to the rumors about labor and birth I'd heard, my mind had since then blocked out the memory of the pain.

"No," Jenny said. "It will hurt this bad for a while, but you can't keep up this level of emotion indefinitely. It will slowly fade. Some days will be worse than others."

"It feels like I'm dying. What if he's the one and this feeling is my heart telling me that?"

My heart felt like a melon thrown off an overpass. She didn't say anything else for a good long minute. We sat in the dark together with my sniffling as soundtrack.

"Tell me I'm going to be okay," I said.

"You will be, sweetie."

28

Happily Ever After

I moved back in with Nyna once more, into the house I'd grown up in, again, still sitting on that hill in San Francisco. The last time I'd lived there it had been with Lior. I knew I had to layer on new memories like Jerusalem layers on stone, a city still open for new life after two thousand years of suffering.

The little brown house looked very much the same from the outside—the same wooden porch and staircase leading to the front door, the same red trim. The row of homes was still a diverse collection of folks; I wasn't the only child who had recently returned to the family nest. The economy had been like that.

I returned to a house occupied most obviously by stuff. In the last few years it had been rented out to a few different families, some of whose detritus still sat in our garage. During that time, Nyna had been filling a larger house across the bay in El Sobrante with our things as well, so when she moved back into the smaller home everything seemed out of proportion, like in "Goldilocks and the Three Bears." A towering armoire greeted me at the entrance.

Set in the small space of the living room, the couch seemed sized for giants.

When not cavorting with San Francisco's delinquents (aka my mom's friends) or sulking on my mother's huge couch, my main activity that autumn was drinking. The years of Lior judging my drinking made me want to prove to him that he hadn't seen anything yet. It did not occur to me that since we weren't in contact, he was not, in fact, watching.

So I became a whiskey connoisseur and learned to work with children hung over.(I don't recommend it, for the record.) Despite my depression, I was not under the illusion that bills pay themselves. I've never understood how the lovesick who actually take to their beds can afford it. I was nannying again within weeks of arrival. I worked, then drank, then hovered around the house among the living, and as long as I kept working everyone assumed I was all right. Drunk but all right.

Twice a year we have to round up the cattle on the ranch. This is so we can take care of things like branding, castration, ear tags, worming, and selecting who stays and who goes to market. It's my job to decide their fate; I'm the Josef Mengele of this beef operation. It is the perfect masochistic role for a vegetarian.

Because I had over the years convinced my closest friends to help me with this task, it had also become a biannual reunion: Jenny flew in from LA, and the rest of my closest friends from high school showed up too. Now that I was back in the Bay Area my presence at round up was a given, which meant that I had to drag myself out of inebriation long enough to drive the two and a half hours north. I took the 101 out from San Francisco, over the Golden Gate Bridge, and into the country.

From the highway, the long ascent up the dusty road took me

winding from the valley, with its carpet of grapes not yet pressed into wine, through grasses that hid starthistle, branches felled from oak mothers, and jackrabbits, to the ridge on which Helen's ailing trailer played sentry to the rest of the land. I parked my car, further beaten up by the road with its many rain-dug pits and the gravel flung from the patch job of repairing them, out in front of the gate; then I slid back the metal piece holding the gate closed and slipped into the fenced area that separated the trailer and barn from the otherwise unfenced front half of the land and kept Helen's geriatric Doberman in the yard.

The dog lumbered out from the trailer, and in the last few seconds before she announced my arrival, my eyes swept the John Deere–green cattle pens and calf table that were waiting for the next day's activities. I spied the ramshackle corral that occasionally held bummer lambs, given to Helen from her neighbors over at the UC Davis field station, and the garden in the front corner, located in the only place where the cows couldn't get in and eat everything. In the opposite corner, the barn where I'd put everything from the back of the moving van, to be sorted later, sat blocked by the rusty pickup truck with its keys perpetually in the ignition. I could imagine it saying, "You learned to drive on me. You almost hit a cow."

Inside the trailer, preparations were underway. Clamps and syringes were being located. Twelve people who'd also made the long, windy drive there were tucked into chairs sprinkled between the living room, dining room and, kitchen. Dinner, something simple like spaghetti and garlic bread, was being made.

When I walked in, people said, "There you are," and passed me between arms for welcoming hugs, a carousel of affection.

This was as close to the feeling of real celebrity as I'd come: a whole crowd of admirers excited to see me. I could sense their protective feelings for me and their circle-the-wagons reaction to my recent trauma when they asked how I was doing. I took advantage of their attention to try and reestablish some sense of identity outside of my relationship. *Who the heck was I, anyway?* I asked folks for their opinions.

"You're talkative. Enthusiastic," said one mullet-sporting lady, Jonas.

"You make people feel special when you're with them. Like they are the only person on earth," said another. On the walls of the trailer were pictures of me growing up through the years—there I was in cowboy hats and boots, in my graduation gown, in a shower cap and nothing else, powdering my own behind. The photos matched up with the person they described.

"You're into history. You like to party. You like strange ice cream flavors," said a third.

"Beach or mountain?" asked Jen, a woman in a baseball cap who was gathering supplies for branding in hand.

"Beach," I automatically answered.

"See that's something right there. Maybe you just need to check out an archive of teen magazines and do all the personality quizzes. You've got plenty of personality. It shouldn't be too hard to figure out who you are."

"You're a stinking vegetarian's what you are," teased Sandy, a friend of the family, in her mellowed Scottish brogue.

As the sole vegetarian in a cattle ranching operation, my position was a great opener for a bad joke. At round up, I looked for ways to help that weren't so scary. I tended to station myself at one of the gates that opened to let the just-tortured calf back into the field, or else I helped coax the calves down the chute and toward the table in the same soothing tones I'd perfected working in daycare.

When the cows had all been brought up from the valley and were ready in the pens, I took my place by the chute. I had dug out a T-shirt from a drawer in the trailer that read in glittery brown print, I'M NOT A PRINCESS, BUT IF THE CROWN FITS . . . and jeans

I didn't mind getting cow shit on as I nudged the calves through the expanse of green-coated metal. At the end of the line, Jenny waited with Daniel Hagerty, another long-time best friend, at the calf table; they both had focused looks on their faces.

Now nearing eighty-five, Helen's job for the day was to sit on one of the rocks grouped in the shade of a feathery leafed tree. But she would not be dissuaded from giving her two cents, and she wandered into the area of the pens where I was standing.

"Miss Kellen, I hope you're paying attention to what's going on and not just petting the calves, because soon enough I want you and your crew to be able to do all this with no one else's help. If you're going to take over this place you have to get more involved and bossy like me."

"I'm being bossy as hell," I declared.

"That's my girl," she said, throwing her arm around my shoulder. I noticed how much lighter it had gotten in age, like a silk shawl draped around me. I thought about how much energy she seemed to have when I was a kid, when she was already middle-aged, and how even now she scrambled over the hills of the land quicker than I did. Her lined face showed no sign of resignation, just stubborn pride projected in my direction. I thought about how I'd squandered much of the time I'd had with Lior, thinking I'd have so much more of it, and vowed to appreciate my time with my aging godmother. We gazed past where people worked in the pens to the valley and the hills behind it, taking in the scene together.

After the cows were done, I walked up the hill from the trailer along the ridge, past the oak tree under which our former equine companions found restful eternity, over toward the prefabricated house that Nyna had recently paid to have dragged up the gnarled dirt road.

When I walked into its cavernous interior I was impressed something like this could be hauled in halves and put together with no more than wiring and foundation as things left to be resolved. I was impressed by the plush tan carpeting, impractical with the intrusive outdoors but still clean and off-gassing at this point. A hint of the formaldehyde they warn about in a small-print sticker on the front window hung as perfume in the air.

My eyes set upon the coffee table and then the table set in the dining room. They were both pieces Lior had packed so ceremoniously into the moving van, the same pieces I had then put into the barn, in the room occupied by the cats that helped keep rodents at bay. I was sure they were happier here, inside. I was sure my mom had done me a favor by dragging them out from the barn, where the heat could have expanded the wood and cracked it.

I walked toward the room Nyna had dedicated as mine. Opening the door, I could see that in it sat the antique bed Lior and I had shared. Running up to Seattle a week before we arrived, my mother had spent her vacation buying antiques, like that bed, from a chatty gay man who was liquidating a mansion. On its headboard was a chipped floral design.

My fingers trailed over the aging wood. My things had taken on a museum-like quality for me. In the corner of the room was my box full of love letters, bursting with promises, proof, evidence— written, signed, sealed, and delivered that this dream was supposed to be mine. Like inflation-struck currency, in a moment it had all become meaningless.

All that good lesbian parenting hadn't done a thing to prepare me for this. But then how does a parent attempt to inoculate a child against the offense of heartbreak?

We'd all bought the snake oil, my lesbians and I, the idea that I was going to be one of the brides in the steady stream of marriages that had coursed through my late twenties. I'd come so close that everyone had started to believe. Nyna had said, "We never thought you'd stick with one guy, especially so young, but after a few years . . ." I felt like a doll put back on the shelf, a returned purchase, a rental video.

I shut the door in my mother's house and headed back down to the group.

On my way, I imagined a day in the future when Lior and I would talk again from a safe distance and he would have thought through his part in what had gone wrong. We would be living in different cities. By then, both of us would have taken different lovers. He would call me and it would all seem super familiar, us on the phone separated by many miles but equally melancholy.

"I just wanted to call and apologize," he'd say. "I've been doing some thinking and I've come to the conclusion that I never really accepted you for who you were. I kept trying to change you." It would make me feel better.

When I got to my mother I asked her, "Why'd you put all of mine and Lior's stuff in your new house?"

"Well, it wasn't holding up very well in the barn, and I thought we might as well put it to use."

She was right, of course. The world charges on. How little all our squealing does to squelch the motion.

Everyone was gathered around long picnic tables eating barbecue and tossing back beers. A buffet of food beckoned from the tailgate of a truck driven into the yard. I took my place among them. From the truck radio we were serenaded with Garth Brooks's "Unanswered Prayers."

Helen came over, her plate piled with food. She folded her still-flexible frame onto the bench that sat on one side of the table. With her weathered hand, she rubbed my back and asked what was on my mind.

"Did you like Lior, Helen?"

"I liked him well enough," she said, "but if he can't figure out how to keep you, well, he can't have been that great. Maybe you were just too much woman for him."

I snorted in response.

I took a walk to settle my post meal stomach. The ranch stretched out on all sides and beneath me. I remembered that this land had been here just as long as Jerusalem but with a lot less drama going on. The quiet called out to me. The pain that gripped my heart faded for the moment into an empty feeling that resembled peace. The land reminded me of who I was. It said, "I remember you naked and muddy in my creek, in this garden. I remember you being dumped from the top of your pony into the thistle. I know you here. You don't have to be anyone else."

I still had my dreams. I told myself this like it was a consolation prize. *Hey, even though you got robbed of your fancy fairy-tale ending, there's at least the rest of your life to live.*

Four Years Later

*J*enny was getting married, and as her maid of honor, it was my job to help her with a variety of wedding-related tasks. I'd asked a mutual friend whether I might consult with her post–bridal outings to debrief.

"I don't want to ruin it for Jenny with my feelings and yet I can't help but be sad sometimes when she talks about the wedding, or worry for her, like it's not a done deal, when she talks about wanting to do things her way. But I don't want to make her paranoid."

"It makes sense, honey," my friend kindly counseled. "Sometimes people getting married don't realize the effect it has on others."

Jenny couldn't help it any more than I could make my heart cease to ache. My heart still hurt the way a broken bone would. It throbbed a year later, two years, then three, then four. Over time it had become less reasonable to talk about it, and so for the rest of the world it had ceased to exist.

It was only those tasks that I remembered doing myself that got to me, like writing the guest list. In my mind I heard myself asking him, "Baby, how many people do you think will be coming from your side?" I remembered listing all my friends on paper while watching the clothing swirl at the laundromat. I had chosen all the centerpieces, the color scheme, the dresses the bridesmaids would be wearing (strapless and fuchsia with chartreuse trim).

I had no such trouble with the tasks that never came. Jenny took me with her to look at engagement rings, in order to describe to her boyfriend the rings she liked, and it didn't get to me at all. I had no pangs of *Where is my ring?* A Persian salesman at one shop even asked, "What about you, darling? Are you married?"

I told him at this point I might never be, but he looked at me like *Why count yourself out of the race this early on?*

"Don't you like the rings?" he asked, flashing a grin.

It was fun to look at them with her and I did want one, but it was because they were so shiny.

"I like the ones with three stones," Jenny said to me as we stared into the glass jewelry case.

At that year's High Holiday services I learned a new meaning for the word *bashert*—the word I'd wrapped around Lior with the understanding that it meant "soul mate." The rabbi associated it with Carl Jung, who, he said, had invented the word "synchronicity," which he described as two things happening at once due to divine intervention.

The rabbi said that *bashert* literally translated to "it was meant to be," not anything about soul mates or people cleaved in half and reunited. I was reminded of a Holocaust poem by Irena Klepfisz, titled "Bashert," in which each line recalls various coincidences— where each coincidence determined whether people lived or died. It was meant to be. I thought about how this new meaning allowed me to keep Lior under that label. I didn't have to give him up. My *bashert*. My "it was meant to be." My "this was all meant to have happened."

He's Just Not That Into You isn't the sort of film where you go into the movie theater expecting to have a life-altering revelation. Maybe the book could be expected to deliver on that level, but the movie was marketed as a lighthearted rom-com with good reason.

Despite its cinematic flaws, I walked out of the dark theater and into the fluorescent haze of the lobby a happier person and a tad bit more self–aware. Somewhere between the opening credits and Scarlett Johansson stealing Jennifer Connelly's husband, I'd had an epiphany.

"That movie just made clear to me what the effect of lesbian parenting is," I said breathlessly to my companion. I wasn't sure I could explain it. It had something to do with being raised by women whose lives didn't revolve around men. I was not quite like the women in the movie, I'd been raised differently.

What if I never got married, never found the right guy? I only had to look to my mothers' lives for the answer, in the way they have found self-satisfaction outside of men—outside of partners, too, for the most part. They are happy for their own sake. Lesbians do not live in spite of or despite of men. They build their lives to their own specifications. I have learned to take comfort in the comfort they find within themselves.

When I look down at my own hand, I now see the slim band of diamonds and rubies encircling my right hand ring finger, given to me by Nyna. She had promised me when I was a child that she would buy me a ruby ring, and she made good on the promise. When she gave it to me she said, "A ring almost as beautiful as you are. So you know you don't need a man to buy you jewelry."

Acknowledgments

As tempting as it is to say I did this all by myself, there are actually a ton of folks who helped me make this happen. Thank you to all the people who read earlier drafts of this book, gave me feedback, or listened to me whine.

Thank you especially to my friends and family who let me use their real names and real lives in these pages (I'm talking to you, Cody, Jenny, Agnes, Ethan, and Moms), and who supported me through the almost decade-length process of getting this book out there in the world. Thanks to CK Humphreys for giving me some much needed attention in the time around my break-up. Thank you to my father, to whom I owe a great deal of myself. To all the guys who had the misfortune of dating me while I was obsessively working on a book about some man who came before them, thank you for your patience and understanding.

Thank you to Tanya Taylor Rubenstein, who helped me with some of the earlier developmental work on the story, and to my friends from that crucial year in Santa Fe, Heather Wright, Zach Sommer, Alia Attallah, Michael Yates, and Megan and Aaron Ashbaugh. I wouldn't have gotten that first draft out without y'all.

I will also be eternally grateful to the UCLA extension writing program—my fellow students, who helped me to workshop my first draft, and in particular my teacher and mentor Samantha Dunn. Thank you to Julian Ornelas, to whom I read large portions aloud while he struggled to stay awake on long, late nights and upon whom I have foisted various unpaid design tasks.

Thank you to the team at She Writes Press, and the legal counsel of Jeremy Daw and Dave Owens, who came generously recommended by Alyson Tufts. Thank you to Julia Jonas for some helpful last minute language massaging. Thank you to Michele Karlsberg for being a publicist extraordinaire. Thank you as well to all the folks who I'm not remembering at the moment, but who contributed to my process and joy. And finally, thank you to my ex, who although tempted at points to sue me, found the generosity of spirit to not stand in my way and who loved me the best he knew how at the time. Thank you.

About the Author

Kellen Kaiser was born in 1981 in San Francisco. As a child, she represented the gay community frequently as a speaker on panels and in the media. Her story has appeared on CNN, in Marie Claire, in the San Francisco Chronicle, and in the Seattle Times. She holds a BFA from NYU. Online, her writing has been featured on Nerve, XOJane, Role Reboot, IncultureParent, and Next Family. When not writing, she also helps run her family's cattle ranch.

Margery   Nyna   Ethan   Kyree   Helen

SELECTED TITLES FROM SHE WRITES PRESS

She Writes Press is an independent publishing company
founded to serve women writers everywhere.
Visit us at **www.shewritespress.com**.

Peanut Butter and Naan: Stories of an American Mother in The Far East by Jennifer Magnuson. $16.95, 978-1-63152-911-5. The hilarious tale of what happened when Jennifer Magnuson moved her family of seven from Nashville to India in an effort to shake things up—and got more than she bargained for.

Loveyoubye: Holding Fast, Letting Go, And Then There's The Dog by Rossandra White. $16.95, 978-1-938314-50-6. A soul-searching memoir detailing the painful, but ultimately liberating, disintegration of a twenty-five-year marriage.

A Different Kind of Same: A Memoir by Kelley Clink. *$16.95,* 978-1-63152-999-3. Several years before Kelley Clink's brother hanged himself, she attempted suicide by overdose. In the aftermath of his death, she traces the evolution of both their illnesses, and wonders: If he couldn't make it, what hope is there for her?

Uncovered: How I Left Hassidic Life and Finally Came Home by Leah Lax. $16.95, 978-1-63152-995-5. Drawn in their offers of refuge from her troubled family and promises of eternal love, Leah Lax becomes a Hassidic Jew—but ultimately, as a forty-something woman, comes to reject everything she has lived for three decades in order to be who she truly is.

The Butterfly Groove: A Mother's Mystery, A Daughter's Journey by Jessica Barraco. $16.95, 978-1-63152-800-2. In an attempt to solve the mystery of her deceased mother's life, Jessica Barraco retraces the older woman's steps nearly forty years earlier—and finds herself along the way.

Fourteen: A Daughter's Memoir of Adventure, Sailing, and Survival by Leslie Johansen Nack. $16.95, 978-1-63152-941-2. A coming-of-age adventure story about a young girl who comes into her own power, fights back against abuse, becomes an accomplished sailor, and falls in love with the ocean and the natural world.

The Gardens

of

Intimacy

by

Barbara Urban

The Gardens of Intimacy, by Barbara Urban
ISBN # 0-89228-173-1
Copyright © 2003

Impact Christian Books, Inc.
332 Leffingwell Ave.,
Kirkwood, MO 63122
314-822-3303
www.impactchristianbooks.com

Cover Design: Ideations and Barbara Urban

Printed in the United States of America

Contents

A Dedication...

This book is specially dedicated to my husband, John, who never tires in providing the perfect building materials for my garden.

Thank you.

A Special Acknowledgment...

*I want to acknowledge my parents,
Ken and Carol Vess,
for their support in the publication
of this book.*

*May your own gardens of intimacy
become His desired habitation.*

Thank you, Mom and Dad.

Introduction

Our lives are meant to grow His spiritual seed—seed that has the potential to transform a broken life into a garden of His delight, bearing spiritual fruit for all to behold. As He prepared the Garden of Eden that He might walk with His creation in it in the cool of the day, so He desires to make a garden out of your life that He might commune with you as a lover and friend.

He is the great gardener of His people's hearts. Have you invited Him to come and tend your garden? He wants to make it one of His gardens.

My Beloved planted a vineyard...

"You who dwell in the gardens,

The companions listen for

your voice—

Let me hear it!"

Song 8:13

Where is my Beloved?

You will find Him frequenting the
gardens of His people's hearts;
that is where you will find Him.

"My beloved has gone to his garden,
to the beds of spices,
to feed his flock in the gardens,
and to gather lilies."
Song 6:2

I am one of His gardens.

Are you?

I. A Garden Enclosed

A garden enclosed
Is my sister, my spouse,
A spring shut up,
A fountain sealed.
Song 4:12

He wooed me under His *apple tree of intimacy* and met me in the garden of my heart. Now we regularly meet there to commune, as did Adam and Eve in the Garden of Eden. He is the great keeper of this garden of mine. I did not know that for such a long time, but He came to show me His desired lordship over my heart, and now we co-labor over this *garden of intimacy*.

It was difficult to meet Him there in the beginning because of all the weeds and briars. I could not see Him easily, and with my garden in such disarray, I found myself uncomfortable in the presence of one so great as He. But He never

15

condemned me for the state of my beleaguered garden. He just kept meeting me and wooing me to eat of His apple tree of intimacy.

> *Like an apple tree among the trees of the woods,*
> *So is my beloved among the sons.*
> *I sat down in his shade with great delight,*
> *And his fruit was sweet to my taste.*

Song 2:3

In our first encounters, He consistently showed me His greatness. I was overcome with awe at His beauty, wondering why someone as great as He would be interested in someone like me. Overwhelmed with the revelation of my true nakedness and inadequacy before Him, He graciously offered me a *covering*, and I gladly crawled under it, prostrate in His magnificent presence.

Feeling that I could never stand in His company again, He gently lifted me to my feet and put a ring on my finger and proclaimed me *His*. I was again prostrate at His feet with adoration and awe at His great gesture of love extended to me in my weakness.

Why? Why did He offer me a king's ransom? Why was I worth so much to Him when previously I was unaware of His importance at all? Why did He love me when I loved Him not? Why did He cover me with that great love and long for my companionship? Who was I that the King of all kings would stand over me with such adoration and care? I could not bring myself to stand in His presence. I was overcome with love for Him who loved me first. I John 4:19 rang true in my heart, *"We love Him because He first loved us."*

His treatment of me was tender and merciful. He had rescued me from the mire of my carnal, godless life, making me not only His servant, but His heir. I suddenly had all of the rights of an heir. My hair was washed, my body bathed and anointed, and the top of my head was kissed with His affirmation as He deposited His Holy Spirit within me. This deposit proved that His word was true and forthcoming. Then He clothed me in His kingly garments, the garments of a royal heir. They were *His* garments. And I was happy to wear them. The Scriptures graphically declare the spectacular nature of this remarkable conversion and the bedazzling adornments that had been bestowed upon me.

"And when I passed by you and saw you struggling in your own blood, I said to you in your blood, 'Live!' Yes, I said to you in your blood, 'Live!' I made you thrive like a plant in the field; and you grew, matured, and became very beautiful. Your breasts were formed, your hair grew, but you were naked and bare. When I passed by you again and looked upon you, indeed your time was the time of love; so I spread My wing over you and covered your nakedness. Yes, I swore an oath to you and entered into a covenant with you, and you became Mine," says the Lord God. "Then I washed you in water; yes, I thoroughly washed off your blood, and I anointed you with oil. I clothed you in embroidered cloth and gave you sandals of badger skin; I clothed you with fine linen and covered you with silk. I adorned you with ornaments, put bracelets on your wrists, and a chain on your neck. And I put a jewel in your nose, earrings in your ears, and a beautiful crown on your head. Thus you were adorned with gold and silver, and your clothing was of fine linen, silk, and embroidered cloth. You ate pastry of fine flour, honey, and oil. You were exceedingly beautiful, and succeeded to royalty."

Ezekiel 16:6-13

I was His treasure, and He was making sure that I knew it. In waves of acceptance, His affirmations washed over me, infusing me with a true gusto for life–*His life,* the life of the kingdom here on earth. He was showing me what it meant to be fully alive, accepting myself and His extravagant love for me.

He seemed to know me through and through –my shortcomings as well as my strengths. To protect me in my vulnerable state, He erected a hedge of protection about me that I might enjoy His communion without the queries of others who did not have my best interests at heart. This hedge was a *lattice wall* around my special garden. Surprisingly, I never felt like a prisoner behind this wall. It was actually a comfort during my many reveries with Him, keeping the wild animals from coming in and terrorizing me.

It was His *song* that often alerted me to His presence. I would hear His song and know He was near, and then I would see Him *gazing* at me through the lattice of my garden, and that gaze was what I lived for–a gaze of unconditional love from my Beloved. It communicated to me that I had become His passion, just as He was becoming mine.

The voice of my beloved!
Behold, he comes
Leaping upon the mountains,
Skipping upon the hills.
My beloved is like a gazelle or a young stag.
Behold, he stands behind our wall;
He is looking through the windows,
Gazing through the lattice.

Song 2:8-9

II. The Briars

Behold, You desire truth in the inward parts,
And in the hidden part You will make me to know
wisdom.
Purge me with hyssop, and I shall be clean;
Wash me, and I shall be whiter than snow.
Psalm 51:6-7

At first we seemed to meet only when *I* desired to meet, or so I thought. I would begin to feel the loneliness of my destitute state and beckon Him to remind me of my new found identity in Him. He was always there to reassure me of my *garments of righteousness*. Yet, I still found myself doubting the effectual nature of these special garments, looking for other coverings that might make me feel more adequate in His presence.

He seemed to leave my garden when I embraced such thoughts, and our sweet communion would abruptly end. But He would always return at my plea for His provision to be upon me. It seems

21

we would wrestle over the coverings of my choosing. For some reason I was unable to put on *His covering* consistently and would resist what I needed so desperately from Him.

I found myself ridiculously attempting to take *off* His garment to put on my own fabrication of a covering–a covering made of mere *dung*. Why did I do this repeatedly? Why couldn't I accept His provision? Its only cost was *my consent*. What prevented this exchange from being complete? Something in me resisted His great provision for me. I secretly believed that I could make my own covering out of my own greatness. I was deceived and struggled with my Kinsman-Redeemer as Jacob too wrestled with Him.

It was during these times of wrestling that I would fall into the briars of my garden, injuring myself even more, sickly aware of the stench of my *dung covering* that I had been fighting so fiercely to preserve. It is then that He would gently show me how to uproot particularly unsightly briars.

The briars all seemed to have their roots in *pride of self*. That deception kept me from believing the good news of what my Lord wanted to freely impart to me. It kept me bound up in the stench of my own provision. It seems the only antidote to this great deception was to embrace His great truth–that He was the *Lamb slain from the foundation of the world for my salvation*.

The simplicity and yet far reaching gravity of that truth baffled me. It caused me to stumble repeatedly. I wanted to make up for my inadequacy. I was like a young child who insists on doing a task on her own without intervention. I didn't really want His help. *I just wanted His affirmation in the midst of my futility.* The truth was that the only antidote for my offensive nature was found in His provision. *I needed Him.*

I came to realize that I absolutely could not commune with Him without crawling under His covering *every time.* There were no exceptions. He would wait for me to submit, and then He would rush in and show me how to pull out the hindering briars that we might sit in comfort and commune together in *peace.*

That was my heart's longing...*to be at peace*

with Him, and there was only one way for that. Unfortunately, I kept resisting that way even when I had experienced its effectual outcome. I desperately wanted to find another way, and my resistance to Him kept me lonely and frustrated in my arrogant wanderings.

But I was tired of living in the briar patch of my garden–*alone*. I had tasted of His companionship and wanted more. I wanted to eat of His apple tree again and knew that I had to crawl under His covering and find Him for whom my heart longed so desperately.

> *By night on my bed I sought the one I love;*
> *I sought him, but I did not find him.*
> *"I will arise now," I said,*
> *"And go about the city;*
> *In the streets and in the square*
> *I will seek the one I love."*
>
> *Song 3:1-2*

I thought *I* had found Him, but it was *He* who had found me–*again*. I humbly sat with Him in His *chambers*, covered in His precious blood. He had captured my heart, and being with Him was becoming a consuming passion.

The king has brought me into his chambers.
We will be glad and rejoice in you.
We will remember your love more than wine.

Song 1:4b

There in His chambers we reasoned together about my many predicaments under sin's enslavement of me. He was gracious and tender toward me, washing my wounds and covering my nakedness each time it was exposed through my pervading rebellion and ignorance.

He was training me in the way of righteousness and showing me how to live and abide in His chambers of intimacy. And I must say that I was most grateful for His attentions. No one had ever shown so much concern for my struggles, and hopes, and dreams. His counsel was merely a whisper away.

"Come now, and let us reason together,"
    Says the Lord,
"Though your sins are like scarlet,
They shall be as white as snow;
Though they are red like crimson,
They shall be as wool."

Isaiah 1:18

25

III. The Rescue

The righteous cry out, and the Lord hears,
And delivers them out of all their troubles.
The Lord is near to those who have a broken heart,
And saves such as have a contrite spirit.
Psalm 34:17-18

Leisurely communing in His chambers, He poured His name forth upon me as a sweet ointment, healing me of my wounds. As His ointment flowed over me, imparting a deeper revelation of His great salvation, a deepening desire to please Him rose within me.

I asked Him what His desires were for me, and He tenderly mentioned His grief over the remaining briars that seemed to continually ensnare me at every turn, blocking my view of Him. He began to expose to me the lies that watered those briars, threatening the precious truth deposited within me. In this gentle fashion, He effectively unveiled to me my prevailing pride in *self* and the deeply rooted thorn bush of *self-exaltation* that had kept me from trusting Him even when He had proven Himself so completely to me.

I understood what He was telling me but did not see a way to get the briars out. They were huge and took up most of my garden. I even wondered if part of *myself* would be disfigured by their harsh removal. He assured me that my visage would indeed change, as would my whole identity and how I saw myself, but it was for the better. I would only be losing my *false identity*, not the true me that was created from the foundation of the world. That sounded harmless and even beneficial. So I assented to the procedure. (I had to come into agreement with everything He desired, or it was not accomplished. We were to be *co-laborers* in the tending of this special garden of mine.)

When He began to show me how He intended to uproot these hideous weeds and thorns, I began to have second thoughts, and even found myself rising up to protect my false view of myself. I hadn't realized how attached I was to it. It had become *me*, and I did not know who I was outside of this distorted identity. It was my comfort zone.

He then assured me that He too had passed this way and had successfully overcome the desires of the flesh. Pursuing God's way over the fleshly life of self is a *choice*. He began to paint a graphic picture of a necessary death to self that had to be orchestrated that the life of the spirit might flourish within the garden of my life. He reminded me of His words in Matthew 10:38-39: *"And he who does not take his cross and follow after Me is not worthy of Me. He who finds his life will lose it, and he who loses his life for My sake will find it."*

My heart was convinced of the need to press on in obedience, but my flesh was rearing up as a wild stallion that has been penned in for the first time. I felt trapped. To go on with Him meant death to my treasured *self-life*, but to keep things the way they were meant *spiritual stagnation*. Yet, I didn't think I had the strength to change. I needed Him to help me in the weakness of my humanity and its many fears.

I desperately turned to Him, begging for His intervention. Astonishingly, I beheld Him in a *crown of briars*–the crown that He had been crowned with at His crucifixion. He assured me that He had full authority to escort me into an overcoming assault against the briars of my garden, for He Himself had single-handedly overcome the *briars of the world system*. He was the good shepherd who could successfully lead me out of the briar patch and into the fragrance of His namesake which is like ointment poured forth to a dying world.

> *Let Him kiss me with the kisses of his mouth—*
> *For your love is better than wine.*
> *Because of the fragrance of your good ointments,*
> *Your name is ointment poured forth;*
> *Therefore the virgins love you.*
>
> *Song 1:2-3*

His stance before me was majestic and reassuring. He really was the good shepherd who leaves the ninety-nine to find the one. At that moment I was the *one*. I had His full attention. How could I refuse His offer of deliverance? I bowed my head and laid my self-life on His altar. As the fire of His presence swooped down upon my offering, the briars of my garden were consumed in an instant, but I did not smell of smoke, nor was a hair singed upon my head. I was liberated, and the view was great!

The briars had concealed the many gifts and talents hidden within the ground of my special garden. I truly had not known who I was. At that moment, I was born anew and could see farther than just my selfish needs for the moment. I could see *Him*, and His beauty was entrancing. I ran to Him and did not let go of His skirts. I was consumed with an overwhelming thankfulness and gratitude for my Deliverer.

I saw Him as a mighty man of valor, rising up in the wilderness of my overgrown garden. He had majestically come to rescue me from myself and my unclean obsessions that separated me from Him.

> *Who is this coming out of the wilderness*
> *Like pillars of smoke,*
> *Perfumed with myrrh and frankincense,*
> *With all the merchant's fragrant powders?*
> *Song 3:6*

IV. His Banqueting House

He brought me to the banqueting house,
And his banner over me was love.
Sustain me with cakes of raisins,
Refresh me with apples,
For I am lovesick.
Song 2:4-5

He had become my great Kinsman-Redeemer, and I could not take my eyes off of Him. In the shade of His presence, I partook of His special *apples of intimacy* and found great delight in them. They were sweet and helped me to forget the poisonous food of which I had been previously partaking. He was now the source of my food and drink. He was the *apple tree* of my delight.

Like an apple tree among the trees of the
woods,
So is my beloved among the sons.
I sat down in his shade with great delight.
And his fruit was sweet to my taste.
Song 2:3

I was eating at *His* banqueting table in the shade of *His* presence, delighting in *His* fruit. How did I come to receive such an invitation? This was the King's table! I was feasting with the King Himself and being transformed with every bite of His precious manna to me. The lies of the enemy concerning who I was and who I was supposed to be were quickly losing their death grip on me. I was becoming *bone of His bone and flesh of His flesh.* I was being immersed in Him!

His words of affirmation sowed special seed in my garden that immediately sprang up in the form of various species of fragrant flowers, blooming in a dazzling array of color. There were towering multicolored hollyhocks, splendid bouquets of fiery red and flaming orange geraniums, and fabulous bunches of pink and purple petunias hovering close to the ground, surrounded by splashes of radiant yellow and orange marigolds.

These flowers were a tangible sign that I was beginning to believe some of the truths that the Beloved was whispering so consistently to me. I was overjoyed that the landscape of my garden had changed so quickly! It was already becoming an inviting place to onlookers, but especially to my Beloved, and He was the one I was most interested in attracting to my garden.

There was only *one* seat in my garden, representing the rulership of my heart. So when He came to visit, I willingly sat at the feet of His rule. He was my Lord, and I was His servant. Even so, He often encouraged me to sit on His lap as would a child, laying my head on His breast. It was in this posture that He introduced me to the Father, and I began to feel comforted and reassured of my identity in the kingdom.

Astonishingly, I found that I was being invited to not just be His servant, but His *friend* and *companion*. I was overcome with awe and wonder at such a proposition. What could be so special about me that such a request would go forth? I was stunned, but also intrigued.

One day, while relaxing comfortably on His bosom, I casually noted that some of the precious seed that flowed from His mouth was falling onto ground that was *still* hard. Disturbed by the waste of such highly valued seed, I purposed in my heart that

the fallow ground of my garden must be broken up.
So naturally, I appealed to the Beloved for His help.
I had no idea of what I was actually requesting...

Sow for yourselves righteousness;
Reap in mercy;
Break up your fallow ground,
For it is time to seek the Lord,
Till He comes and rains righteousness on you.
You have eaten the fruit of lies,
Because you trusted in your own way,
In the multitude of your mighty men.
                                        Hosea 10:12

V. Furrowing the Fallow Ground

Break up your fallow ground,
And do not sow among thorns.
Circumcise yourselves to the Lord,
And take away the foreskins of your hearts,...
Jeremiah 4:3b-4a

It wasn't long after my request for more of my garden to be furrowed that my life began to manifest various pressures. My relationships began to be strained, and I was feeling exceptionally irritable. My time with the Beloved in the garden began to be less frequent and more hurried when I was there. Circumstances in general were pressing on me; I was anxious about life. Quite frankly, I didn't have time to sit with the Lord in my garden because I had too much to do. In addition, when I did come away to visit with Him, He was often not there. He must have been busy too. *Or so I thought.*

The night times became particularly lonely for me. I was accustomed to communing with Him late into the night. That was our special time. But now, when I did pull myself away to find Him, He was no where to be found. Had I done something wrong? Why wasn't He in the garden? My unrequited longing fueled my desperation. I had to see Him. My seeking began to be more in earnest as I sought Him night and day, even asking others if they had heard from Him.

> *The watchmen who go about the city found me;*
> *I said, "Have you seen the one I love?"*
> *Scarcely had I passed by them,*
> *When I found the one I love.*
> *I held him and would not let him go.*
> *Until I had brought him to the house of my*
>   *mother.*
> *And into the chamber of her who conceived me.*
>   *Song 3:3-4*

I finally found him after searching my heart and falling into a heap in *repentance*. My heart was broken over my lack of diligence in pursuing Him consistently. Realizing how short-sighted I had been, when I found Him again, I couldn't release Him from my grasp. I clung to Him as a desperate lover. There was nothing that could compare to Him and His embrace. I was ashamed at my previous lack of concern for spiritual things in the midst of my busyness. He was life itself, and I had shirked Him. He had given me so much, and I had wanted so much more from Him. Yet, my desire for Him was so easily overshadowed by the cares of life.

While I was clutching Him greedily to my chest, I noticed the condition of my garden. It had changed. In the places where many of the briars had been cleared away, new thorns and weeds had quickly taken their place. When did this happen? Had I forgotten the truths that He had sown within me already? And how did the enemy's seed grow so fast?

The Beloved explained to me that the enemy's seed is watered by our anxiety and care for the things of this life. All things must be laid at His feet, the Master's feet, or we will be weighted down by our own anxiety. The laying down of burdens has to happen *daily* and sometimes hourly. If we do not purpose to go to the garden to lay them down and thus diligently "pull the weeds" of the enemy seed out of our ground, it will quickly sprout up and overtake the good seed, choking the life out of it.

As He explained this principle to me, I reflected on how easily I had prioritized the cares of life over my time with the Master in the garden. I failed to weed the garden of my heart by laying my burdens daily at His feet and aligning my body, soul, and spirit to His desires and ways. Resorting to living life out of my flesh, *my carnality had overtaken my spiritual life and subdued it.* Thankfully, He used my desperation to awaken me to my everlasting need for Him. And that is when my search for Him was resurrected, *after* the cares of life had worn me down.

Why did it take such a total collapse of all energy in me to finally realize my need for Him? What type of deception, or *briar*, still lurked in the garden of my heart, convincing me that I could live fairly well without the Beloved's life-giving input?

> *Do not let your heart turn aside to her ways,*
> *Do not stray into her paths;*
> Proverbs 7:25

I continued to repent of my deep-seated carnality and short-sightedness as I lay my head on His shoulder. He did not condemn me, but He was quieter than usual. He was more instructional in His manner, showing me my heart and the consequences of those bad seeds that were so

40

diligently *watered* by my poor choices. I was reminded of the truth of Proverbs 16:9, *"A man's heart plans his way, but the Lord directs his steps."*

After looking into my heart and assessing my weaknesses, *together* we weeded the garden, pulling out each weed that had sprung up. Then we attended to the stronger weeds and thorns in the harder ground–*the unfurrowed ground*. These did not come up so easily, and I found myself desperately crying over my predicament. Why wouldn't they come up? I had decided I didn't want them anymore. Wasn't that enough?

I felt my heart breaking more and more over my sin and hard-heartedness in regard to the Master's kingdom. As my tears flowed from a heart of repentance, the ground began to loosen up, and the Master and I began to pull up the weeds and thorn bushes with joy. We sang robustly as we pulled them out by *the roots*. I must admit that I felt a few tinges of pain as the larger ones were pulled out. I guess they were more deeply rooted in my heart than I had imagined. But their absence definitely made me feel clean and ready for the Beloved to plant anew His holy seed.

The Master and I spent days and even weeks just on this section of the garden. When we finally finished, the area we were working on surprisingly unearthed a peculiar stone path hidden under the broken up dirt. The path had been hidden there all this time beneath the briars and thorns that had previously defined my life. I was amazed. Where did the path lead? And was it *my* path, or another's? It was an intriguing disclosure, inspiring many queries—queries that would lead me on a journey of *discovery*.

> *You will show me the path of life;*
> *In Your presence is fullness of joy;*
> *At Your right hand are pleasures forevermore.*
> *Psalm 16:11*

VI. The Garden Path

Show me Your ways, O Lord;
Teach me Your paths.
Lead me in Your truth and teach me,
For You are the God of my salvation;
On You I wait all the day.
Psalm 25:4-5

The Master and I gently brushed away the dirt from some of the stones that made up the path. They were *ancient stones*, and had been there a long time. They looked like they had been walked on by others through the years. I wondered who those people were and how they had tended their gardens when they were alive.

A few of the stones had primitive directional markings and even Scripture references inscribed on them. The Master stood by as I explored them with interest. The thought that others had passed this way made my journey even more interesting. So I was not the only one? There were others. Did they fail the Master repeatedly as I had? Did they find His covering difficult to keep on because of their own need to produce a covering of their own making? Did they find the walk of faith as difficult as I did? Who were these people?

The references engraved on the stones seemed to bring some light to these questions; for they all pointed to men and women in the Holy Scriptures –men and women who had failed on occasion, but who had also walked the walk of faith with diligence and repentant hearts. Their histories began to sing to me of their triumphs of faith; for they were actually testimonies of God's faithfulness to each of them. I began to reflect on my own victories and how they too were reflections of God's faithfulness to me in my hour of need. There seemed to be images of the Beloved in each of the stories hidden there on the stones. He had imprinted Himself in each of their lives, crafting them not just as servants, but as friends and lovers–

> *...of whom the world was not worthy. And all these, having obtained a good testimony through faith, did not receive the promise, God having provided something better for us, that they should not be made perfect apart from us.*
>
> *Hebrews 11:39-40*

Pondering again His invitation to become a friend and lover of His, I began to consider it as a plausible reality. I realized that it was *His* faithfulness to *His* word to me, coupled with a consistent "yes" in my heart that would actually accomplish this great transformation. It was not dependent on *my performance*, but on the "yes" that I am required to steward in my heart. The Beloved would do the rest. And His commitment to transforming me would be a direct reflection of His commitment to having a bride worthy of Him.

What an astounding offer this was! And others had even gone before me! But how do I take my first steps? The Master pointed to the garden again and reminded me that as I faithfully stewarded the garden of my heart, keeping the soil soft and fertile, He would be able to mold me easily into a faithful friend and lover for His good pleasure.

I was eager to take my first steps on this wondrous path, and wondered if it would lead me to the same places that it had led the others before me, or would it be unique in some ways? The Master reminded me that since the path was an expression of a person's heart, it would naturally have its own idiosyncrasies that characterized aspects of a person's temperament and giftings in the kingdom. That excited me even more–*a unique path.* He then assured me that the many failures of humanity through the ages had manifested distinct patterns, and more than likely I would fit into a few of those *patterns* whether I realized I possessed such propensities or not.

I didn't let that last bit of information daunt my enthusiasm. Maybe I could learn from the mistakes others had made before me and save myself from the heartache of such failures. Reflecting on that *great cloud of witnesses* watching me from the heavenlies, I set out to study my predecessors and see if I might learn something from their struggles.

> *Therefore we also, since we are surrounded by so great a cloud of witnesses, let us lay aside every weight, and the sin which so easily ensnares us, and let us run with endurance the race that is set before us, looking unto Jesus, the author and finisher of our faith, who for the joy that was set before Him endured the cross, despising the shame, and has sat down at the right hand of the throne of God.*
>
> *Hebrews 12:1-2*

VII. Clearing the Air

The heart is deceitful above all things,
And desperately wicked;
Who can know it?
I, the Lord, search the heart,
I test the mind,
Even to give every man according to his ways,
According to the fruit of his doings.
Jeremiah 17:9-10

After brushing away the dirt from the stones we had discovered, I began to study some of the people who had passed by this way prior to me. One thing that stood out to me was God's grace and mercy toward each of them. I had experienced that side of my Lord as well. He consistently waited patiently for my heart to cry out in true repentance so He could pour out His mercy to me in abundance.

The Lord is good to all,
And His tender mercies
are over all His works.
Psalm 145:9

47

As I reminisced about the sacrifices these others had made for the sake of His kingdom, I wondered what He would ask of me. Surely, He had requests of me that would be *sacrificial*.

That evening while walking with Him in the garden, admiring some of the new plants that had sprung up from my obedience to Him, I asked Him about the *sacrifice* that I was intended to make for Him. He said it was not time to reveal that, for I would not embrace it. I was offended by that observation. Had I not devoted my life to Him, even giving up my former identity and pastimes? Surely He didn't know me as well as I knew myself! Proclaiming my virtues, I pleaded with Him to tell me. He seemed to only grow more quiet. I gave up, and left the garden disheartened.

The next day I got into an angry dispute with one of my friends. I was thinking hateful thoughts of revenge and decided to tell the Lord how I had been bitterly mistreated. Maybe He would avenge me.

While railing against this person who was formerly cherished by me, I noticed a deepening sadness in the Master's eyes. I finally was silent, sensing a growing stench of sin that was beginning to choke me. Flowing from within, I was literally *defiling* my garden. I could hardly even see the Master because of the haziness of the air. The smell was equally putrefying and smothering.

I cried out for Him to rescue me from my repugnant state. Immediately, a brilliant light pierced the blinding haze, illuminating Him before me in overwhelming beauty and grace. He said nothing, but He looked at me with such affectionate eyes of unconditional love and adoration that I was brought to my knees by His gracious response to my ugliness. He had completely forgiven me, and I was free to enjoy His affirmation once again. But I didn't deserve it! And I knew it. His grace and mercy to me were mystifying. I fell on my face and exclaimed as did Isaiah,

> *"Woe is me, for I am undone!*
> *Because I am a man of unclean lips,*
> *And I dwell in the midst of a people of*
> *   unclean lips;*
> *For my eyes have seen the King,*
> *The Lord of hosts."*
>
> *Isaiah 6:5*

The Master bent down and reminded me that I was clean *only* because of His provision, not because of anything I might say or do to make up for my sin. I was suddenly conscious of that hidden desire –*to be able to make up for my sin*. I *still* was resisting His covering for me. Yet I knew that the Scriptures clearly taught of the absolute cleansing offered by the Master's blood sacrifice.

> *But if we walk in the light as He is in the light, we have fellowship with one another, and the blood of Jesus Christ His Son cleanses us from all sin. If we say that we have no sin, we deceive ourselves, and the truth is not in us. If we confess our sins, He is faithful and just to forgive us our sins and to cleanse us from all unrighteousness. If we say that we have not sinned we make Him a liar, and His word is not in us.*
> I John 1:7-10

I was guilty. Not only had I not accepted His righteousness freely, but I was judging others, speaking horrendous things about them, all in a self-righteous attitude. Yet, I bore no righteousness outside of Him, and I was outside of Him when I refused His sacrifice. My heart was smitten with the vanity of my heart.

The Lord then reminded me that as I had been forgiven much, so I needed to extend the same grace and mercy to others. I had been taught that spiritual truth, but never realized how little I truly believed it. Now because of the lavish show of undeserved grace and mercy that had been poured out on me, I understood it in a more applicable fashion. I saw how many times I had violated this principle–*daily*. I did not love others as He desired me to love them. I had judged them and decided that I was better than they. How foolish I had been! And how far from God's heart. I thought I had loved God with all of my heart and soul, but it was really *me* I was continuing to love.

> *He who says he is in the light, and hates his brother, is in darkness until now. He who loves his brother abides in the light, and there is no cause for stumbling in him. But he who hates his brother is in darkness and walks in darkness, and does not know where he is going, because the darkness has blinded his eyes.*
>
> *I John 2:9-11*

No wonder I couldn't see the nature of my path! I was blinded by my own deceptions that were hidden in my heart. I began to speculate about how many other misconceptions and lies were keeping me from abiding in Him and finding my way on His path of life for me.

> *My flesh and my heart fail;*
> *But God is the strength of my heart*
> *and my portion forever.*
> *Psalm 73:26*

At this point the Master pointed out to me that the exposing of that one deception had cleared the air so much that not only could I see the path more clearly, but I could see myself more clearly as well. What I saw was a person who desperately needed to stay in the embrace of the great Kinsman-Redeemer, because outside of His covering I was lost and without hope in a dying world.

The worship within me for Him increased to a new level of intensity. I was so grateful to Him for His goodness to me. How could I repay Him? He reminded me that some day I would indeed sacrifice unto Him, but it would be a sacrifice of *His choosing*, and my flesh would take no glory in it. That was the sacrifice that I was not ready to know about yet, and now I knew why–I was deceived about the level of commitment I had for Him in my heart. My resolve was not nearly as radical as I had once thought. My failure reminded me of some of the failures of those who had passed this way before me; pride was a major contributor in all of their failures as well. I had to live a life of humility, but how? If I had hidden pride, how could I live humbly?

The Lord assured me that He knew how to instill humility in His children. He had a gleam in His eye that caused me to wonder what other "exposures" of my decrepit self-nature were in store for me. At any rate I wanted them all out of me, as painful as that might be. It had to be done. This was part of His chastening of His children.

> "My son, do not despise the chastening of the
> Lord,
> Nor be discouraged when you are rebuked by
> Him;
> For whom the Lord loves He chastens,
> And scourges every son whom He receives."
> Hebrews 12:5-6

I knew that if I endured chastening I would indeed pass from my role as His servant to His *friend*. And it was His friends who were made ready to live sacrificial lives unto Him, serving His will and desires and not their own.

I beseech you therefore, brethren, by the mercies of God, that you present your bodies a living sacrifice, holy, acceptable to God which is your reasonable service. And do not be conformed to this world, but be transformed by the renewing of your mind that you may prove what is that good and acceptable and "perfect" will of God. For I say, through the grace given to me, to everyone who is among you, not to think of himself more highly than he ought to think, but to think soberly, as God has dealt to each one a measure of faith.

Romans 12:1-3

I wanted that, but now I knew that I was not ready to do it. That was all right. He would make me ready. He was my divine caregiver, and I had to trust Him. After all, He seemed to know my heart better than I did.

I now understood how my path would be clarified. It would come through my maturity in His kingdom. As I matured, I would naturally understand what He was calling me to do. I couldn't wait for that incredible revelation to unfold, for I was extremely anxious to see where my special path would lead...

VIII. The Gated Entry Way

Strive to enter through the narrow gate,
for many, I say to you, will seek to enter
and will not be able.
Luke 13:24

Striding hand in hand through the garden, the Master and I were relishing the many sights and aromas that had erupted in my little *garden of intimacy*. Intoxicated by the fragrance of the jasmine flowering amidst the flourishing gardenias beside the path of stones, we were mesmerized by the stunning sight of some blue hydrangeas in full bloom, lounging in the shade. The Master was commenting on their intense hue, and I was noticing the abundance of blossoms on these vibrant shrubs. Watered by my *tears of intercession* for others, these flowers represented the growth of *compassion* in my life. I had no idea I was "watering" such precious treasures in my garden.

The tremendous amount of new growth had

dramatically changed the garden's appearance, reflecting the many changes in my personal life as well. In fact, my regenerated life bore little resemblance to the beggarly, lackluster life of sin that I was trapped in just a few years ago. I was a living testimony of 2 Corinthians 5:17, *"Therefore, if anyone is in Christ, he is a new creation; old things have passed away; behold, all things have become new."*

I liked what I saw. He was making my garden into *His* garden. As a growing reflection of Him and His kingdom, it was becoming an invitation for Him to come and inhabit this special garden of intimacy. He was creating a place for Himself to rest and abide. So as I learned to abide in Him, He would abide in me. In that respect, His provision for *rest* actually extended to Himself; for His great salvation purchased a people in whom He could rest. *"For he who has entered His rest has himself also ceased from his works as God did from His"* (Hebrews 4:10).

It was usually in the cool of the day that the Master and I would survey the condition of the *garden of my heart*, leisurely strolling through it, arm in arm, talking quietly. His companionship was causing my self-esteem to grow. Since I was beginning to value myself based on my relationship with Him and the innate qualities He had hidden within me, my identity was not as controlled by what others thought of me. I was becoming at ease with my new found identity in Him, and it felt good.

It was during one of our strolls that the Master pointed out a hidden area of the garden that I had not seen before. It was behind a *gated entry way*. I don't know how I had missed a gated entry way in my own garden, but I had. I would imagine it was because my focus had previously been on the ground, and now I was beginning to lift my eyes in gratitude and worship to Him. This allowed me to survey the *land of my inheritance*–a land of which I had been strangely ignorant for most of my life. I suspected that the special stones in the path were connected to the final conquest of this land, but I was still waiting for the unveiling of such mysteries.

This gated entry was overshadowed by some straggly looking yellow roses striving to hold onto their possession–the trellis upon which they clung. Dramatically communicating their desperate need to be trimmed and fertilized, they bore a faint aroma.

The sight of their tremendous struggle disturbed me; for they had truly been neglected. What did they represent? The Master explained to me that they covered the entry way to a secret part of my heart to which even *I* had not been privy. My curiosity was significantly stirred. How could I have places in my heart that I was not even aware existed?

The Master invited me to peer over the gate and see what was behind it. I wasn't impressed. It was an empty plot of ground. Discouraged, I decided I wasn't all that interested anymore. But the Master assured me that precious seed had been sown in that part of my garden before the foundation of the world. That rejuvenated my curiosity, but when I went to open the gate, it was locked. Why? There wasn't anything behind the gate, so why lock it?

The Master then explained to me that the key to opening the gate was to be found in tending the climbing roses that overshadowed the gate. With my curiosity sufficiently piqued, I quickly took out some clippers, intending to begin some pruning, but *fear* suddenly arrested me in my intentions. I didn't know from where it had come.

A *fear of the unknown* had stayed my hand; and in order to prune these roses, I would have to overcome that fear. But how do I overcome something that I can't see? If it is a fear of the unknown, how do I convince myself that the unknown need not be feared? I was baffled. Then the Master reminded me that the key to overcoming sin is found in abiding in Him and His testimony. I would need to sit down and reflect on this. So we went to our seat, and I situated myself on His lap as a child in her father's lap, with our heads touching.

How was I to overcome this newly disclosed fear? That question hung about me like a dark cloud. It seemed like I was supposed to know the answer to this, but I didn't. I knew *He* was the answer, but that is all I knew. I had no revelation of what that meant or how that was to be applied to my life.

The Holy Spirit began to whisper hints to me, as fleeting thoughts about specific truths came to my mind. One of those thoughts brought to mind Jesus' Sermon on the Mount in which He encouraged us to take no thought for tomorrow, for tomorrow shall worry about itself.

"Therefore I say to you, do not worry about your life, what you will eat or what you will drink; nor about your body, what you will put on. Is not life more than food and the body more than clothing?

"...Therefore do not worry, saying, 'What shall we eat?' or 'What shall we drink?' or 'What shall we wear?' For after all these things the Gentiles seek. For your heavenly Father knows that you need all these things. But seek first the kingdom of God and His righteousness, and all these things shall be added to you. Therefore do not worry about tomorrow, for tomorrow will worry about its own things. Sufficient for the day is its own trouble."

Matthew 6:25, 31-34

I knew this truth and *thought* that I had sufficiently dealt with my self-reliance, but in all honesty, I didn't really exhibit the life of faith exemplified in the Scriptures. I had laid an aspect of my self-reliance on His altar, but in actuality, I was still quite self-reliant and rather proud of it. Frankly, I *liked* the empowerment that I felt when I knew I was doing things for myself. Was that a bad feeling? How did it impede my growing intimacy with Him? Did He not like a *little* self-reliance in His servants? Did He not have more important things to avail Himself? It seems like He would be grateful that He did not have to dote over me concerning such petty things as food and clothing.

As I ruminated over these thoughts, I became aware that the Master had extended His hand to me. He wanted me to give Him my trust, abandoning myself to His desires, causing me to literally be dependent upon Him for everything. Could I relinquish *control*? What did He offer in return?

He pointed to the secret part of my heart guarded by the straggly yellow roses, languishing about the entry way. Did I really want to know what type of seed was planted in that vacant space in the garden of my heart? It seemed like such a lavish price to pay for something I could not see or judge. I had to trust Him. I guess that was the whole point –that I would come to truly trust Him, not just for salvation but for my *quality of life*. Could I do that? I was used to getting *my way*. Did He want me to have my way? I had a hunch that He wanted to effect more changes than I was ready to make.

I got up from His lap and walked over to the gated entry way. Peering over the gate and through the thorny, bedraggled roses hanging about in disarray, something in me rose up. It was an insatiable desire to know everything about myself and who I was created to be. I *had* to know what type of seed had been planted in my soil. There must be a way to *compromise* on this issue of control. I turned to inquire after a more diplomatic solution, but the stern look in His eye silenced me. I had to *choose*.

I couldn't do it then. I had to weigh my options. So I left the garden. For days and then weeks, I came into the garden burdened with my decision. Why couldn't we go back to the way things were before I saw the secret place in my garden? I wanted to forget it altogether. Could I? No. It was a part of the garden that now consumed me.

Finally, after weeks of deliberating, I realized that self-reliance was the breeding ground for my blinding unbelief and my paralyzing fear of the unknown. Repulsed by my delusions, I took my *self-reliance* and laid it at His feet. I couldn't look at it lying there. It had been part of me, and it looked just like me lying on the ground at the Master's feet. As I was weeping over my new "death" to self, my *fear of the unknown* left me, and I felt the Master nudge me over to the gated entry way. He handed me the clippers, and I began to prune those neglected yellow roses. Sobbing the entire time, I pruned them severely at His instruction, and was amazed to see the gate slowly open.

I took my first step into the new land of acquisition, and was stunned to note that the same stones we found on my path, passed through here as well. They looked less worn in here however, as if few had passed here. In fact, the stones looked less like stones in a path and more like huge *gemstones*.

There were *twelve* of them glistening before me. I didn't know what they represented, but I immediately stood on each of them in turn, delighting in knowing that I had the authority to do so. So I did, and I did it with glee. I was strangely aware that I was standing on the foundation of something that was soon to be erected–something that would come from the building materials of my own life in Him. It was a prophetic moment, and I soaked it in. These were *stones of identity* in Him, and they were part of who I was.

I delighted over these stones for several days, frequenting the gated area with a giddy wonder. This was now a place of discovery, and I was entranced with it. Daily, my tongue began to prophetically declare the exalted importance of each of these enigmatic stones.

"O you afflicted one,
Tossed with tempest, and not comforted,
Behold, I will lay your stones with colorful
*   gems,*
And lay your foundations with sapphires.
I will make your pinnacles of rubies,
Your gates of crystal,
And all your walls of precious stones.
All your children shall be taught by the Lord,
And great shall be the peace of your children.

In righteousness you shall be established;
You shall be far from oppression, for you
*   shall not fear;*
And from terror, for it shall not come near you.
Indeed they shall surely assemble, but not
*   because of Me.*
Whoever assembles against you shall fall for
*   your sake.*

"Behold, I have created the blacksmith
Who blows the coals in the fire,
Who brings forth an instrument for his work;
And I have created the spoiler to destroy.

No weapon formed against you shall prosper,
And every tongue which rises against you in
judgment
You shall condemn.

This is the heritage of the servants of the Lord,
And their righteousness is from Me,"
Says the Lord.

Isaiah 54:11-17

IX.   A Sure Foundation

Therefore thus says the Lord God:
"Behold, I lay in Zion a stone for a foundation,
A tried stone, a precious cornerstone,
a sure foundation;
Whoever believes will not act hastily.
Also I will make justice the measuring line,
And righteousness the plummet;
The hail will sweep away the refuge of lies,
And the waters will overflow the hiding place."
Isaiah 28:16-17

My time in the garden was spent more and more in the new gated area. Intensely curious about the twelve stones, I spent much time sitting on them, lying on them, walking around them, inspecting them, and even polishing them. I was enamored with these stones.

One sunny day, while statuesquely posed on one of the stones, the Master suddenly appeared in front of me, standing on one of the other stones. With awe and utter amazement, I beheld Him in

His beauty. Gloriously transfigured before my eyes, I was overwhelmed by a tangible sense of His great love for me, as well as for all mankind. *He was love.* The reality of that abstraction became something I could "stand" on. It gave me security and confidence. It empowered me to love others because the reality that I was loved first had overcome my furtive self-loathing and creeping insecurities. *"But God demonstrates His own love toward us, in that while we were still sinners, Christ died for us" (Romans 5:8).*

The reality of His love toward me, even in my times of rebellion, loosed me to receive that love as genuine and unconditional. It caused me to stand on His love as a sure foundation of my place in Him as His heir. Giving my identity in Him a framework, I had a basis for relationship with Him. His love for me as evidenced in His sacrificial death grounded me in Him.

> *...that you, being rooted and grounded in love, may be able to comprehend with all the saints what is the width and length and depth and height—to know the love of Christ which passes knowledge; that you may be filled with all the fullness of God.*
> *Ephesians 3:17b-19*

This was not my only experience on the stones. Others followed, with each revealing an aspect of the Master's character that set me free of specific deceptions that had led to uncanny fears. The Master was literally becoming the foundation that I stood upon. I was beginning to *stand* in His presence as I learned to abide in each of His character traits. *"For no other foundation can anyone lay than that which is laid, which is Jesus Christ" (I Corinthians 3:11).*

One particularly memorable experience was when His righteousness was revealed to me. It left me at peace with His decisions for my life. I felt free to rest in Him and truly cease from my labors. His righteousness reigned, and I could either reap the benefits of that truth by abiding in His righteousness by faith, or I could reap the judgments that assail us when we separate ourselves from His righteousness.

Suddenly, the truth of this reality liberated me to *rest in Him*. I did not feel the same compulsion to stir up my own righteousness, for it would not be in agreement with His and would only release judgments upon me. *I was only safe in His righteousness.* What a day of liberation that was!

As for me, I will see Your face in righteousness; I shall be satisfied when I awake in Your likeness.

Psalm 17:15

The Master was transforming me into His image as I beheld Him according to the truths of who He is. More than that, by standing on the truths of who He is, I was able to stand in His presence and talk with Him as a *friend*. I noticed that as I stood upon each of these traits, the color of the stone representing that trait began to emanate from within me. *He was taking up His abode in me!*

As this transformation of our relationship unfolded, I went from being His servant to being His *friend*. I was standing on the truth of who He is, and that empowered me to stand before Him in His righteousness.

It is at this juncture in our relationship that He took my hand and led me to a shady place next to a pomegranate tree in a far corner of the gated area, near the *twelfth* stone. Beside the tree were two chairs slightly facing one another. Gesturing toward them, He invited me to sit with Him.

We talked as we had never talked before–*face to face*. The colors of the stones swirled around us and emanated from within us. We were communing around these truths which defined Him and now me in *Him*. As such, they were the *foundation* of our blossoming *friendship*. I realized that we were actually communing as *friends* who have things in common to discuss. His words to His disciples about them being His friends were now words He spoke to me.

> *No longer do I call you servants, for a servant does not know what his master is doing; but I have called you friends, for all things that I heard from My Father I have made known to you.*
>
> *John 15:15*

My foundation in Him had led me to *friendship with God*. And it is out of this foundation that the walls of my life in Him would be built; for this foundation exhibited the *government of God* in my life which is where the twelve stones had led me. Establishing Him and all that He is as the essence of my life in His kingdom, they provided a basis for true friendship with God. This reality caused me to reflect on the new Jerusalem whose foundation, too, is of precious stones–*twelve* layers of them.

The foundations of the wall of the city were adorned with all kinds of precious stones: the first foundation was jasper, the second sapphire, the third chalcedony, the fourth emerald, the fifth sardonyx, the sixth sardius, the seventh chrysolite, the eighth beryl, the ninth topaz, the tenth chrysoprase, the eleventh jacinth, and the twelfth amethyst.

Revelation 21:19

X. Weeding... in the Wrong Places

Therefore you are inexcusable, O man,
whoever you are who judge, for in whatever
you judge another you condemn yourself;
for you who judge practice the same things.
Romans 2:1

The summer was in full bloom, and it was a busy time for me. Not only were my cultivated shrubs, perennials, and annuals blooming, but the *weeds* were thriving as well. The only solution was to pull them out by the *roots*, but that was not always easy, especially if they were growing too closely to my prized specimens. Sometimes, if a weed wasn't dealt with in its infancy, it had to be left to grow, so as not to endanger the other plants around it.

I greatly despised having to let some of the weeds grow in and about my treasures. But it was my own fault. The Master had warned me time and again to deal ruthlessly with any weeds that sprang up in the garden, and to deal with them at the *root.*

One particular weed that kept popping up was *judgment*. This was a sly weed. Appearing much like the *sprouts of discernment* that I prided myself on cultivating, I often overlooked these impostors until it was too late . When this would happen, often the *judgment weeds* would entwine themselves menacingly around one or more of my cultivated plants, keeping true fruit from coming forth. What was even more discouraging, is that I rarely saw these counterfeits at all.

It was the Holy Spirit who began to alert me to the subtle differences in appearance and *fragrance*, causing the faint distinctions in aroma to ultimately alert me to the counterfeits. These *scents* were compromising my garden, keeping fruit from coming forth–fruit that my Beloved longed to see in me.

Having to live with some of the more mature judgment weeds assailing my garden was a humiliating judgment all its own. I kept vowing that I would never be in that predicament again, but lo and behold another weed would begin to make itself known at a point in its growth when I could do nothing but let it grow alongside the legitimate seed. Becoming increasingly frustrated and feeling very isolated in my struggle, I began wondering if anyone else was having this same problem.

One day, while surveying my garden, looking intensely for any new sprouting weeds, my eye happened to land on a friend's garden. And what do you think I saw? *Weeds!!* Everywhere, weeds! There were not only seedlings of weeds sprouting, but even mature weeds which were actually beginning to go to seed! I was amazed at how easy it was to spot the weeds in *her* garden as opposed to my own. I couldn't let this gift go to waste. So I raced over to her aid and began glibly pointing out these pesky weeds that truly compromised her garden before the Lord.

She was thrown into a cloud of condemnation and despair. I assured her that she need not fear. I would help her to pull them out because I had great experience in this area. So we set to work.

My friend seemed appreciative at first. But then as my zeal picked up momentum, and I began attacking the mature weeds, dragging them out along with her precious cultivated plants, she became agitated. Frankly, it was just so much easier to pull *her* weeds out as opposed to my own. So I guess I was a little on the zealous side, but I assured her that this process had to continue or the whole garden would be compromised by their invasion. She assured me that if I did prevail, *there wouldn't be a garden*. We exchanged words, and I left in a huff. She didn't understand how gifted I was at *"seeing"* these things. After all, I just wanted to help.

When I finally made it back to my own garden, I was stunned by the amazing overgrowth of weeds, thorns, and thistles. If I didn't know better, I would say that they had grown twice as fast while I was away. In fact, my garden looked even worse than my friend's garden did! How did this happen to me? I had been such a diligent gardener. And now look at it—

> *And there it was, all overgrown with thorns;*
> *Its surface was covered with nettles;*
> *Its stone wall was broken down.*
> *When I saw it, I considered it well;*
> *I looked on it and received instruction:*
> *Proverbs 24:31-32*

Coming out from behind some particularly tall, haunting looking weeds, the Lord looked at me with a raised brow. I knew what He was thinking,

"How did you let the garden get to this state of disarray?" I informed Him of my humanitarian efforts, thinking He would be impressed with the extensive use of my "gift." But He surprised me with a different response.

He leaned over and gently pulled a large piece of *debris* out of my eye, speaking the truth of Matthew 7:1-5 over me:

> *"Judge not, that you be not judged. For with what judgment you judge, you will be judged; and with the measure you use, it will be measured back to you. And why do you look at the speck in your brother's eye, but do not consider the plank in your own eye? Or how can you say to your brother, 'Let me remove the speck from your eye'; and look, a plank is in your own eye? Hypocrite! First remove the plank from your own eye, and then you will see clearly to remove the speck from your brother's eye."*

Immediately, I was stricken by the poignancy of the truth He had spoken. I had actually *fed* the weeds in my garden through my own *judgments*, making even more work for myself; and to top it all off, I *thought* I could actually *help* the Holy Spirit by pointing out the weeds in my friend's garden. My presumption was revolting. How did such self-deception ensnare me? And how could I keep it from happening again?

The Lord reminded me that it is the Holy Spirit who leads us into all truth. Without His teaching and counsel, I would surely be duped again by my own arrogance and pride. At that moment I felt the Holy Spirit put me in remembrance of Romans 12:3:

> *For I say, through the grace given to me, to everyone who is among you, not to think of himself more highly than he ought to think, but to think soberly, as God has dealt to each one a measure of faith.*

The Master stood by as the Holy Spirit continued to counsel me, bringing truth after truth to life in me. My delusions about myself were beginning to break off, and I felt humbled by the truth. It felt good. *Humility is much lighter to wear than the overbearing weight of pride and presumption.*

Tears of repentance began to flood the garden, and as they did I noticed that their effect on the weeds was most intriguing. They caused the weeds to loosen their hold in the ground so that I could more easily pull them from the ground, *roots and all*. I was so encouraged by this that I quickly ran about the garden looking for weeds that were "ready" to be removed.

To accomplish this, I had to greatly humble myself, contritely bending over each weed to test its strength against my tears. After exhausting myself at this, I noticed that I had on a new garment, kind of scruffy looking and brown. It was a *garment of humility*. The Holy Spirit had put it on me in place of my pride and arrogance that had previously fueled my presumptuous, defiling judgments.

> *Likewise you younger people, submit yourselves to your elders. Yes, all of you be submissive to one another, and be clothed with humility, for*
> *"God resists the proud,*
> *But gives grace to the humble."*
> *I Peter 5:5*

It felt refreshing and reassuring to wear this homely garment, especially since I knew the Holy Spirit had graced me with it, and it wasn't my own covering. It had come from Him.

By humility and the fear of the Lord
Are riches and honor and life.
Thorns and snares are in the way of the
perverse;
He who guards his soul will be far from them.

Proverbs 22:4-5

XI. Fall's Fetching Farewell

"While the earth remains,
Seedtime and harvest,
Cold and heat,
Winter and summer,
And day and night
Shall not cease."
Genesis 8:22

There was a hint of *change* in the air—a chill that causes the leaves to begin to *blush*, painting the trees with splashes of tawny golds, fiery reds, and blazing oranges. The splendor of the color captivated my gaze and transfixed it upward. The view was like an abstract painting that changed daily. I was enraptured. Aside from the glory of the profusely blooming chrysanthemums, the only thing that could pull my gaze away from this extravagant show of color was a visitation of the Lord Himself to my garden.

One breezy day, He came out from behind a

large tree surrounded by some brilliantly tinted sun-yellow and burnt-orange chrysanthemums. My eyes were drawn to His feet for some reason, maybe it was the splash of color about them. He had on *boots*, instead of sandals. It occurred to me that summer was really over. *Winter was coming!*

Picking one of the bright sun-yellow flowers, the Beloved placed it gently in my hair. He reminded me to live in the present and to not miss any of its surprises, but to also anticipate tomorrow, full of faith and hope. I assented and took His outstretched hand.

We sauntered over to our chairs beside the pomegranate tree and sat down next to each other, looking eye to eye. I could tell that He had something important to tell me. He began explaining to me the importance of respecting the seasons by *preparing* my garden to weather each season productively. I didn't quite understand.

Then He showed me a bag of bulbs and some bulb fertilizer. I didn't feel like planting. It was time to enjoy my labors from the spring and summer which were such busy seasons in the garden. But

He persisted in His desire for the bulbs to be planted.

Finally, I assented, but with reservations. Why couldn't we wait to plant everything in the spring and do all of our sowing at one time? Again He explained to me that these bulbs were not like seed that is cast. Carefully placed in special places, these bulbs were to be buried deep in the ground, hidden away from all speculations about them until their surprising eruption at another time.

Amazingly, these bulbs represented special promises from Him to me. If I failed to plant them and hide them away in the furrowed ground of my heart, they would never come forth and manifest their beauty. Thus was my heart smitten by the importance of their planting.

As the Lord eloquently poured His promises out on me, I assigned each of them to a specific bulb, and He and I picked the perfect spot for each one to be hidden. We labored together, and when we were finished, I felt very full, like I was pregnant—*pregnant with the holy seed of His words to me.*

I couldn't wait to see what these promises

would look like when they broke through the ground and bloomed for all the world to see. What a day that would be!! Lounging in our garden chairs, we gazed lovingly at one another with hope. Life was stirring within me, reminding me of Peter's words.

Grace and peace be multiplied to you in the knowledge of God and of Jesus our Lord, as His divine power has given to us all things that pertain to life and godliness, through the knowledge of Him who called us by glory and virtue, by which have been given to us exceedingly great and precious promises, that through these you may be partakers of the divine nature, having escaped the corruption that is in the world through lust.
I Peter 1:2-4

It wasn't long after this awesome experience that the weather changed, *dramatically*. It had gotten much colder, and the beautiful leaves had become more of a brownish tan color, flailing and twisting their way to the ground in agonized deaths–all at the whim of fall's brisk breezes. I was greatly disappointed by this new spectacle, for it left the trees looking so bare and lifeless.

I began to feel despondent over the garden's sudden metamorphosis. What had happened to all of its color and life? It seemed like only yesterday that it had enraptured me with its vitality. Now it looked like it was dying. In fact, the freeze of the night before had caused the bountiful begonias to wilt and shrivel up next to the ground. One day, they were vibrant; the next day, they were a shrunken fragment of plant pulp. I was aghast at this loss. Where was the Lord? Surely He could bring the flowers back to life with His touch.

Suddenly, there He was. He didn't seem as disturbed by all the death and destruction as I was. After pleading with Him to intervene, He smiled and simply said, "Winter is coming."

That's it? Winter is coming? Why does winter have to come? I hate the winter. It is so cold and dreary. I don't feel like doing anything in the winter. I am just too cold! And worst of all, we won't be able to meet in the beauty of the garden. What shall we do?

He smiled at my dramatics over a mere season, and then reminded me that it was necessary. If winter didn't come and take the hidden bulbs through a freeze, they would not come forth. It was that simple.

But why did things always have to *die* before they came forth in glory? He simply retorted, "That is the way in the kingdom. I even had to pass that way. But death was swallowed up in my victory. Don't you remember?" He then proclaimed I Corinthians 15:36 to me. *"Foolish one, what you sow is not made alive unless it dies."*

I took my rebuke and glumly joined Him in moving the piles of leaves around that they might help to insulate the shrubs from the harshness of winter that was on the way—regardless of my overriding dislike for it. I would submit to winter's blast, but only for a *season*; for each season comes from the Lord.

You have set all the borders of the earth;
You have made summer and winter.
                    Psalm 74:17

XII. Winter's North Winds of Adversity

If you endure chastening, God deals with you as with sons; for what son is there whom a father does not chasten?
Hebrews 12:7

Though I had willingly submitted to this *winter season*, I had no idea what I was going to face. As the temperature dropped and the winter winds stripped the trees of their remaining dried up shriveled leaves, I could sense the indisputable chastening of the Lord that was upon me. I too felt stripped and barren. It was a harrowing time of seeming rejection and alienation, and I felt more alone than I had ever felt.

Struggling against the harsh winter winds, I would daily make my way to the garden, plodding through piles of leaves and dead branches. Bundled in layers of warm clothes, I would traverse the familiar paths, calling for my Beloved to come to me. But I could not find Him. I was as the Shulamite in the *Song of Songs*, searching for Him, but not finding Him.

> *I opened for my beloved,*
> *But my beloved had turned away and was gone.*
> *My heart leaped up when he spoke.*
> *I sought him, but I could not find him;*
> *I called him, but he gave me no answer.*
> Song 5:6

I was truly lovesick for His attentions. Why would He not talk to me? What had I done to cause Him to turn away from me? Slouched in my garden chair situated in the *gated area of friendship*, I stared absently at His empty seat next to me, day after day.

My friends were similar to Job's friends, telling me that repentance was in order if I ever wanted to commune with the Son again. So I searched my heart again and again, crying out to Him to have mercy on me.

Others felt that I was being punished by the Lord, which is why He had turned His back on me. Was that so? I certainly was worthy of any punishment, but I thought His provision was ever upon me, saving me from His judgments.

I was greatly wounded by the opinions of these in regard to my situation. As they speculated about secret sin in my life, I groaned from deep within, overwhelmed with shame over their presumption. I had lost their respect. They disdained me as one who is spiritually deranged.

> The watchmen who went about the city
>   found me.
> They struck me, they wounded me;
> The keepers of the walls
> Took my veil away from me.
> I charge you, O daughters of Jerusalem,
> If you find my beloved,
> That you tell him I am lovesick!
>   Song 5:7-8

I began to search the Scriptures for comfort and answers to my dilemma. I even returned to the ancient stones on the path in my garden, contemplating each Scripture referenced, looking for a clue about my predicament. I wondered if the *great cloud of witnesses* who had preceded me were interested in my plight. Did they ever feel abandoned by the Lord? Then I remembered that the Lord experienced abandonment on the cross. Was I entering into His sufferings? Is that what this season was all about?

My God, My God, why have You forsaken Me?
Why are You so far from helping Me,
And from the words of My groaning?

O My God, I cry in the daytime, but You do
     not hear;
And in the night season, and am not silent.
                                        Psalm 22:1-2

As the weeks passed, my friends were not calling as often. I guess I wasn't very interesting to be around. It didn't matter. What consolation could they possibly give anyway? They weren't the ones I wanted to see. I was despondent and lonely for my Lord's companionship.

Adversity had now become my companion. Every day brought new hardships and challenges to overcome—*without* the seeming companionship of my Lord. The lowliness of my state was pathetic and uninspiring to those watching, and I was as disgusted with myself as others were. *Oh, how the mighty have fallen!*

But I am a worm, and no man;
A reproach of men, and despised by the people.
All those who see Me ridicule Me;
They shoot out the lip, they shake the head,
     saying,

*"He trusted in the Lord, let Him rescue Him;
Let Him deliver Him, since He delights in
Him!"*

Psalm 22:6-8

My grieving increased as I considered the lost promises that were buried in the once furrowed ground of my heart. What had become of them? No longer feeling pregnant with God's words, I actually felt *barren* and devoid of all life in the spirit. I felt forsaken. I was even more grieved that my offenses with God were causing an iciness in my heart, causing the ground in my heart to harden. How could I prevent this? Was there no escape?

Lying in my bed with tears blurring my eyes, I decided to reread the testimony of those who had lived by *faith* and not by sight. And there was the key—*faith*. It is the only way to please God.

*But without faith it is impossible to please
Him, for He who comes to God must believe
that He is, and that He is a rewarder of
those who diligently seek Him.*

Hebrews 11:6

Something in me awakened. I was stirred by the truth. At my lowest point, I resolved that I would continue to praise Him, as did Job—*"though He slay me.*" What was my alternative? I had already found the one I love, and I couldn't release Him, even when His voice was far from my ear and His touch absent from my senses. I would praise Him regardless, for the testimony of His faithfulness does indeed pervade the creation.

That day, I chose to stand on the foundation of who He is–Creator of Heaven and Earth–by faith. *I would live and die by faith.* And if I should happen to die in the wilderness, I would do it full of faith, knowing that my promises were hidden in Him. Just as those described in the book of Hebrews did not receive the promises in their life times, but were made partakers by *faith*, so it would be an honor to be counted among them.

> *These all died in faith, not having received the promises, but having seen them afar off were assured of them, embraced them and confessed that they were strangers and pilgrims on the earth.*
> *Hebrews 11:13*

I simply chose to believe my Lord over the lies of the enemy. He said He would never leave me nor forsake me, and I released that truth into the air. Though the heavens were as brass and suffocating grey clouds hovered ominously over my head, I chose that day to trust Him regardless of my circumstances or my disappointments with Him. He was my God, and I would praise Him.

> *But You are holy,*
> *Enthroned in the praises of Israel.*
> *Our fathers trusted in You;*
> *They trusted, and You delivered them.*
> *They cried to You, and were delivered;*
> *They trusted in You, and were not ashamed.*
> *Psalm 22:3-5*

It was shortly after this momentous decision, a few days later, that I felt a renewed surge of faith rise up within me concerning what I had spoken. Sitting in my cold, isolated chair in my impoverished and forsaken garden, I actually felt something stir within me–*faith and hope*. I had stirred up my *faith*– faith in those things that I knew to be true about my Lord–and *hope* was born anew.

Unexpectedly, I heard a whisper. It was my Lord. My heart leapt for joy. I couldn't see Him, or touch Him, but I heard Him whisper in my ear, *"I am here."* That was enough. Tears overcame me– tears of joy and tears of grief over my lovesickness for Him. How I longed for more of Him, but I knew that for now, I needed to rest in the knowledge that *He was with me*. I was not alone.

Distracted by a flash of red out of the corner of my eye, I looked more intently and was amazed to discover three blood-red flowers beaming up at me in prophetic splendor on a small camellia bush beside my chair. What a shocking contrast to the garden's dreariness! I was stunned by the significance of their appearance. They were a sign of *hope*—a sign that the Father, Son, and Holy Spirit had been beside me even in the midst of winter's most frigid assault on my life. They were proof that my garden wasn't dead after all.

I felt instantly rejuvenated with faith, hope, and love for my Redeemer and His extravagant provision for me. At that moment, a ray of sunshine unexpectedly broke through the clouds to confirm my experience. As the light poured warmly over my head, I pondered John 1:4: *"In Him was life, and the life was the light of men."*

As the light of His revelation broke in upon me with great shafts of piercing light, I came to understand that though His chastening during this harsh winter season had ruthlessly exposed my fear of man and my desire to protect my godly reputation, it had also shown me who my first love was–*Him*. He was the one for whom my heart beat, and He was worth the suffering that I was intended to endure. With this in mind, there were specific things that *needed to die* in my garden, making room for the new seed that would be sown in the next season.

It was encouraging to know that in the midst of my misery and self-pity, He had sufficiently prepared me to endure this test, enabling me to ultimately choose Him over my own self-preservation. That choice released another piece of my heart to Him. My Lord was right. *Winter is necessary.* It reveals the hidden places of our hearts, preparing them to house the seed of His promises.

Now no chastening seems to be joyful for the present, but painful; nevertheless, afterward it yields the peaceable fruit of righteousness to those who have been trained by it.

Hebrews 12:11

XIII. The Voice of the Turtledove

To everything there is a season,
A time for every purpose under heaven:
A time to be born,
And a time to die;
A time to plant,
And a time to pluck what is planted;
Ecclesiastes 3:1-2

Winter had been long and weary, and I was searching for any sign that this treacherous season was coming to an end. Pacing about the garden, I would listen and look intently for any possible indication that my Beloved had returned.

The days were becoming a bit warmer, and the sky even seemed bluer. So I decided to start clearing away some of the dead leaves and sticks. Maybe if I made the garden *look* more presentable, the Lord would want to return to it and visit with me. So I set to work.

For several days I raked leaves and cleared

out dead branches. While busy clearing the paths, I noticed some little buds of growth on the trees. Something was happening in this seemingly dead place. I was surprised to find that many of the plants and trees that I was convinced were dead, weren't at all. They had made it through winter, just as I had, and they had something new to bring forth. They were preparing for spring.

I began to wonder if I too had something new to bring forth from my winter season of chastening. What would the fruit of this season look like in the spring and summer? I knew there would be fruit–that is the sure product of chastening that is endured to the end.

In the midst of my reflections, it happened. I heard Him who stirs my heart. His *song* was floating on the breeze. It was the *song of the turtledove*, a prophetic call that made my heart race with expectancy, for it signaled not just His presence but the beginning of a new season in the kingdom. I looked about frantically to see where He was. He was calling to me from outside the walls of my enclosed garden.

Was He wooing me to come *outside* the garden walls? Without a second thought, I ran to Him and fell at His feet. I said nothing. I couldn't. I was just elated that I was with Him again. In the many times that I had contemplated our next meeting, I always thought that I would question Him concerning His seeming abandonment of me; but now in His presence, I seemed to know its purpose. The futility of attempting to manipulate God for my purposes had been exposed to me, and I had been forced to *wait* on Him. He is worthy of our waiting. Is it not our privilege to wait on one so majestic?

> *Wait on the Lord;*
> *Be of good courage,*
> *And He shall strengthen your heart;*
> *Wait, I say, on the Lord!*
> *Psalm 27:14*

The reality of His sovereign rule over me and His vast creation humbled me. I lay limp at His feet in adoration of Him. The establishment of His sovereignty in my life had changed my perspective of Him. I had presumed upon our relationship, thinking that I knew Him better than I actually did. Now I was seeing Him afresh, and He was even more glorious. I felt as Job when he exclaimed,

"I have heard of You by the hearing of the ear,
But now my eye sees You.
Therefore I abhor myself,
And repent in dust and ashes."

Job 42:5-6

After awhile, He gently lifted me to my feet, and He began to entreat me with His desire.

My beloved spoke, and said to me:
"Rise up, my love, my fair one,
And come away.
For lo, the winter is past,
The rain is over and gone.
The flowers appear on the earth;
The time of singing has come,
And the voice of the turtledove
Is heard in our land."

Song 2:10-12

He commenced to tell me of other gardens that were His. He wanted to show me these gardens. I assented, full of curiosity. So we made our way to the mountains to acquire a view. In the high places, I could see what He saw—*many* gardens. They were all His, and He frequented them all. Each of them had a unique quality all its own, causing Him to delight in each of them. As we stood arm in arm admiring the many gardens of His kingdom, I thought of Song 6:2:

My beloved has gone to his garden,
To the beds of spices,
To feed his flock in the gardens,
And to gather lilies.

So this is where He spends His time when He's not with me. I felt a little jealous and began comparing the other gardens to mine. Knowing my heart, He cautioned me against such presumptuous comparisons and reminded me that my place in Him was not based on how I measured up to others. He measured me by whom I was created to be. "Your comparisons are not valid in the kingdom. You measure by the world's standards and not by the measurement of the heart." I bowed in assent, but still felt a twinge of jealousy stirring within me.

I asked Him why all the gardens were not in a winter season as was my garden. He informed me that each garden has its own seasons and times, and those times and seasons are ordained by Him and the choices of those who tend each garden. It seems that each garden also has different purposes, specializing in specific plants and trees. In addition, each garden's size is determined by the *calling* of that particular garden and its level of *maturation*. It would appear that *maturity brings an increase of land.*

It was at this turn in the conversation that the Beloved divulged to me that it was time for the boundaries of my garden to be *extended*. It had been made apparent through my chastening that I was ready to tend more land; and with spring coming, I needed to prepare that land for sowing. I was quite exhilarated by this unexpected reward, for it meant that the land of my inheritance had just been increased.

> *Wait on the Lord,*
> *And keep His way,*
> *And He shall exalt you to inherit the land;*
> *When the wicked are cut off, you shall see it.*
> *Psalm 37:34*

The Master then went on to tell me that the new ground in my garden would be made ready for the sowing of seeds of intercession for *all* of His gardens. He wanted me to enter into new levels of prayer for the corporate people of God represented in the many gardens we were viewing from the mountain tops.

I wasn't sure how I felt about this. I really wasn't that excited about seeing all the other gardens. Now, out of my own *barrenness*, the Master wanted me to devote time and energy to sowing seed into these gardens. Ultimately, He was asking me to *tend another person's garden*.

"Sing, O barren,
You who have not borne!
Break forth into singing, and cry aloud,
You who have not labored with child!
For more are the children of the desolate
Than the children of the married woman,"
     says the Lord.
"Enlarge the place of your tent,
And let them stretch out the curtains of your
     dwellings;
Do not spare;
Lengthen your cords,
And strengthen your stakes.
For you shall expand to the right and to the left,
And your descendants will inherit the nations,
And make the desolate cities inhabited...

For a mere moment I have forsaken you,
But with great mercies I will gather you."
     Isaiah 54:1-3 & 7

XIV. Spring's Sudden Surprises

For as the earth brings forth its bud,
As the garden causes the things that
are sown in it to spring forth,
So the Lord God will cause righteousness and
praise to spring forth before all the nations.
Isaiah 61:11

After visiting with the Lord on the mountain tops, I returned back to my garden to look for more sprouts of new growth. The Beloved had proclaimed that the winter was past and the flowers were here. So I wanted to see for myself. Sure enough, close to the ground, scattered along my path, were several tiny crocus bulbs blooming. What an inspiring sight! They didn't seem to mind the still lingering frigid air. Their vibrant purples, blues, and yellows announced to the world that spring was definitely coming. They were a pleasant surprise, catapulting my hope and expectation to a new level.

Then as I looked closer, I saw other bulbs beginning to break through the ground. This excited me even more. My hard work in the fall had paid off, and some of the promises that the Beloved had helped me to bury in my garden were beginning to break through. *Change was in the air, and I liked it.* It was time for winter to be over, and it was.

I felt inspired to begin the preparations of my new land which was situated down in a valley. There was no real view, but it was quiet and beautiful just the same. Different flowers seemed to grow down there, as it was much lower in altitude.

Surveying the land, I surmised that the numerous rocks scattered about the land would need to be attended to first. So I began carrying them off to the side, deciding to pile them on top of one another, creating an *altar*. It turned out that there were *twenty-four* of these rather large rocks.

A daunting project, I could have used some help, but I had the impression I was supposed to do this on my own. Albeit, the familiar counsel of the Holy Spirit was ever in my ear, encouraging me with the revelation that even the *preparations* of the land were an essential aspect of my supplications for the covenant people of God.

> *Go through,*
> *Go through the gates!*
> *Prepare the way for the people;*
> *Build up,*
> *Build up the highway!*
> *Take out the stones,*
> *Lift up a banner for the peoples!*
> *Isaiah 62:10*

Did the stones themselves carry significance in regard to my intercession? Meditating on this and the fact that the stones needed to be moved to a more suitable place, their number intrigued me, reminding me of the twelve tribes of Israel as well as the twelve disciples. In addition, the twenty-four elders of Revelation 5 came flashing across my mind with that whole prophetic scene concerning the Lamb of God in the throne room.

> *Now when He had taken the scroll, the four living creatures and the twenty-four elders fell down before the Lamb, each having a harp, and golden bowls full of incense, which are the prayers of the saints. And they sang a new song, saying:*

"You are worthy to take the scroll,
And to open its seals;
For You were slain,

And have redeemed us to God by Your
blood
Out of every tribe and tongue and
people and nation,
And have made us kings and priests
to our God;
And we shall reign on the earth."
Revelation 5:8-10

While laboring over the stones, the *song of the twenty-four elders* became a prophetic declaration in my mouth for the people of God. As I proclaimed the truth of this song, a groaning began to come up from within me, and I could sense the Holy Spirit's agreement with this proclamation of truth.

Likewise the Spirit also helps in our weaknesses. For we do not know what we should pray for as we ought, but the Spirit Himself makes intercession for us with groanings which cannot be uttered. Now He who searches the hearts knows what the mind of the Spirit is, because He makes intercession for the saints according to the will of God.

Romans 8:26-27

Laboring over the stones with specific prayers of prophetic proclamation from the Scriptures, I strategically situated each stone one upon the other. It seemed as though I was calling for a dramatic change in the corporate body of believers, declaring their ordained position under God's soon to be established government. Intriguingly, the secret of these destined positions seemed to flow out of the truth of the *song of the twenty-four elders*. I was convinced that my labor bore profound prophetic significance in regard to the unfolding destiny of the covenant people of God.

Taking several days to accomplish, I was quite overwhelmed by the final completion of this unusual feat. Sensing a need to mark the occasion, I felt led to pour out a libation before the Lord on this new altar in my burgeoning *garden of intercession*. So I took some water, consecrated it as a prophetic picture of God's desire for His covenant people, and poured it out over this majestic pile of twenty-four stones, calling for the truth of God's desire to go forth with power, wooing His people to align themselves with His prophetic purposes for the hour. In a mysterious way, I sensed that the *esoteric identity of God's people* was being released, and the prophetic *unveiling of the Bride* for this hour was in process.

> " 'For I will pour water on him who is thirsty,
> And floods on the dry ground;
> I will pour My Spirit on your descendants,
> And My blessing on your offspring;
> They will spring up among the grass
> Like willows by the watercourses.'
> One will say, 'I am the Lord's';
> Another will call himself by the name of Jacob;
> Another will write with his hand, 'The Lord's,'
> And name himself by the name of Israel."
> Isaiah 44:3-5

An intense rumbling began to stir from deep within my spirit, accompanied by the literal rumble of thunder in the distance. I felt God's affirmation raining down upon me as never before—in the spirit and in the natural—for it had begun to *rain*. It was as if I had unplugged a fountain of truth, and it was raining down upon *all* of the gardens of His kingdom, preparing them to fulfill their destiny hidden in Him from the foundation of the world. A new age was coming.

> For as the rain comes down, and the snow
>   from heaven,
> And do not return there,
> But water the earth,
> And make it bring forth and bud,

*That it may give seed to the sower
And bread to the eater,
So shall My word be that goes forth from
My mouth;
It shall not return to Me void,
But it shall accomplish what I please,
And it shall prosper in the thing for which I
sent it.*

Isaiah 55:10-11

Looking at this strange altar, I knew that much had been accomplished; for the removal of the stones had profoundly prepared the ground for sowing, even more so than any plowing would have done. The Holy Spirit was teaching me how to intercede with prophetic insight and proclamation. It was a novel experience for me, and I welcomed it.

Ascending back up the hill to my *garden of intimacy*, I was thrilled to discover that the Lord was waiting for me. He was sitting in the gated area beside the pomegranate tree–our place of communion. We discussed the significance of the stones and what I had been led to do. Overjoyed, the Lord informed me that the profound significance of this act would provide the basis for all ensuing prayers to which I would give myself in the coming months.

I wasn't sure I understood all of what the Lord meant, but I believed that I had just been a part of something bigger than myself, and it felt remarkable. Reflecting on all of this, my gaze was captured by some bright yellow daffodils bobbing their heads in the breeze. Giddy with delight, I sauntered over to these glorious beauties, leaning over them with admiration. They were a welcome sight, inspiring awe and gratitude to the Maker whose astonishing creativity consistently left me speechless. Spring was definitely manifesting its share of surprises. It was going to be a fruitful season.

> *And He said, "The kingdom of God is as if a man should scatter seed on the ground, and should sleep by night and rise by day, and the seed should sprout and grow, he himself does not know how."*
> *Mark 4:26-27*

XV. A Garden Stowaway

Now the serpent was more cunning than any beast of the field which the Lord God had made...
Genesis 3:1

Spring had officially sprung in a spectacular display of color and fragrance. Smothered in stunning fuchsia blossoms, the azaleas were aggressively pushing their way through the lattice wall and tantalizing all who walked by. Interspersed between them, the lavender blooms of the rhododendrons competed for the view afforded by this same lattice wall. Between the two of them, they presented a dazzling extravaganza of color on the inside of the garden, as well as on the *outside*.

Because of the irresistible beauty of these stunning shrubs positioned around the perimeter of my garden, I was receiving new visitors who were stopping by almost daily to admire the garden. Some of them I got to know on a more intimate level, and we actually shared experiences with one another about the Lord and His many surprises. Others, merely visited the garden once out of curiosity, failing to return. I never really knew if my garden had impacted them or not.

Those who did make return visits were often looking for something from me. I found that these people usually wanted some type of impartation or prayer from me that would bring some new level of breakthrough in their spiritual progression. Many times, the Lord would give me a special word for them or a prophetic prayer to pray, and they would leave satisfied. At other times, I felt powerless to give any relief. It really was up to the Lord as to what type of ministry came forth in these visits.

One sunny day, while sowing seed and planting gladiola bulbs near the peach trees blanketed in luscious creamy white blossoms, an old friend stopped by to see me. Looking up from my bent over position, I squinted up into a face that appeared rather care-ridden. We embraced and took a leisurely stroll through the garden.

Assuming she wanted to see what the Lord and I had done in the garden, I began sharing with her about the significance of the multi-colored bulbs blooming in the flower beds and God's faithfulness to His promises. I even unraveled the tale about the gated area and how the Lord had helped me to overcome my fears that I might fellowship with Him in that special area of my heart.

Enjoying the fragrance of the honeysuckle vines near the gated area where the once straggly yellow roses now bloomed profusely, I noted that my friend showed little interest in what the Lord and I had accomplished. In fact, she seemed almost pained by it all. I wasn't sure how to respond to this, other than to quit talking about the Lord and His great exploits in my life–*immediately.*

She informed me that I shouldn't boast about what the Lord is doing in my life because it is a sign of pride. I didn't respond to this analysis, but sensed that *jealousy* was beginning to rear its head. As a defense, I began to focus our discussion on my friend's life, asking questions about her own garden of intimacy. In fact, I suggested that we walk over to her garden. So we did. As we were leaving, I failed to notice a small green snake that slithered out from my friend's handbag, falling onto my garden ground.

Upon arriving at her garden, I immediately noticed its startling impotence. It looked more like a barren wilderness than a garden. She must be in a winter season, I thought. I was going to ask her about that, but she began telling me of the many activities in which she was engaged. She was definitely a busy person, but her garden showed *no* fruit for her labors. How could this be?

Her life seemed to be a contradiction. She talked about the Lord's work, but her own garden showed no evidence of the Lord's touch. Did He come here to commune? I wasn't so sure. So I decided to ask her about her personal times with the Lord. She seemed quite evasive in her answers, and quickly focused the discussion back on the things she *did* for the Lord, as opposed to her personal time with Him *alone*, away from everyone. I was distressed by her seeming lack of intimacy with the Lord.

The futility of our conversation led me to ask her blatantly if the Lord ever visited her garden. Offended by my brashness, she informed me that the Lord didn't visit every garden like He did mine. I thought, how do you know that? I tried to approach the topic from another perspective–*the Lord's*. I insisted to her that it is the Lord's desire to be intimately involved in *all* of His children's lives. Instead of encouraging her, this prospect seemed to only frustrate her more. She insisted that she had tried to spend time with the Lord, but He never came.

Remembering my early experiences with the Lord, I asked her if she had submitted to His blood covering. She rolled her eyes and informed me with a superior attitude that she had indeed asked him to come into her heart. Again, I asked her about the *covering*. She conveyed to me in no uncertain terms that the covering was there because she had asked Him for it. I quickly noted that if she didn't take off her own covering *daily*, she couldn't submit to *His*, preventing her from entering into a growing intimacy with Him.

Definitely angered by my last comment, she accused me of trying to take her salvation away from her. I insisted that I was merely trying to ascertain if she was actually partaking of the Lord's great provision for her because her garden testified of something else.

Finally, overwhelmed by her defensiveness, I

told her that I needed to get back to my own garden, and we parted. I walked back to my garden bewildered. Did she know the Lord, or just about Him?

Heading straight to the gated area of my garden, I found the Lord waiting for me. I began to tell Him about my friend, but He didn't seem too interested in talking about her with me; instead, He reminded me that my judgments are *unjust*, for I simply do not see the struggles of the heart as does He. So we talked about the progress in *my* garden, and how pleased He was in the display of color and fragrance that the garden was manifesting.

We were then interrupted by *another* visitor. He too was an old friend. I left the Lord and went to greet him. Excitedly, he revealed to me that he had just been made a deacon at his congregation. I was a little offended by this, because as his friend, I knew *all* of his shortcomings. I also knew that he hadn't weathered the same winter storms that I had. In addition, he didn't spend enough time in his garden. Little did I know that beside me, under a fabulous pink flowering rhododendron, the green snake of jealousy was curled up, listening eagerly to our conversation.

After sharing his news, he left in a flurry of excitement. I was left stewing over his disclosure. I had been faithful to the Lord for many years now, weathering His many chastenings of me. In fact, the Lord had given me promises concerning leadership amongst His people, but nothing had manifested thus far. Why did my friend get chosen? Was I not faithful to the Lord?

As my judgments and rationalizations began to take form, I felt something creep up my leg. I jumped with a start, and shaking it off, observed that it was a tiny green snake. Where had *that* come from? It slithered off, and I darted back to the gated area to find the Lord.

Thankfully, He was there. I shared my complaints, and He listened. When I was finished, all He said was that I was *comparing* again, and that comparison inevitably leads to either *jealousy* or *pride*, and both are sins.

Jealousy? Why would I be jealous of this friend of mine whose garden was not nearly as fruitful as mine? He responded by saying, "I don't know. Why are you jealous of what *little* he has? Does he really have something you want?" I thought about that last question, and after considering it, decided that he really didn't have anything that I wanted. He had a *position*, but he didn't have the intimate relationship that I was craving. I was forced to admit that a position is not what I desired. I longed for Him.

> *For we dare not class ourselves or compare ourselves with those who commend themselves. But they, measuring themselves by themselves, and comparing themselves among themselves, are not wise.*
> *I Corinthians 10:12*

At this revelation, He ordered me to hunt the snake of jealousy down and put it under my feet where it belonged, so that its deceptions could not distort my priorities again. I asked Him how I was supposed to find a snake amidst so much abundant growth. He informed me that He would walk with me, and the truth of His words would force the snake to show itself.

So we started out, hand in hand. The Lord

spoke of the glories of His kingdom, and I looked intently for the snake to respond to His truth. Sure enough, out slithered that little green snake. I instinctively put my foot down on its head with a vengeance and declared:

> *"And the God of peace will crush Satan under your feet..."*
>
> Romans 16:20a

XVI. Summer's South Winds of Affirmation

Then He spoke to them a parable: "Look at the fig tree, and all the trees. When they are already budding, you see and know for yourselves that summer is now near. So you also, when you see these things happening, know that the kingdom of God is near."
Luke 21:29-31

Spring had been an incredibly productive season. I had been consumed with the sowing of seed in both of my gardens—my *garden of intimacy* and my *garden of intercession*. It seemed that the more time I spent with the Lord, the more seed sprang up, and not just flower seed, but shrubs, and trees, and herbs. There were things growing that I hadn't even planted! Their seed had been there since the foundation of the world, and the holy utterances of the Beloved had watered them, causing them to literally spring forth out of response to His life-giving words.

Faithfully sowing spiritual seed in the lives of the numerous visitors who frequented my garden of intimacy, I had also been sowing spiritual prayers into the many gardens of His kingdom while laboring in my garden of intercession. It was quite remarkable to observe the relationship between these two gardens. They seemed to be connected spiritually; for as my garden of intimacy abounded, so did my garden of intercession as well, causing my supplications to be that much more powerful.

Together, the Holy Spirit and I had planted this special garden of intercession. We would go there in the mornings when the sun was just beginning to peer over the mountain tops, pouring yellow rays of light onto the valley below, illumining the fiery red poppies that carpeted the slope of the hill on the way down to the valley.

The garden itself was circular, strategically bordered by *twenty-four pomegranate trees*. They represented the priestly ministry of the covenant people of God, specifically those called to leadership who function as *gatekeepers and watchmen* over the gardens of God's people–which in this particular prophetic picture was represented by twenty-four rows of *grapevines*. I was tending a vineyard! Amidst the pomegranate trees, several varieties of herbs were thriving, emitting pungent and aromatic odors.

It was in this vineyard that my supplications went forth for the corporate people of God. I paced the rows of vines *daily*, praying the power of the Scriptures over the many gardens of God's kingdom. I couldn't see these gardens, but at times, it was as if I could. In fact, it almost felt like I was actually walking in some of these gardens, declaring the prophetic proclamations which the Spirit of God would raise up from within me. And maybe I did visit these gardens. Who is to say if I was *seeing* a vision, or *experiencing* one? At times, I felt like Paul when he confessed,

> *And I know such a man—whether in the body or out of the body I do not know, God knows —how he was caught up into Paradise and heard inexpressible words, which it is not lawful for a man to utter.*
> *II Corinthians 12:3-4*

Not every day in the vineyard was sensational, but many were that and even more. The Holy Spirit led me into numerous prophetic experiences which often involved the altar of twenty-four stones which had become the foundation of my supplications. In fact, recurrently the Holy Spirit would instruct me to literally stand upon this pile of rocks. It was as if I were perched on a *wall*. I felt like I was on the wall that surrounds Jerusalem, for the Scriptures tell us that the Lord has indeed set watchmen on the walls of this spiritual city.

> *I have set watchmen on your walls, O Jerusalem;*
> *They shall never hold their peace day or night.*
> *You who make mention of the Lord, do not keep*
> *silent,*
> *And give Him no rest till He establishes*
> *And till He makes Jerusalem a praise in the*
> *earth.*
> *Isaiah 62:6-7*

I was beginning to take on the Lord's perspective of His gardens, wanting them all to come to maturity that their beauty, deposited within them before the foundation of time, would manifest the glory of their Maker. As such, I grieved over their failures and extended seasons of chastening that I became aware of through the Holy Spirit, for they could have been avoided through simple obedience.

At times the grief of the Holy Spirit over the

disarray of these other gardens would well up within me uncontrollably, throwing me to the ground in convulsions accompanied by tears and loud outcries. Those were exhausting times which drained me spiritually and physically, but when I ascended the hill to meet with my Beloved in the gated area of our friendship, He had a way of restoring me with a kiss. *"Let him kiss me with the kisses of his mouth— for your love is better than wine" (Song 1:2).*

Our times beside the pomegranate tree in the gated area had matured and deepened quite remarkably, causing our friendship to progress into a *love affair.* He was completely overcome by the fragrance of the *incense of my supplications;* for they bore the scent of heaven. Holding my hands and gazing into my eyes, He repeatedly extolled my virtues.

Your plants are an orchard of pomegranates
With pleasant fruits,
Fragrant henna with spikenard,
Spikenard and saffron,
Calamus and cinnamon,
With all trees of frankincense,
Myrrh and aloes,
With all the chief spices—

Song 4:13-14

It occurred to me that the aroma the Beloved detected from me was actually *His scent*; for He had been soaking me in the spices of His presence every moment we were together. Remarkably, my supplication for the other gardens caused His aroma to be released to an even greater degree. He was smelling Himself in me. *I had begun to smell like Him!*

One afternoon, the Beloved took my hand and told me it was time to go to a new place with Him. I was exhilarated. We walked down the hill and into the valley, past my garden of intercession toward a mountain on the other side. At the base of the mountain a lone *budding fig tree* greeted us. A peculiar sight, we paused and then began our climb.

The mountain itself was very rocky, and the summer's south winds were much stronger on the mountain; so He held me close as we made our ascent. I felt a little apprehensive because of the height, but His embrace assured me. In addition, the south wind caused the fragrant indescribable scent that we were both emitting to be even more noticeable.

Finally, we came to a *cleft* in a huge rock on the side of this mountain. Inside this quaint little niche was a bench for two hewn out of the rock, so we cozily sat down on it next to one another. Nestled in an embrace of love and adoration, the Beloved began to sing passionately over me. His song floated on the air along with His fragrance.

> *You have ravished my heart,*
> *My sister, my spouse;*
> *You have ravished my heart*
> *With one look of your eyes,*
> *With one link of your necklace.*
> *How fair is your love,*
> *My sister, my spouse!*
> *How much better than wine is your love,*
> *And the scent of your perfumes*
> *Than all spices!*
> *Your lips, O my spouse,*
> *Drip as the honeycomb;*
> *Honey and milk are under your tongue;*
> *And the fragrance of your garments*
> *Is like the fragrance of Lebanon.*
>   *Song 4:9-11*

Enraptured by His attentions to me and overcome with a consummate adoration for Him, I sang a song of affirmation in return. Amazingly, my voice sounded as beautiful as His, floating on the air along with the special fragrance I was emitting

–His fragrance.

> *My beloved is white and ruddy,*
> *Chief among ten thousand.*
> *His head is like the finest gold;*
> *His locks are wavy,*
> *And black as a raven.*
> *His eyes are like doves*
> *By the rivers of waters,*
> *Washed with milk,*
> *And fitly set.*
> *His cheeks are like a bed of spices,*
> *Banks of scented herbs.*
> *His lips are lilies,*
> *Dripping liquid myrrh.*
> *His hands are rods of gold*
> *Set with beryl.*
> *His body is carved ivory*
> *Inlaid with sapphires.*
> *His legs are pillars of marble*
> *Set on bases of fine gold.*
> *His countenance is like Lebanon,*
> *Excellent as the cedars.*
> *His mouth is most sweet,*
> *Yes, he is altogether lovely.*
> *This is my beloved,*
> *And this is my friend,*
> *O daughters of Jerusalem!*
> *Song 5:10-16*

We were lost in our reverie for one another, and the fragrances that swirled about us were utterly intoxicating. It was an exhilarating experience that seemed to take us outside the dictates of time and space.

At one point, the Beloved directed my gaze away from Him to the prophetic view below us. It was not a view of the many gardens of His kingdom that He had shown me before, but a single *vineyard*. This was the maturing vineyard of His people, whose fruit would be *the Bride*—those who had entered into intimacy with the Son. I was stunned and amazed. *From this would come the Bride?*

XVII. The Longings of Lovers

Now let me sing to my Well-beloved
A song of my Beloved regarding His
vineyard:

My Well-beloved has a vineyard
On a very fruitful hill.
He dug it up and cleared out its stones,
And planted it with the choicest vine.
He built a tower in its midst,
And also made a winepress in it;
So He expected it to bring forth good grapes,
But it brought forth wild grapes.
Isaiah 5:1-2

We sat in the *cleft of the rock* peering down at this beleaguered vineyard. "Hidden in the tangle of vines is My bride," He beamed. I was hardly impressed, but the Beloved looked at her differently. He admired her as He admired me—with lavish devotion and prophetic anticipation. Perplexed, I wondered if maybe I looked like this too, and didn't know it.

His vineyard had been planted many years ago after instituting His covenant with Abraham and then establishing the Twelve Tribes of Israel as His *covenant people*. Delivering her from her enemies, He nurtured her in the wilderness before taking her into her promised land where He defeated her enemies. But she went into rebellion, forcing Him to discipline her with His judgments.

"And now, O inhabitants of Jerusalem and
*   men of Judah,*
Judge, please, between Me and My vineyard.
What more could have been done to My
*   vineyard*
That I have not done in it?
Why then, when I expected it to bring forth
*   good grapes,*
Did it bring forth wild grapes?
And now, please let Me tell you what I will
*   do to My vineyard:*
I will take away its hedge, and it shall be
*   burned;*
And break down its wall, and it shall be
*   trampled down.*
I will lay it waste;
It shall not be pruned or dug,
But there shall come up briers and thorns.
I will also command the clouds
That they rain no rain on it."

For the vineyard of the Lord of hosts is the
*   house of Israel,*

And the men of Judah are His pleasant plant.
He looked for justice, but behold, oppression;
For righteousness, but behold, a cry for help.
                                    Isaiah 5:3-7

Prophets were sent to work in this vineyard, but were miserably mistreated. The Beloved then told me that the Father sent *Him* to attend to this vineyard, but they rose up against Him as well, *rejecting Him.*

Hear another parable: There was a certain landowner who planted a vineyard and set a hedge around it, dug a winepress in it and built a tower. And he leased it to vinedressers and went into a far country. Now when vintage-time drew near, he sent his servants to the vinedressers, that they might receive its fruit. And the vinedressers took his servants, beat one, killed one, and stoned another. Again he sent other servants, more than the first, and they did likewise to them. Then last of all he sent his son to them, saying, "They will respect my son." But when the vinedressers saw the son, they said among themselves, "This is the heir. Come, let us kill him and seize his inheritance." So they took him and cast him out of the vineyard and killed him.
                            Matthew 21:33-39

I could see the sadness in the Beloved's eyes as He told the story of His vineyard's rejection of Him. But He brightened considerably as He mentioned the Gentile nations and their joyful acceptance of His freely offered salvation. As such, the Gentiles had been *grafted in* as heirs of His kingdom, enlarging His vineyard.

> *Then I will sow her for Myself in the earth,*
> *And I will have mercy on her who had not*
> *   obtained mercy;*
> *Then I will say to those who were not My*
> *   people,*
> *"You are My people!"*
> *And they shall say, "You are my God!"*
> *   Hosea 2:23*

Concerning the Jews, He informed me that *"God has not cast away His people whom He foreknew... Even so then, at this present time there is a remnant according to the election of grace"* (Romans 11:2a & 5). Though there has always been a remnant of the faithful, the majority of the Jews have been blinded for a season that all nations might enter into this great salvation.

> *For I do not desire, brethren, that you should*
> *be ignorant of this mystery, lest you should*

*be wise in your own opinion, that blindness
in part has happened to Israel until the
fullness of the Gentiles has come in.*

Romans 11:25

"The fig tree has budded," He sighed, "and
the time of the Jews has come again." I thought of
the budding fig tree that greeted us at the foot of
the mountain. *"And they also, if they do not continue
in unbelief, will be grafted in, for God is able to graft
them in again" (Romans 11:23).*

He then gestured toward two gnarled olive
trees that surprisingly grew out of the side of the
mountain on either side of the cleft. As a prophetic
picture, these represented those Jews and Gentiles
who have chosen to be grafted into His kingdom as
a people called by His name—*Israel*. Zechariah saw
this mystery of the two witnesses.

*Then I answered and said to him, "What
are these two olive trees—at the right of the
lampstand and at its left?" And I further
answered and said to him, "What are these
two olive branches that drip into the
receptacles of the two gold pipes from which
the golden oil drains?" Then he answered
me and said, "Do you not know what these*

are?" And I said, "No, my lord." So he said,
"These are the two anointed ones, who stand
beside the Lord of the whole earth."
                                    Zechariah 4:11-14

Pondering the two olive trees staunchly standing before me, I heard the Lord tell me that His heart ached for the two to come into agreement with one another. It was time for the sibling rivalry to end.

> *For you are all sons of God through faith in*
> *Christ Jesus. For as many of you as were*
> *baptized into Christ have put on Christ.*
> *There is neither Jew nor Greek, there is*
> *neither slave nor free, there is neither male*
> *nor female; for you are all one in Christ Jesus.*
> *And if you are Christ's, then you are*
> *Abraham's seed, and heirs according to the*
> *promise.*
>   *Galatians 3:26-29*

We sat for a time in silence, looking at the love of His life—*His vineyard.* He had given His life for her perfection, and yet, she looked in such disarray. Why? Sadly, the Beloved relayed to me that it was because of her failure to submit fully to the provision of His sacrifice, causing her to be under His continuing chastisement. She had chosen to live out of her own understanding, arrogantly *tending* her own vines, resisting His headship. In essence, the Gentiles were making the same presumptuous errors that the Israelites had made, incurring similar judgments.

> *Israel empties his vine;*
> *He brings forth fruit for himself.*
> *According to the multitude of his fruit*
> *He has increased the altars;*
> *According to the bounty of his land*
> *They have embellished his sacred pillars.*
> *Their heart is divided;*
> *Now they are held guilty.*
> *He will break down their altars;*
> *He will ruin their sacred pillars.*
>   *Hosea 10:1-2*

Intriguingly, it will be the re-grafting in of the Jews that will cause the vines to flourish, inspiring an even greater harvest in the nations. *"For if their being cast away is the reconciling of the world, what will their acceptance be but life from the dead?" (Romans 11:15).*

As those harvested from *all* nations choose to enter into genuine intimacy with the Beloved, they will surely come to *abide* in Him—the *true vine*. Immersed in His desires, they will come to understand that His vineyard is made up of Jew *and*

Gentile, and these two witnesses in the earth uniquely comprise His peculiar covenant people, *Israel*. It is the living out of this truth that will bring forth the coveted fruit of the vine–the obedient *remnant* of Jew and Gentile who have been mysteriously hidden away in this struggling vineyard. It is these who are destined to be revealed as the Beloved's unblemished *bride*.

> *I am the true vine, and My Father is the vinedresser. Every branch in Me that does not bear fruit He takes away; and every branch that bears fruit He prunes, that it may bear more fruit... Abide in Me, and I in you. As the branch cannot bear fruit of itself, unless it abides in the vine, neither can you, unless you abide in Me. I am the vine, you are the branches. He who abides in Me, and I in him, bears much fruit; for without Me you can do nothing.*
>
> *John 15:1-2 & 4-5*

My spirit was stirring, and I knew that my new perspective of His vineyard and His great desire for her was going to have a dramatic impact on my continuing intercession for His people. I now had more understanding of the *twenty-four stones* that had to be moved and piled on top of one another as an altar. The two witnesses in the earth were prophetically destined to become *one* living testimony of a covenant people who have *overcome* their enemies by the blood of the Lamb. Change was indeed coming to His vineyard; for the fig tree had miraculously *budded.*

I felt His desire becoming *my* desire. I wanted what He longed for–a vibrant fruitful vineyard to present to the Father. I pledged to give myself to His longing, for His desires had become my desires. *"I am my beloved's, and his desire is toward me" (Song 7:10).* How could I resist the one I love and His great longing for His bride? Am I not part of that desire? Am I not one of the vines in this great vineyard of His? *How I longed to be counted as one of the hidden remnant who would manifest as His spotless bride...*

XVIII. Tending His Vineyard

I went down to the garden of nuts
To see the verdure of the valley,
To see whether the vine had budded
And the pomegranates had bloomed.
Song 6:11

After our time on the mountain, I was anxious to return to my garden of intercession. Overjoyed at the discovery that my vines and pomegranates were blooming, I anticipated a spectacular harvest. Fruit would be forthcoming. To add to my projected harvest, I decided to sow the new revelation I had received about the Bride into the many gardens of the kingdom. So I set to work.

I was quite zealous in my delivery of the news of the Beloved's vineyard, thinking people would be clamoring to their knees in *repentance*. But that didn't happen. My message also failed to bring forth any *unity* in the brethren. In fact, the only thing they seemed to consistently unify around was their hatred for my *message*. I was confused. Didn't they see the truth? How could they deny it? It was right there in the Scriptures. The Lord had shown me Himself. Yet, they seemed to gnash their teeth in disgust at me, dismissing me with various derogatory labels, identifying me as a fanatical heretic–someone dangerous to the *unity of the brethren*.

After several weeks of this, I shook the dust off of my feet and knew how some of the prophets felt. The people of God just didn't understand. They were blind. But why was I so surprised? The Lord had shown me the impoverished state of His vineyard –*straggly and weak*. They were definitely the epitome of that picture.

I had the truth, and they didn't. In fact, I was sure that I was the *only* one with the truth–the only one who hadn't bowed the knee to pagan ideas that continued to fuel the carnality of the covenant people of God. Thoroughly disgusted, I found myself deeply offended with the blatant indifference and insensitivity of God's people to the truth.

Retreating to my garden of intimacy, I self-righteously purposed in my heart that I would not waste my energy on the brethren anymore; however, my preponderance upon the hard-hearts of God's people was abruptly arrested by the shocking sight I soon stumbled upon. I was appalled to see the yellow roses on the gated entry way covered with despicable bugs. They had stripped off all of the yellow petals and were hungrily starting on the leaves. Looking around more intently, I noticed that many of my plants were blighted by *pestilence*!

Not seeing the Beloved anywhere, I ran down to the valley to see my garden of intercession. It too was blighted! The fruit that had begun to grow was gone or shriveled up. What had caused this?

I collapsed in a heap near the twenty-four stones piled near the entrance to the garden. I lay there for quite some time, weeping and feeling sorry for myself. Before long, the garden was full of the stench and pale green mist of *self-pity*. I had seen it before and knew what it was. I needed to find the Lord.

So I went back up the hill to my garden of intimacy and waited for Him in the gated area. After a season of reading the Scriptures, He walked up to me. I dramatically shared with Him the state of my gardens as well as the state of His vineyard that had treated me so badly and had probably caused this pestilence by their hatred for me.

He listened, but did not talk back. I knew what that meant. I was not speaking the *language of the kingdom*. I had begun to speak the *language of Egypt*—the language of this world, a language of doubt, suspicion, and unbelief. I finally grabbed my head between my hands and cried out for Him to save me from my ways and to show me *His* ways. *"'For My thoughts are not your thoughts, nor are your ways My ways,' says the Lord"* (Isaiah 55:8).

He responded to my cry and began to show me the error of my way. Referencing my ministry to the brethren that had failed so miserably, He noted that I had discarded His *garment of humility*, putting on a counterfeit *garment of revelation*—my newly acquired revelation about the Bride and His languishing vineyard. This counterfeit garment was based in *pride* and offered NO protection from the attack of the enemy. In fact, it served as a giant invitation to the enemy.

I had allowed the knowledge of this revelation to puff me up. *"Knowledge puffs up, but love edifies" (I Corinthians 8:1b).* The pride that quickly took over, disqualified my ministry, causing people's hearts to be closed to me; for there was no love in my message, only judgment. *I had judged the brethren based on my current revelation of the kingdom.* That was an unrighteous judgment.

In addition, I had failed to make appropriate supplications that a way might be made in the spirit for the message to be heard. Failing to plow the ground of those other gardens through Holy Spirit-inspired intercession, I had wrongly presumed that they were actually *ready* to hear the message that I had been given.

I failed to recognize that the Beloved had graciously made me ready to receive that revelation; otherwise, I would not have had ears to hear it either. Because of my presumption and critical spirit, I had invited not only rejection from the people, but a pestilence upon my own garden. And since my sin was against God's people, my punishment would be even greater than if I had just carried this judgment in my heart. I had sown seed that wasn't ready to be sown yet, bringing premature judgments on the brethren to which they should not have been exposed; for they had heard truth for which they were now responsible.

The Beloved had shown me His struggling vineyard so that I would begin to pray for the *hearts* of His people to be made ready for a closer encounter with Him. *I had not done that.* I presumed the Lord wanted me to help the Holy Spirit; so I told the people what was *wrong* with them. They weren't ready for that message. They needed to hear about what a meticulous caregiver the Beloved is for His vineyard and how long-suffering and gracious He is to those who cry out for help.

The Beloved had indeed shown me that side of Himself, but I had not revealed that aspect of Him to the brethren. I made them think that He was mad at them, but that wasn't true. *I was the one mad at them*.

I so wanted the Bride to come forth, and they seemed to be standing in the way. Ironically, it was misrepresentations of God that were actually standing in the way, and I had miserably misrepresented the Lord. *I had become part of the problem.*

I was greatly grieved. My view of the kingdom was still so very short-sighted. Persisting in interpreting the ways of the kingdom through the lens of *this world*, I had resorted to *manipulation* to try and coerce the people into repentance. (Manipulation is just another word for witchcraft.) I was using my soul power to get a response out of the people. I got a response all right, but not the one for which I was looking.

The Lord seemed to know I was going to make this mistake. He wasn't taken off guard by my behavior at all, but He still seemed sad over my lack of genuine faith in *His ways* which were apparently still not *my ways*. Though His rebuke was firm but gentle, for some reason, this time, I felt the *pain* of my sin against Him. We were so much closer now, and I wanted to please Him, not because of a fear of rejection, but out of a lover's desire in me that wanted to please and honor *His desires*. Unfortunately, I *thought* I was honoring His desires, but I had been puffed up by the awesome nature of the revelation He had given me, and my pride had blinded me to

His desires. I had confused my desires with His, thinking that *my* thoughts and desires were actually *His*, but that was not so.

I asked Him what could be done about my garden. He said that pruning was in order after defilement of this kind had been permitted into the garden. So we took the pruning shears and started on the yellow roses. I was pained, but not nearly as grieved as when we had to prune the vines in my garden of intercession. That act brought me to tears. *My harvest was gone.*

Soon after this, the air began to change temperature—dramatically. I knew what was coming —another *winter season*. I quickly prepared the garden for winter's blast, raking the leaves around the base of the trees and shrubs to shield them from the cold.

Coming faster than I had anticipated, within a few short days, the frost of winter had settled over both gardens. Overnight, they were transformed, looking greatly diminished and chastened—all because of my *presumption*. I wanted to learn this lesson well, so that I wouldn't have to repeat it.

This winter season was different from my previous ones. My relationship with the Lord was much closer, so when I didn't sense Him near me, I *knew* that He was, regardless. However, after several weeks, I started feeling *lonely* for the Beloved's companionship. I wanted to lean my head on His breast. In addition, my message had caused the brethren to greatly misunderstand me, so I was living in even greater isolation, bearing the reproach of their judgments. I was forced to find encouragement from the Scriptures concerning my plight.

> *Listen to Me, you who know righteousness,*
> *You people in whose heart is My law:*
> *Do not fear the reproach of men,*
> *Nor be afraid of their insults.*
> *For the moth will eat them up like a garment,*
> *And the worm will eat them like wool;*
> *But My righteousness will be forever,*
> *And My salvation from generation to*
> *generation.*
>
> *Isaiah 51:7-8*

I paced the garden of intercession even more than usual, hoping it would bring a breakthrough; but the frigid air persisted. Both gardens were miserable sights. I decided I needed another view. So I went to the *mountain of our ascent* and began to climb.

The winter wind was howling menacingly on the side of the mountain, and just when I thought I should give up because of the difficulty, I sensed a trace of His fragrance in the air. I looked about frantically with excitement, but He was no where to be found. Then it occurred to me that this aroma was coming from *me*. It was His deposit within me, reminding me that He ever abides in me as I abide in Him.

Enraptured as if He were standing before me, I was amazed that my fragrance was emitted in the *chastenings of winter* as well as in the *affirmations of summer*. I found myself thanking the Lord for the winter winds of chastening, for they revealed His abiding presence in me and provided evidence of His great work within me.

> *Awake, O north wind,*
> *And come, O south!*
> *Blow upon my garden,*
> *That its spices may flow out.*
> *Let my beloved come to his garden*
> *And eat its pleasant fruits.*
> *Song 4:16*

The fragrance of my Beloved strengthened my desire to make it to the *cleft in the rock* on the mountain. Buoyed by the thought that He was with me, I felt as skillful as a deer making the ascent.

The Lord God is my strength;
He will make my feet like deer's feet,
And He will make me walk on my high hills.
                                              Habakkuk 3:19

Before I knew it, I was there. I stood for a moment by each of the gnarled olive trees, thinking of the importance of what they represented in the kingdom. Then I went over to the cleft and curled up on the bench. Still lost in my Beloved's aroma wafting through the air, I fell asleep in a reverie of thought about Him.

While the king is at his table,
My spikenard sends forth its fragrance.
A bundle of myrrh is my beloved to me,
That lies all night between my breasts.
My beloved is to me a cluster of henna blooms
In the vineyards of En Gedi.
                                              Song 1:12-14

At one point I was awakened by the voice of my Beloved. His song was floating upon the air. I felt my heart enlarging, making room for my increased desire for Him. Where was He? My heart cooed back to Him, beckoning for Him to come and eat in my garden of spices.

> *I sleep, but my heart is awake;*
> *It is the voice of my beloved!*
> *He knocks, saying,*
> > *"Open for me, my sister, my love,*
> > *My dove, my perfect one;*
> > *For my head is covered with dew,*
> > *My locks with the drops of the night."*
> > > *Song 5:2*

Falling in and out of my slumbers, I longed for His appearance. Then, thinking I was still dreaming of Him, I opened my eyes to behold my Beloved actually standing over me. He had been admiring me while I slept, and His song erupted anew.

> *I have come to my garden, my sister, my*
> > *spouse;*
> *I have gathered my myrrh with my spice;*
> *I have eaten my honeycomb with my honey;*
> *I have drunk my wine with my milk.*
> > > *Song 5:1*

Overcome with joy, I embraced Him eagerly.

He held me and whispered in my ear that I had *passed my test.* This season of chastening had served its purpose. He had given me a single vision for Him and only Him, and this reality had sufficiently manifested itself through the time of testing. Even in the face of loneliness and being misunderstood by the brethren, I had sought Him alone for affirmation and solace. "Well done," He smiled, breaking into song again.

> *Behold, you are fair, my love!*
> *Behold, you are fair!*
> *You have dove's eyes.*
> *Song 1:15*

Sitting down beside me, we looked out over the vineyard—the vineyard I had injured. He took my hand and told me I was ready to *tend His vineyard.* Stunned by this comment, I quizzically looked in His eyes to try and understand what He meant. He motioned for me to lay my head on His breast, and then gently instructed me to pray over His vineyard that which I perceived in His heart.

I began to hear specific Scriptures that prophetically describe His cherished Jerusalem and her perpetual place in His heart. I declared their power over that languishing vineyard, joining my heart to His. *We were tending His vineyard together.*

> *Thus says the Lord of hosts:*
> *"I am zealous for Zion with great zeal;*
> *With great fervor I am zealous for her."*
> *Thus says the Lord:*
> *"I will return to Zion,*
> *And dwell in the midst of Jerusalem.*
> *Jerusalem shall be called the City of*
> *Truth,*
> *The Mountain of the Lord of hosts,*
> *The Holy Mountain."*
> *Zechariah 8:2-3*

As we labored over His vineyard of promise, it occurred to me that I had actually been tending this vineyard for quite some time through my supplications for the gardens of His people, as they were each represented in this vineyard. The Holy Spirit had led me to tend this special vineyard before I even knew what it was. I had always felt that my prayers were part of something bigger than I knew.

Thinking back on how I had been tutored by the Beloved and His Holy Spirit, I realized how incredibly diligent they are in tending each individual garden as well as the corporate vineyard of the brethren from which the long-awaited Bride will emerge. His people are certainly a priority, and the proclamations He urged me to declare over His vineyard revealed His heart toward His people—one of great love and compassion. He is truly the great vinedresser of His vineyard.

> *In that day sing to her,*
> *"A vineyard of red wine!*
> *I, the Lord, keep it,*
> *I water it every moment;*
> *Lest any hurt it,*
> *I keep it night and day."*
>   *Isaiah 27:2-3*

XIX. The Budding
of His Vineyard

Come, my beloved,
Let us go forth to the field;
Let us lodge in the villages.
Let us get up early to the vineyards;
Let us see if the vine has budded,
Whether the grape blossoms are open,
And the pomegranates are in bloom.
There I will give you my love.
Song 7:11-12

We tended the vineyard of His heart's desire *daily*. It was our passion, and we looked intently for any sign of new life and the prospect of a fruitful season. In fact, I had taken on the Beloved's desire so completely, that it was *I* who prevailed upon Him each day that we might attend to His vineyard and prophetically beckon its fruit to come forth.

We had become virtually inseparable, and our times of prayer and prophetic proclamation over the vineyard of His people had intensified our bond. In fact, the proclamations themselves were profoundly disclosing even more of the Beloved's attributes and desires, causing me to know Him more fully. As I became increasingly acquainted with Him and the magnificence of who He is, I also became that much more aware of who I am in *Him*. My identity in Him was taking on new dimensions of expression, causing our spirits to call out to one another as *deep calls to deep*.

We would walk the rows of vines down in the valley in my garden of intercession, entreating the vines to awake from their *slumber* and shake off the cares of this life. Proclaiming the Lord's provision for them through *repentance*, we would disentangle any of the vines from the invasive weeds trying to distract them and point the vines in the right direction that they might grow unhindered onto the arbor. (The arbor represented the Beloved's "wedding canopy" of provision for the vines of His people, encouraging them to cling to Him.)

> *And do this, knowing the time, that now it is high time to awake out of sleep; for now our salvation is nearer than when we first believed. The night is far spent, the day is at hand. Therefore let us cast off the works of*

darkness, and let us put on the armor of light. Let us walk properly, as in the day, not in revelry and drunkenness, not in lewdness and lust, not in strife and envy. But put on the Lord Jesus Christ, and make no provision for the flesh, to fulfill its lusts.
                                        Romans 13:11-14

Up on the mountain was where our most powerful pronouncements were made. We would routinely call for the nations to give up the *sons of the kingdom*–Jew and Gentile–whose destinies are hidden in Him. Much of the time we focused on the Jews who still need to return to the land of Israel, for they are the sign of His promise in the earth. When He fulfills His promises to the Jews, it is a sign that *all* of His promises to those of every kindred and nation will come to pass as well; for His kingdom is open to *all* peoples and nationalities, but salvation is to the Jew *first* as a sign of God's covenant with them.

Fear not, for I am with you;
I will bring your descendants from the east,
And gather you from the west;
I will say to the north, "Give them up!"
And to the south, "Do not keep them back!"
Bring My sons from afar,

And My daughters from the ends of the earth—
Everyone who is called by My name,
Whom I have created for My glory;
I have formed him, yes, I have made him.
                                    Isaiah 43:5-7

I was discovering that God is an awesome *promise keeper*, and this essential aspect of His nature was revolutionizing how I thought about myself and other people groups of the earth. If God is a promise keeper, then there is no need for the Gentiles to be jealous of the Jews or the Jews to be jealous of the Gentiles; for God has made elaborate provision for peoples of all nations to come under the banner of His love. No one has been overlooked.

Look to Me, and be saved,
All you ends of the earth!
For I am God, and there is no other.
I have sworn by Myself;
The word has gone out of My mouth in
        righteousness,
And shall not return,
That to Me every knee shall bow,
Every tongue shall take an oath.
He shall say,
"Surely in the Lord I have righteousness
        and strength.
To Him men shall come,
And all shall be ashamed

Who are incensed against Him.
In the Lord all the descendants of Israel
Shall be justified, and shall glory."
                              Isaiah 45:22-25

I especially enjoyed our pronouncements over Jerusalem, the city where He will establish His peace in the earth. Given her history, I relished being a part of God's prophetic proclamations over that controversial city; for she has truly been *"a very heavy stone for all peoples" (Zechariah 12:3)* as the nations have repeatedly fought over her, often not leaving one stone upon another, failing to honor God's sovereign claim on her destiny.

For Zion's sake I will not hold My peace,
And for Jerusalem's sake I will not rest,
Until her righteousness goes forth as brightness,
And her salvation as a lamp that burns.
The Gentiles shall see your righteousness,
And all kings your glory.
You shall be called by a new name,
Which the mouth of the Lord will name.
You shall also be a crown of glory
In the hand of the Lord,
And a royal diadem
In the hand of your God.
You shall no longer be termed Forsaken,
Nor shall your land any more be termed
          Desolate;

But you shall be called Hephzibah, and your
*   land Beulah;*
For the Lord delights in you,
And your land shall be married.
For as a young man marries a virgin,
So shall your sons marry you;
And as the bridegroom rejoices over the bride,
So shall your God rejoice over you.

Isaiah 62:1-5

I would often sense the jealousy of the Lord rising as we would prophesy over this prophetic city. His vengeance was ready to pour out on His enemies. The only thing that seemed to stay His wrath was His great desire for His bride to come to fullness, and many who were destined to be part of her company were still hidden in the nations, ignorant of who they were called to be. So the Lord waited for the fullness of His kingdom to come.

I am zealous for Jerusalem
And for Zion with great zeal.
I am exceedingly angry with the nations at ease;
For I was a little angry,
And they helped—but with evil intent.
"Therefore thus says the Lord:
'I am returning to Jerusalem with mercy;
My house shall be built in it,' says the Lord of
*   hosts,*

'And a surveyor's line shall be stretched out over Jerusalem.' "

Zechariah 1:14-16

The Beloved so longed for Jerusalem's fullness that He had set watchmen on her figurative walls, and I was one of them. In fact, one night He took me by the spirit to the actual walls of Jerusalem. The spiritual reality above the city was a hotbed of activity, but all scattered at our approach. He set my feet down on the walls and in unison our voices sang out over the city:

Your watchmen shall lift up their voices,
With their voices they shall sing together;
For they shall see eye to eye
When the Lord brings back Zion.
Break forth into joy, sing together,
You waste places of Jerusalem!
For the Lord has comforted His people,
He has redeemed Jerusalem.

Isaiah 52:8-9

Jerusalem's fullness will ultimately be a picture of the Bride. She is the place the Beloved has chosen to abide in the earth; and the place of His spiritual habitation is His covenant people–His bride. No wonder this city has been fought over so vehemently;

and no wonder our proclamations seemed to shake the earth, stirring up great storms in the unseen realm. *She is the diadem in His hand.*

At times we would pray on the mountain all night. I loved those times, lying in His arms, hidden away in the cleft of the rock on the side of the mountain. Occasionally, these would be melancholy nights of weeping over Jerusalem and those Jews who were still blind to His true Messianic identity. He allowed me to enter into His sufferings over this, bearing His burden with Him, carrying a measure of His heartache. Those were the times when we became a bundle of *myrrh* to one another, enduring the *dark night of the soul* on behalf of those who had not entered into covenant with Him yet.

Our fellowship in the garden of intimacy continued to thrive as did the garden itself. Delighting in one another beside the pomegranate tree laden with fruit, He took great pleasure in showing me new aspects to my identity in Him and the uniqueness of who I was created to be. He truly delighted in all of His creation, and I was no exception. There were secrets buried within me from my very inception, and He longed to disclose their mysteries to me. I just loved beholding Him. *He was all fair, and I couldn't take my eyes off of Him.*

Then one day, it happened. I had awakened with a burning desire to go to the *mountain of our ascent.* Encountering the Beloved in the gated area of my garden of intimacy, I grasped Him by the hand and urged Him to accompany me to the mountain; for we must *"see if the vine has budded."*

We had seen new growth in the vineyard for quite some time now, but still no buds. So we scrambled to the mountain for a view. Though I led Him gleefully down into the valley, it was actually *His desire* leading us, for His desire had unquestionably become *my desire.*

As we passed my garden of intercession, we were amazed to see the pomegranate trees and vines blooming profusely. Energized with expectancy, we were then greeted by the surprising appearance of *fruit* on the fig tree at the foot of the mountain. A gasp of wonder escaped my lips. Scurrying up the mountain with the agility of hinds' feet, our hearts were focused on one thing–*His vineyard.* Had she too budded? Our hearts were soaring with such intense expectancy that at one point, we were actually airborne, flying around the mountain as an *eagle!*

We both caught sight of her at once. Her dew-covered buds sparkled like diamonds in the morning sun. She was a captivating sight. The promise of fruit was upon her vines, conveying to us that the *hidden ones* were being prepared for their unveiling as the *Bride of the Beloved*. Reflecting on the significance of this sight and what it meant, the motley vineyard sparkling with hope reminded me of Jerusalem with all of her violence and upheaval and pervasive barrenness, but now the promises were coming forth, and a spotless bride would soon emerge. *She was the diamond that twinkled in His eye from time eternal.*

XX. The Harvest is Ready!

And another angel came out of the temple,
crying with a loud voice to Him who sat on
the cloud, "Thrust in Your sickle and reap,
for the time has come for You to reap, for the
harvest of the earth is ripe." So He who sat
on the cloud thrust in His sickle on the earth,
and the earth was reaped.
Revelation 14:15-16

It wasn't long after the budding of the vineyard that the callings and anointings on the brethren began to increase, instantly promoting many who had been hidden away. It had a curious effect on the vineyard, causing parts of it to actually rise up in jealousy and accusation against these budding ministries.

This persecution from the brethren seemed to literally force the fruit of the vine to come forth, unveiling the *remnant* who had been set aside to be groomed as the Bride. Their obvious consecration inspired many of the brethren to actually gnash their teeth in jealousy and hatred against them.

The religious spirit was giving full expression to its hatred for those submitted to the leading of the Holy Spirit. Ironically, this persecution from the brethren only served to hasten the maturation of the Bride. Having been fully prepared for her unveiling, she was ready for this assault. *"...These are the ones who follow the Lamb wherever He goes. These were redeemed from among men, being firstfruits to God and to the Lamb" (Revelation 14:4).*

I found myself being thrown in the midst of these unrighteous judgments of the brethren, and though it was grievous to be labeled a heretic, the Beloved's affirmation was ever in my ear, and it was His voice that I lived to hear. So even though their rejection was indeed painful, I knew that I would *overcome* the great accuser of the brethren, for the Beloved's provision was my sustenance, not man's opinion of me.

> *Then I heard a loud voice saying in heaven, "Now salvation, and strength, and the kingdom of our God, and the power of His Christ have come, for the accuser of our brethren, who accused them before our God*

*day and night, has been cast down. And they
overcame him by the blood of the Lamb and
by the word of their testimony, and they did
not love their lives to the death."*
                    Revelation 11:10-11

The Bride's progressing maturation caused
another spectacle to happen. Her burgeoning beauty
had torn the "veil" that was over the eyes of the
Jews, causing many of them to flee to the provision
of the Son's sacrifice. This caused the vineyard to
thrive in many places, expanding to the north, the
south, the east, and the west.

Intriguingly, the influx of Jews into the
kingdom released a peculiar grace for the *harvesting
of the nations*. The people of God were busier than
ever–teaching, preaching, pastoring, delivering,
prophesying, and leading these new little lambs to
the Son of God, their Redeemer. There didn't seem
to be enough workers to keep up with the incredible
growth of the vineyard. It was an exciting time.

I was overjoyed to be planting, watering, and
harvesting God's seed in a continuous flow of
anointing. Waiting for this type of ministry my whole
life in God, I had accomplished more in just one

year than in the last several years of struggling to accomplish something in God's troublesome vineyard. Though His vineyard was still problematic, the power of His anointing made it all worthwhile, and the prayers of the saints were even more empowered, effecting great changes in the earth.

> *Then another angel, having a golden censer, came and stood at the altar. He was given much incense, that he should offer it with the prayers of all the saints upon the golden altar which was before the throne. And the smoke of the incense, with the prayers of the saints, ascended before God from the angel's hand. Then the angel took the censer, filled it with fire from the altar, and threw it to the earth. And there were noises, thunderings, lightnings, and an earthquake.*
>
> *Revelation 8:3-5*

The beauty of the Bride and her righteous acts, coupled with the power of her prayers caused not just particular sections of the vineyard to gnash their teeth, but the whole *world system*. The spirit of this world was beginning to lash out against the undefiled purity of the saints, causing them to live *outside* the mainstream of society—for the most part. This actually ended up being God's provision for the saints. Their separation protected them from many of the judgments of God which were beginning to fall on the unrighteous; for evil had matured, and the time had come for wickedness to reap its judgments.

> *And another angel came out from the altar, who had power over fire, and he cried with a loud cry to him who had the sharp sickle, saying, "Thrust in your sharp sickle and gather the clusters of the vine of the earth, for her grapes are fully ripe." So the angel thrust his sickle into the earth and gathered the vine of the earth, and threw it into the great winepress of the wrath of God. And the winepress was trampled outside the city, and blood came out of the winepress, up to the horses' bridles, for one thousand six hundred furlongs.*
>
> *Revelation 14:18-20*

The winepress of God was most effectual, causing people's hearts to fail them. The message of the kingdom was the only hiding place, but many refused to acknowledge the provision of the Son even in the midst of such turmoil and distress. Their hard hearts would not soften.

The time finally came for the harvesting of the grapes from the Master's vineyard. *This was the long-awaited fruit of the vineyard that represented the Bride.* These grapes, too, were destined for God's winepress, but not the *winepress of judgment*–the *winepress of persecution* which reaps the blood of the grape from the lives of the believers.

As such, many of the saints were destined for *martyrdom.* The fruit of their lives was to be squeezed that new wine could be collected for the Marriage Supper of the Lamb. Others, who were not destined to die a *martyr's death,* lived a *martyr's life,* suffering greatly for the King. The Bride was destined to drink the *cup of His sufferings* that her fruit would pass through God's great winepress and be collected for the great wedding feast. These were those *"who did not love their lives to the death" (Revelation 12:11b)*– the extravagant lovers of God who follow the Lamb, regardless of the sacrifice.

> *When He opened the fifth seal, I saw under the altar the souls of those who had been slain for the word of God and for the testimony which they held. And they cried with a loud voice, saying, "How long, O Lord, holy and true, until You judge and avenge our blood on those who dwell on the earth?" Then a white robe was given to each of them; and it was said to them that they*

should rest a little while longer, until both the number of their fellow servants and their brethren, who would be killed as they were, was completed.

Revelation 6:9-11

XXI. The Fruit of the Vine: The Bride

*"Let us be glad and rejoice and give Him
glory, for the marriage of the Lamb has come,
and His wife has made herself ready."
And to her it was granted to be arrayed in
fine linen, clean and bright, for the fine linen
is the righteous acts of the saints."
Revelation 19:7-8*

The time finally arrived for the Bride to be
presented to the Son. She had made herself ready
with the white linen of her righteous acts prepared
for her through the Son's own sacrifice. Her
obedience to His lordship had released His provision
for her wedding apparel.

It was a glorious time, and I was most amazed
to find myself in the company of so many others
who had been dressed in fine linen as myself. We
had been caught up by the *desire* of the Bridegroom
who could not resist being apart from us any longer.
We were now in His presence at the great *Marriage*

Feast of the Lamb.

Our majestic Groom was preparing to partake of the cup–*the cup of the fruit of the vine of His bride.* He had told His disciples at His Passover celebration with them that He would not drink of the fruit of the vine again until this great day. And here it was.

> *"But I say to you, I will not drink of this fruit of the vine from now on until that day when I drink it new with you in My Father's kingdom."*
>
> *Matthew 26:29*

The first miracle of His earthly ministry had been the turning of water into wine at the wedding feast in Cana of Galilee (John 2:1-11). Thus it was fitting that the prophetic transformation of the water of His words in His people be manifest in the fruit of the vine of His bride. She had become the new wine for the wedding feast. It was His crowning achievement. It was for this cup that He sacrificed Himself. He desired a bride, so He purchased her with His own blood.

With great joy the Son presented this prophetic cup of the fruit of the vine to His Father.

It was the long-awaited *wine of the Bride*–the wine of all wines. As He extended it toward His Father, He gestured to the great company of believers standing beside Him, clothed in white linen–*His bride*. The Bride and the Groom beamed at one another. Their wedding day was finally here. Her place of rest was beside Him for all of eternity; and His place of rest was beside her.

The Son partook of the cup and extended it to the Bride. Great rejoicing ensued with an exuberant outburst of dancing and singing. It was the day we had all been anticipating–the consummation of the betrothal of the ages; the marriage of God to His covenant people. At last, the great promise had been fulfilled.

> *"And it shall be, in that day,"*
> *Says the Lord,*
> *"That you will call Me 'My Husband,'*
> *And no longer call Me 'My Master,'*
> *For I will take from her mouth the names*
>   *of the Baals,*
> *And they shall be remembered by their*
>   *name no more...*
> *"I will betroth you to Me forever;*
> *Yes, I will betroth you to Me*
> *In righteousness and justice,*

In lovingkindness and mercy;
I will betroth you to Me in faithfulness,
And you shall know the Lord."

Hosea 2:16-17 & 19-20

After the wedding feast we were called to accompany the Son in His judgment of the nations. Instantly, we were all on horses, riding beside our Lord as His bride and companion for eternity.

Now I saw heaven opened, and behold, a white horse. And He who sat on him was called Faithful and True, and in righteousness He judges and makes war. His eyes were like a flame of fire, and on His head were many crowns. He had a name written that no one knew except Himself. He was clothed with a robe dipped in blood, and His name is called The Word of God. And the armies in heaven, clothed in fine linen, white and clean, followed Him on white horses. Now out of His mouth goes a sharp sword, that with it He should strike the nations. And He Himself will rule them with a rod of iron. He Himself treads the winepress of the fierceness and wrath of Almighty God. And He has on His robe and on His thigh a name written:

KING OF KINGS
AND
LORD OF LORDS.

Revelation 19:11-16

The fire of His mouth consumed His enemies before our eyes. His judgments are righteous and true, and His enemies could not stand under them.

> *Then the beast was captured, and with him the false prophet who worked signs in his presence, by which he deceived those who received the mark of the beast and those who worshiped his image. These two were cast alive into the lake of fire burning with brimstone. And the rest were killed with the sword which proceeded from the mouth of Him who sat on the horse. And all the birds were filled with their flesh.*
> *Revelation 19:20-21*

Shortly after this spectacle, we found ourselves at the auspicious *Judgment Seat of Christ*. Hearing the words, *"Well done, thou good and faithful servant,"* were the words for which we had all been longing to hear our whole lives. The pronouncement of those words made every hardship and tear shed on earth worthwhile. It was at this time, that we each became cognizant of the weight of our *jeweled* crowns of reward resting majestically upon each of our heads. Instinctively, we threw them at His feet in utter abandoned adoration of Him, joining in the song of the twenty-four elders.

> *Whenever the living creatures give glory and honor and thanks to Him who sits on the throne, who lives forever and ever, the twenty-four elders fall down before Him who sits on the throne and worship Him who lives forever and ever, and cast their crowns before the throne, saying:*
>
> *"You are worthy, O Lord,*
> *To receive glory and honor and power;*
> *For You created all things,*
> *And by Your will they exist and were created."*
>
> *Revelation 4:9-11*

XXII. The Sacred Reign of Bride and Groom

Now I saw a new heaven and a new earth, for the first heaven and the first earth had passed away. Also there was no more sea...
And God will wipe away every tear from their eyes; there shall be no more death, nor sorrow, nor crying. There shall be no more pain, for the former things have passed away.
Revelation 21:1 & 4

After the judgments of the Lord, we were assigned places in the earth to rule and reign during the establishment of the Beloved's Messianic kingdom on earth. His government is righteous and true, and we were an expression of that government in the earth. This period further prepared us for the final unveiling of the *New Jerusalem* which followed His *Final Judgment*.

We all gazed in wonder at the unprecedented beauty of this holy city, for she was a prophetic picture of our own consummate union with the Son.

183

Not realizing the stunning beauty that had been deposited within each of us by our Redeemer, we had become the *precious stones* in the walls of this gleaming prophetic city before us, and He was the *cornerstone* of its great foundation. His beauty had become our beauty, and we had been made into the perfect companion for the Son.

> *Then I, John, saw the holy city, New Jerusalem, coming down out of heaven from God, prepared as a bride adorned for her husband. And I heard a loud voice from heaven saying, "Behold, the tabernacle of God is with men, and He will dwell with them, and they shall be His people. God Himself will be with them and be their God."*
> *Revelation 21:2-3*

At the sight of the New Jerusalem, the Son began dancing and singing over the beauty of His bride. His prophetic declarations rang in our ears. It was His song for the Bride. I remembered the Beloved pronouncing this prophetic declaration repeatedly during our supplications for Jerusalem, and now He was singing it over those of us who had been counted worthy to be His bride. We were His *New Jerusalem*, without spot or wrinkle, a city of peace for our King to abide in.

Sing, O daughter of Zion!
Shout, O Israel!
Be glad and rejoice with all your heart,
O daughter of Jerusalem!
The Lord has taken away your judgments,
He has cast out your enemy.
The King of Israel, the Lord, is in your midst;
You shall see disaster no more.
In that day it shall be said to Jerusalem:
    "Do not fear;
    Zion, let not your hands be weak.
    The Lord your God in your midst,
    The Mighty One, will save;
    He will rejoice over you with gladness,
    He will quiet you with His love,
    He will rejoice over you with singing."
                    Zephaniah 3:14-17

The Lord of Hosts is a crown of glory and a diadem of beauty to the remnant of His people, just as the Bride is the Groom's diadem, a crown of glory in His hands. In this respect, the Lord and His people are a diadem of precious gems to one another. Crowned by *His* attentions and *His* elaborate provision for her, the Bride's beauty is an expression of the Son's beauty. Quite simply, her beauty is His, and His beauty is hers.

In that day the Lord of hosts will be
For a crown of glory and a diadem of beauty

To the remnant of His people
Isaiah 28:5

Zechariah specifically compares the *remnant* to jewels in a crown. Their beauty is such that they are fitted for a crown and lifted over His land, reminding us of the New Jerusalem as she descends from above as a banner of His love—for her perfection testifies of His faithfulness to His promises.

> *The Lord their God will save them in that day,*
> *As the flock of His people.*
> *For they shall be like the jewels of a crown,*
> *Lifted like a banner over His land—*
> *Zechariah 9:16*

Through His provision, Jerusalem had been transformed into a royal diadem in His hands, fulfilling Isaiah's prophetic picture of her. She is His crown; His great accomplishment in the earth— the sign that He has succeeded in preparing Himself a worthy companion.

> *You shall also be a crown of glory*
> *In the hand of the Lord,*
> *And a royal diadem*
> *In the hand of your God.*
> *Isaiah 62:3*

The beauty of the Bride was captivating, and her place in the heart of God was indescribable. Her prophetic destiny had captured His heart throughout time. She was His place of rest–His inheritance. *"Blessed is the nation whose God is the Lord, the people He has chosen as His own inheritance" (Psalm 33:12).* As she had chosen to abide in Him and clothe herself in His beauty, so it was possible for the Lord to rest in her –His inheritance. *She wears His beauty, and she is all fair.* She is His glory, His crown. She is His elaborate provision for His Sabbath rest that He prophetically declared He would take on the seventh day of creation.

> *Then one of the seven angels who had the seven bowls filled with the seven last plagues came to me and talked with me, saying, "Come, I will show you the bride, the Lamb's wife."*
>
> *And he carried me away in the Spirit to a great and high mountain, and showed me the great city, the holy Jerusalem, descending out of heaven from God, having the glory of God. Her light was like a most precious stone, like a jasper stone, clear as crystal. Also she had a great and high wall with twelve gates, and twelve angels at the gates, and names written on them, which are the names*

*of the twelve tribes of the children of Israel:
three gates on the east, three gates on the
north, three gates on the south, and three
gates on the west. Now the wall of the city
had twelve foundations, and on them were
the names of the twelve apostles of the Lamb.*
Revelation 21:9-11

Thus was the Sabbath rest of creation
initiated; for the great wedding of the Lamb and
His Bride had been consummated and peace would
be the enduring fruit of this sacred union—forever...

*The twelve gates were twelve pearls: each
individual gate was of one pearl. And the
street of the city was pure gold, like
transparent glass. The city had no need of
the sun or of the moon to shine in it, for the
glory of God illuminated it. The Lamb is its
light. And the nations of those who are saved
shall walk in its light, and the kings of the
earth bring their glory and honor into it. Its
gates shall not be shut at all by day (there
shall be no night there). And they shall bring
the glory and the honor of the nations into
it. But there shall by no means enter it
anything that defiles, or causes an
abomination or a lie, but only those who are
written in the Lamb's Book of Life.*
Revelation 21:21-27

About the Author...

Integrating the arts in a variety of ways, Barbara Urban ministers in the United States and overseas, speaking at conferences and setting up specialized retreats and seminars which focus on our pursuit of intimacy with the great Bridegroom of our souls. Her ministry, *Shulamite Creations*, is dedicated to instilling a passion for intimacy with the Beloved. The Lord specifically uses Barbara to host Feasts of the Lord in which she invites believers to peer into the inner courts of God's presence, leading them into prophetic experiences which are full of kingdom pictures concerning our life hidden in Messiah. Referencing the Hebraic roots of the faith, she unfolds the richness of Yeshua's blood which ever speaks on our behalf, making full provision for us to hear and obey the Lord within the context of an intimate love relationship with Him.

Barbara's first book, *The Dance of the Shulamite*, invites us to passionately chase after intimacy with the Beloved; for it is this holy pursuit which will lead us into our mysterious identity as His covenant people. This is the call of the Bride– a call to love-sick abandonment, clothed in His overcoming blood. This is the call of our lives– to become friends and lovers of God.

Barbara's ministry is committed to educating Jew and Gentile about who the true Israel of God is and how our prophetic intercession for natural Israel will help to unfold the mystery of a united Israel who will be an empowered, overcoming bride, made up of all nations, abiding in Messiah Yeshua who is the true land of the Bride's inheritance.

For more information about setting up retreats and seminars,
contact Barbara Urban of *Shulamite Creations*
by email at
shulamite@mindspring.com

189

Shulamite Creations' Ministry Retreats and Seminars

"The Veiling of the Bride" Retreat

This unique and life-changing women's retreat explores the feminine identity of the Bride of Messiah through the prophetic participation in an actual ancient Jewish wedding ceremony. Participants are invited to discover the richness of their identity as the Bride for whom our Messiah will surely return. He is indeed in the process of "veiling" His bride's beauty until her prophetic "unveiling" at the great wedding day of the ages.

"The Bride's Priestly Ministry" Retreat

Geared for men and women, this retreat explores the many aspects of the Bride's priestly ministry through a study of the priestly garments worn by the old covenant priests. Be challenged to worship the Lord in new expressions of service. Creating a prophetic tabernacle of meeting for you to explore, participants are encouraged to walk out the realities of these spiritual truths in creative and inspiring ways.

"Speaking the Language of Judah" Seminar

This seminar explores what the "language of Judah" is and how we can more fully immerse ourselves in the ways of Messiah's kingdom. The "language" of this kingdom conveys the cultural priorities of a kingdom that is very different than the cultures of this earth. As such, the seminar explores the prophetic aspects of this kingdom which are designed to impact our world and cause His kingdom to reign on earth as it does in heaven. In the process, prophetic gesturing and artistry as a language are explored as powerful expressions of Messiah's kingdom culture.

"Ministry in the Secret Place" Retreat

This retreat leads believers into the "secret place" of their hearts— a place where they meet with Messiah as friends and lovers. To facilitate this reality, a captivating "secret place" is erected with veils, disclosing His "throne." His ministry to us and our ministry to Him are both explored with inspiring prophetic pictures, inviting us to frequent this place with an utter abandonment to His desires.

For information e-mail: *shulamite@mindspring.com*

Shulamite Creations' Feasts of the Lord

Shulamite Creations hosts unique prophetic re-enactments of the Feasts of the Lord...

Pesach (Passover)

Passover is the prophetic proclamation of Messiah's sacrifice as the Lamb of God, slain from the foundation of the world. Barbara Urban has written her own Passover Haggadah, "Yeshua's Passover," highlighting Messiah Yeshua's fulfillment of this feast. Through the course of the Passover Seder, our understanding of Yeshua as our Jewish Messiah is unveiled with greater clarity, enriching the Scriptures to us.

Shavuot (Pentecost)

Shavuot is the picture of Yeshua betrothing Himself to His bride– His people. The great betrothal gift that seals the betrothal is the giving of the Holy Spirit to His bride. This feast unveils the beauty of our betrothal to Him and the joy of being consecrated to the one we love– Messiah Yeshua.

Rosh HaShanah (The New Year)

Rosh HaShanah carries with it wonderful bridal images, calling us to awake from our carnal stupors and prepare ourselves for our Bridegroom's anticipated return. Themes of repentance and self-examination are explored as ritual re-enactments are attended to with prophetic insight concerning the cycles of the kingdom and our journey in God.

Sukkot (Feast of Tabernacles)

Sukkot is the wonderful picture of Messiah fulfilling His promise to create a tabernacle for Himself to dwell in, and that tabernacle is His bride, made up of all nations, abiding in Him. The re-enactment of this feast carries passionate pictures of bridal intimacy and bridal fulfillment for the individual believer as well as for the corporate church. Sukkot prophetically communicates the culmination of God's romancing of a bride throughout time and the fulfillment of His desire to rest in a people called by His name.

191

Impac **Chris** **ian Books**

332 Leffingwell Ave., Suite 101
Kirkwood, MO 63122

AVAILABLE AT YOUR LOCAL BOOKSTORE, OR YOU MAY
ORDER DIRECTLY. Toll-Free, order-line only M/C, DISC,
or VISA 1-800-451-2708.

Visit our Website at *www. impactchristianbooks.com*

Write for *FREE* Catalog.